THE SECRET HISTORY
OF
CHEMICAL WARFARE

THE SECRET HISTORY
OF
CHEMICAL WARFARE

N.J. McCAMLEY

Pen & Sword
MILITARY

First published in Great Britain in 2006 by
PEN & SWORD MILITARY
an imprint of
Pen & Sword Books Ltd
47 Church Street
Barnsley
South Yorkshire
S70 2AS

A CIP catalogue record for this book is
available from the British Library

Typeset in 10/12 Sabon by Concept, Huddersfield, West Yorkshire
Printed and bound in England by Biddles Ltd

Pen & Sword Books Ltd incorporates the Imprints of
Pen & Sword Aviation, Pen & Sword Maritime,
Pen & Sword Military, Wharncliffe Local History,
Pen & Sword Select, Pen & Sword Military Classics and Leo Cooper

For a complete list of Pen & Sword titles please contact
PEN & SWORD BOOKS LIMITED
47 Church Street, Barnsley, South Yorkshire, S70 2AS, England
E-mail: enquiries@pen-and-sword.co.uk
Website: www.pen-and-sword.co.uk

Contents

Introduction

The term 'chemical warfare' can, without some form of qualification, encompass a vast range of weapons from tear gas, through the choking gases like chlorine and the vesicant blistering agents like mustard gas, to the instantly fatal nerve gases such as sarin or 'VX', and may too justify the inclusion of chemical defoliants like Agent Orange and phosphorous, used either as an incendiary or as a component of marker smoke. In either of the latter roles the primary purpose of phosphorous weapons is not to inflict personal injury, although that is frequently the collateral effect. In order to contain this book within manageable bounds, interest is strictly confined to those agents formulated specifically to harass, maim or kill combatants and so will make no further mention of military insecticides, defoliants – although they figured with great contention throughout the Vietnam War – psycho-chemicals (from the same period) or the broad range of marking and concealing smoke-cloud generators.

For a similar motive, this book is heavily weighted with developments made in the field of chemical warfare between the years 1915 and 1956, the years which, coincidentally, mark Britain's initial adoption and final rejection of chemical weapons as a legitimate mode of war. We have stretched the boundaries a little to follow the final refinement of the nerve agent 'VX' which, in reality, was chemical warfare's last spasm and which was so horrifyingly toxic that, by so terrifying its possessors, effectively brought about its own death.

All the agents that we will discuss in the following pages fall neatly into a series of simple categories which will be described shortly. Although chemical weapons are generally thought of as 'poison gas' they can, in fact, take many forms. Their common feature is that they all do their work by being inhaled as a gas, vapour, aerosol or in the form of liquid droplets, or else are absorbed in similar form through the surface of the skin. Some, at normal temperature and pressure, are gases, but most are liquids, a few of which do their damage in liquid state while others first evaporate.

Chemical agents are generally categorized as either 'harassing' or 'casualty'. Harassing agents are designed to inconvenience temporarily or disorientate the victim, causing him perhaps to don a respirator and other protection, with all the disruption of military effectiveness that that involves, or else perhaps to evacuate rapidly a disputed area.

Harassing agents can be further subdivided into *lachrymators* (tear gases) and *sternutators* (sneezing gases).

The purpose of casualty agents, on the other hand, is to cause serious, long-term physical injury to the victim rendering him permanently useless as a battlefield asset. Casualty agents do not, by definition, have to kill their victims, but frequently do. To some extent it is regarded better if they do not, for a seriously wounded soldier is more of a liability than a battlefield corpse. Casualty agents can be further subdivided but the distinction between subdivisions can become blurred. In action they are either *respiratory* or *cutaneous*. Respiratory agents, as their name suggests, damage the lungs in the process of respiration while cutaneous agents act through contact with the skin. Cutaneous weapons, like mustard gas, are 'vesicants' or blistering agents which cause horrific, disabling lesions on the surface of the skin. Aerosolized mustard gas may, however, be breathed in, in which case it acts as both a respiratory and vesicant agent, destroying the delicate lining of the lungs.

Amongst the respiratory agents may also be included hydrogen cyanide which, when inhaled, does no immediate physical damage but prevents the blood from transporting oxygen, and causes death within a few minutes. The nerve gases represent a final group of agents that might be classified firstly as *fatal* agents because their sole purpose is to kill, which they do with marked efficiency. The nerve gases may be described as respiratory or cutaneous because death ensues with equal rapidity whether the vapour is inhaled or the tiniest droplet allowed in contact with the skin.

Within the bounds outlined above it is time, like the introduction of a Shakespearian play, to introduce the cast of characters – no heroes, but malefactors all. The following list of poison gases gives brief details of all the major chemical warfare agents employed during the period covered by this book. It is not an exhaustive list, however, for any number of more minor players are introduced as we proceed through their history and there are many more which, having been briefly investigated and found to be of dubious military utility, were left by the wayside.

CS Gas (2-chlorobenzalmalononitrile)
CS is now widely used by law-enforcement agencies as an effective riot-control agent but was initially developed as a military harassing agent. Some 7,000 tons of CS were used by the United States during the Vietnam War. It is an easily prepared chemical which was produced by several commercial manufacturers in the United States for less than $10 per kilogram in the 1960s.

The effects of CS on the human body are immediate and include stinging pain from exposed skin, constricting pains in the chest, coughing, retching and emissions from the eyes and nose. Lengthy exposure to higher dosages can give rise to long-term skin damage and, if inhaled, to serious lung lesions.

Phosgene

Phosgene (carbonyl chloride) is an easily liquefied colourless gas with a hardly distinguishable odour of new-mown hay. It was widely used throughout the First World War as a lung irritant and stocks were maintained by the armed forces of many countries throughout the inter-war years, into the Second World War and beyond. A major attraction of phosgene, apart from its military effectiveness, is that it is a ubiquitous, widely used intermediary in many civilian chemical processes and is manufactured commercially at the rate of several hundred thousand tons annually. Its broad range of industrial applications led to the development of remarkably efficient manufacturing processes enabling production at a very low unit price, a situation reflected in the fact that in 1969, when the United States Army disposed of its remaining stocks by selling them back to the chemical industry, the price paid was the market rate of just 3 cents per kilogram.

The physiological effects of phosgene are deceptive and insidious. Although just a very small dose may prove fatal the inhalation of relatively large doses can go virtually unnoticed in the first instance except for a transient irritation of the throat. The symptoms become manifest many hours – sometimes a full day – after first exposure and by that time such traumatic, irreversible damage has been done to the lungs that death is virtually inevitable. The walls of the alveoli of the lungs break down allowing blood plasma to escape into the lungs, which gradually fill with a bloody froth; breathing becomes shallow and spasmodic and the victim finally drowns in his own body fluid. Death is a frightful affair; the victim, weak from oxygen starvation, his chest constricted as his lungs cease to function, gasps for breath in an extremity of panic, spewing a vile, blood-tinged exudate from his mouth until unconsciousness and then death overtakes him.

Diphosgene (trichloromethyl chloroformate) has similar characteristics to phosgene but, existing in the liquid state, is rather more persistent in its action.

The Blood Gases

Principal amongst this class of chemical are *hydrogen cyanide* and *cyanogen chloride*, of which the former is the most lethal and was most widely used during the First World War. Although the killing power of cyanogen chloride is somewhat lower it has advantages over hydrogen cyanide in certain circumstances, particularly due to the facts that it is somewhat less inflammable and, unlike hydrogen cyanide, can produce disabling effects in sub-lethal doses. Such doses of hydrogen cyanide have no discernible effect on the human physiology. Lethal doses of both agents result in death within minutes and both, due to their low molecular weights, are difficult to filter effectively from the air. Millions of tons of hydrogen cyanide, cyanogen chloride, potassium cyanide and sodium cyanide are produced cheaply and easily each year by the commercial chemical industry as intermediaries in numerous chemical processes and for a myriad of other industrial applications including the electro-plating process.

The effect of hydrogen cyanide upon the human body is peculiar. It is easily absorbed into the bloodstream but, at low dosage, has little or no adverse effect as it is rapidly destroyed by the body's detoxifying system. Once the dosage threshold is reached at which the chemical is absorbed into the bloodstream more quickly than it can be detoxified, the effect is instantaneous and death occurs within sixty seconds. Cyanide acts by inhibiting the enzyme in red blood cells that controls the transport of exhaust carbon dioxide from body tissue to the lungs, causing histotoxic hypoxia. The consequences of a fatal dose are immediate and distressing. Upon inhalation the victim becomes dizzy and disorientated within a few seconds. Hydrogen cyanide has a faint but distinctive odour of bitter almond but by the time the victim has recognized the smell it is too late, the cyanide will already have stimulated his respiratory system and he will be involuntarily gasping for oxygen, quite unable to hold his breath in order to avoid further inhalation of the poison. Within thirty seconds he will be overwhelmed by physical weakness and he will be wracked by violent convulsive spasms. Before a further thirty seconds have passed the victim will cease breathing and by then he will be beyond all hope of medical resuscitation. Intravenous injection of sodium thiosulphate or methylene blue can be an effective – indeed almost miraculous – antidote to cyanide poisoning, but only if administered within twenty seconds or so of exposure.

Although, as we have seen, cyanogen chloride has certain advantages over hydrogen cyanide it is a less effective killing agent and is less insidious in its action. Unlike cyanide it advertises its presence by its pungent smell, by its immediate and powerful irritation of the respiratory tract and by its lachrymatory action. Sub-lethal doses, however, can cause massive and disabling damage to the lungs similar to that produced by phosgene. Although initially rejected by the United States Army as an inferior agent to phosgene it was subsequently found to be very effective in penetrating Japanese gas masks under humid, tropical conditions. Over 11,000 tons were manufactured by the United States during the Second World War and packed into 500 lb and 1,000 lb bombs. Although only pilot quantities were produced, Germany maintained standby facilities to produce 20 tons of cyanogen chloride per month.

Mustard Gas

Mustard gas (Bis 2-chloroethyl sulphide) is a powerful vesicant agent developed as a military poison during the latter part of the First World War. Relatively easily manufactured, it was produced in huge quantities and was responsible for the majority of gas casualties during that conflict. Production resumed in many countries in the late 1930s and, although none was used by any belligerent during the Second World War, hundreds of thousands of tons were stockpiled, much of which remained in national inventories until at least the 1970s. At that time the United States, for example, finally destroyed its residual stock estimated at 25,000 tons.

Mustard gas is not a gas at all but a viscous, oily liquid with a relatively high freezing point. It does not readily vaporize in cold weather and thus poses little danger to the lungs under moderate or adverse climatic conditions, but if the ground is warm then high vapour concentrations can accumulate and the danger is consequently much greater. Mustard gas in aerial bombs or aircraft spray tanks is susceptible to thickening or freezing at high altitudes and additives are required in these circumstances to depress the freezing point.

Mustard gas is not a commercial chemical with any potential peacetime application, although certain of its intermediaries and by-products (notably ethylene glycol) are used in industry. Consequently it was necessary to develop from the first principles of chemistry suitable manufacturing techniques, and to design production plants which, due to the nature of the processes involved, were necessarily required on a large scale. Most of the mustard gas used during the First World War was manufactured by the relatively simple Levinstein process which had been developed in Germany during the War using sulphur monochloride as the starting point. While the Levinstein process supplied mustard gas cheaply and easily in huge quantities throughout the latter years of the First World War, there were a number of concerns raised about the suitability of the end product. The agent produced was impure, heavily contaminated and of greatly varying quality from batch to batch. Its greatest military failing, however, was that even during short-term storage solid impurities settled out of suspension into a dense sludge at the base of filled shells, thereby seriously upsetting the ballistic properties of the projectiles. Various techniques of purification were developed, though none were thoroughly effective. Despite this, the Levinstein process continued to be the primary source of mustard gas produced in both the United States and the USSR throughout the

Second World War. Meanwhile, in the United Kingdom, government chemists at the shadowy Sutton Oak research station (of which we will read more later) had been developing since 1936 what proved to be a far superior method of manufacture using sulphur dichloride as the base material. Simultaneously both Britain and Germany were also working on improvements to a third method of mustard gas synthesis based upon thiodiglycol. The Germans had developed a thiodiglycol process during the First World War and had begun quantity production before adopting instead the much simpler though ultimately less satisfactory Levinstein method. During the years immediately preceding the Second World War, the United Kingdom built factories to manufacture mustard gas using both the sulphur dichloride process (codenamed 'Pyro') and the thiodiglycol or 'Runcol' method in parallel. By 1941, however, the 'Pyro' process had become the preferred method of production and much of the 'Runcol' capacity was closed down. Detailed descriptions of the British mustard gas plants and processes can be found in Chapter 6.

In its early, impure form mustard gas was brownish in colour with a distinctive odour of horseradish, but that produced during the Second World War by the improved 'Pyro' and 'Runcol' processes was colourless and virtually odourless which made it much more difficult to detect. This absence of obvious identifying characteristics, coupled with the typical six- to twelve-hour delay before the symptoms of exposure first appeared, made mustard gas a particularly insidious poison.

Because of its low vapour concentration under temperate conditions it is unlikely that an atmospheric concentration will be inhaled sufficient to cause any harmful effects upon the lungs. However, if aerosol droplets are inhaled – and it had been the overriding ambition of chemical weapon designers since mustard gas first made its debut in the theatre of war to develop means of dispersing the agent as an aerosol cloud above large masses of enemy personnel – then the effects are catastrophic. Rapid destruction of lung tissue ensues, almost invariably resulting in fatal pulmonary oedema for all who inhale the deadly cloud.

The most pronounced and militarily significant effects of mustard gas are upon the eyes and skin, particularly where it is warm and moist such as the armpit or groin. Several hours after initial exposure the eyes become red, sore and painful, exhibiting symptoms similar to those of acute conjunctivitis. Even at relatively low doses victims are temporarily blinded for a week or more. Larger dosages produce much longer lasting and severe effects which in some cases are still evident more than twenty years after exposure. The initial effects of skin contact are similar to sunburn; the affected area develops a red, itchy rash which rapidly swells to form thin-skinned, chronically painful blisters that can become very extensive and are liable to serious infection when they burst. The blisters and accompanying pain may take many weeks to subside and thereafter the victim may suffer continued, often lifelong, hypersensitivity to mustard gas. In humid weather conditions the potency of mustard gas increases five-fold.

Lewisite

Lewisite (beta-chlorovinyldichloroarsine) is a dark, oily liquid with a distinct odour of geranium. It was first synthesized by a research team headed by Captain Winford Lee Lewis at the Washington Catholic University laboratories of the US Chemical Warfare Service in the spring of 1918.

The initial symptoms of lewisite poisoning are much more immediate than mustard gas. Contact with the eyes causes instantaneous, excruciating pain while skin contamination results in a similarly immediate nettle-like stinging sensation. Inhalation of minute quantities of lewisite results in violent coughing and sneezing accompanied by vomiting and an asthma-like tightening of the chest. Because of its arsenical properties, lewisite also acts as a systemic poison causing pulmonary oedema, low blood pressure and subnormal body temperature.

The development of lewisite was a response to the United States Army's utter lack of preparedness for chemical warfare when it entered the First World War in 1917. America had no experience of the effects of chemical weapons and no home manufacturing facilities for mustard gas which, by the closing stages of the War, was the most widely used and recognized as the most effective of the war gases. Unwilling to rely upon its English and French allies for supplies of vesicant gas, the US administration decided to develop its own agent which, it confidently predicted, would be considerably more potent than anything in current use. Large-scale production, based upon weak theoretical presumptions and slapdash laboratory analysis, began in the autumn and the first shipments arrived in France in November 1918. Its deficiencies measured against mustard gas soon became apparent to men in the field but was never acknowledged by the US military authorities and throughout the interwar years and into the Second World War lewisite continued to be vaunted by the Americans as a super-power chemical agent of devastating power and effectiveness. Indeed, it was reported in the American press that 'an expert has said that a dozen lewisite air bombs of the greatest size in use during 1918 might with a favourable wind have eliminated the population of Berlin.' This was, of course, nonsense, but it suited the ambitions of America's interwar chemical industry and the proponents of increased chemical warfare preparedness within the US military establishment to propagate these stories.

It was, however, not just political, military and economic expediency that promoted lewisite's unwarranted reputation. Many American scientists, basing their opinion upon earlier, flawed research, genuinely believed in the superiority of lewisite and these opinions were reinforced by the shortage of investigative laboratory capacity during the 1930s which curtailed further research. So it was, then, that immediately after the attack on Pearl Harbor in November 1942, which precipitated the United States into the Second World War, the US Chemical Warfare Service embarked upon the construction of a series of large-scale lewisite plants, still ignorant of the agent's lacklustre performance. Not until many hundreds of thousands of dollars had been squandered on the production of some 20,000 tons of lewisite was it realized, following a programme of rather more systematic analysis, that its properties did not warrant this scale of effort.

Apart from the fact that it was a child of its own research organization, the United States Chemical Warfare Service was initially attracted to lewisite in preference to mustard gas because of its additional systemic effects and because of its apparently enhanced vesicating properties. In the field, however, it was found that sufficiently high concentrations of lewisite for the systemic effects to become significant were rarely achieved, and, whilst it caused somewhat more extensive blistering to appear more quickly than mustard gas, the burns ultimately were less severe and more short term in their effects. Crucially, too, mustard gas readily penetrated clothing and even the leather of military footwear which lewisite did not. Mustard gas was also much more resistant to decomposition by moisture in humid conditions; conditions which, indeed, enhanced the effectiveness of mustard gas.

Despite its shortcomings, lewisite was manufactured by several other belligerents apart from the United States, including Russia, France, Japan and the United Kingdom. The UK manufacturing plants were standby facilities only and no weapons were ever charged with the agent although it was considered as a freezing-point depressant when added to mustard gas for high-altitude bombs and spray tanks. Russia and Japan also took advantage of the anti-freeze qualities of lewisite when admixed with mustard gas.

Chlorine

Chlorine, which under normal temperature and pressure is a greenish-yellow gas, slightly heavier than air, was the first chemical weapon used on a large scale in wartime. First used by Germany at Ypres in April 1915, it was a crude but, initially at least, a reasonably effective weapon that killed by asphyxiation. It could be argued that the fatal effects of chlorine relied more upon the laws of physics than upon chemistry. Being just slightly heavier than air it formed a blanket of low, hanging vapour that displaced air and thus the oxygen that was essential to support the life of its victims. Like water, chlorine gas found its own level, flowing into the trenches and dugouts where soldiers sought shelter but where they then faced the alternatives of asphyxiation if they stayed, or the prospect of death in a hail of machine-gun bullets if they attempted to climb out and above the deadly green cloud.

There were, of course, chemical effects but these were to some extent secondary to the simple act of asphyxiation. In contact with the moist lining of the lungs chlorine is hydrolyzed to hydrochloric acid which is a powerful irritant and destroyer of tissue, so if the victim exposed to chlorine attack escaped death by choking he would suffer terrible and long-term lung damage which would render him a liability on the battlefield and militarily useless for many months. For the user there was a welcome psychological bonus to chlorine, too, in that the advancing cloud of swirling green gas some 8 or 10 feet high, advancing inexorably across no-man's-land on a front often several miles in width, could readily evoke absolute terror in the troops under attack.

Why was chlorine selected by the German High Command from the almost infinite array of chemical agents, ranging from simple elemental gases to immensely complex organic compounds available from the nation's chemical industry? The answer lies in the nature of that industry in the early years of the twentieth century. In those years Germany led the world in the field of industrial chemistry; it was the monopoly producer and supplier of many of the most pivotal basic chemicals upon which the rest of the world's putative chemical industries relied and the great German industrial combination of I.G. Farben was a virtual monopoly within that monopoly. Chlorine, although an important element in its own right, with a myriad of industrial applications, was also a by-product of other more important basic processes and its supply, both in Germany and in the United Kingdom, frequently exceeded demand. In Germany it was suggested by Fritz Haber – the future Nobel Laureate, inventor of the revolutionary Haber process for the synthesis of ammonia and, since 1911, head of the Kaiser Wilhelm Institut fur Physikalische Chemie und Elektrochemie in Berlin – that this excess of chlorine could be well used as a weapon of war. Its credentials were impressive. Chlorine was already being produced in enormous quantities at minimal cost and production volumes could easily be boosted; it was, as we have seen, endowed with all the right physical attributes of a suffocating agent, and was easily compressible to the liquid state for transport. It was also a potent systemic poison – less than 2.5 mg per litre of air was fatal. The full story of chlorine in war is explored in Chapter 1.

BBC (Bromobenzyl Cyanide)

An important lachrymatory agent (i.e. a tear gas) widely used throughout the First World War. Stockpiles were also held by most combatants during the Second World War.

The 'G' Agent Nerve Gases: Tabun, Sarin and Soman

The development of the so-called 'V' agent nerve gases in the mid 1930s represented a quantum leap forward in the potency of chemical weapons. With their capacity to kill instantaneously in even the most minute doses and the difficulty in detecting their presence before their evil work was done, the 'G' agents brought the prospect of unimaginable horror to both the battlefield and to unprotected (and largely unprotectable) civil populations.

The 'V' Agent Nerve Gases: 'VX' and its Analogues

Continued post-Second World War industrial research into the same family of organophosphorous insecticides that gave birth to tabun, sarin and soman, led to the discovery of the most vile of all chemical weapons, the nerve agent codenamed by the Americans 'VX' (Ethyl S-2-di-isopropylaminoethylmethylphosphonothiolate). The organophosphate 'G' and 'V' agents are of such fundamental importance that the whole of Chapter 7 is devoted to their development.

Chapter 1

Gas in the First World War

Ever since general awareness of the nature of modern chemical warfare became widespread during the early years of the First World War it has engendered international opprobrium and disgust. The public perception is of men in their thousands dying hideously tortured deaths, laid waste in swathes by an invisible hand, their bodies bloated and blackened, or still living but on the edge of extinction, 'their faces, arms and hands,' according to a report in the *London Times* in 1915, 'a shiny grey-black colour, with mouths open and lead-glazed eyes, all swaying backwards and forwards trying to get breath ... all these poor black faces, struggling, struggling for life'.

Fuelled by this sort of propaganda, and without rational thought, politicians, commentators and most ordinary men and women were inculcated with the belief that there was something archetypically evil about chemical warfare, something underhand, unethical, unsporting and ungentlemanly; the sort of activity that no civilized nation worthy of its place on the world stage would descend to. The media whipped up a frenzied whirlwind of terror that still eddies around us today. Chemical weapons were vilified as indiscriminate weapons of appalling power, weapons of mass destruction that threatened to destroy entire populations at a stroke, civilians and military alike. That there was not a jot of evidence to support these assertions was, however, a question that was never addressed.

The inescapable fact is that throughout the First World War chemical weapons were responsible for the deaths of just a few thousand combatants while conventional weapons routinely killed men in their millions. Arguments that conventional weapons are more humane in their modes of dealing death are fatuous. Indeed, to suggest that a mutilated conscript, his young life ebbing away in a stinking, polluted crater on the battlefield of Ypres, his shattered limbs scattered across an acre of battlefield, his bowels ripped open and his red raw guts lying in the mud, might raise his bleeding stumps to the heavens in gratitude that his dreams and ambitions were torn away by shrapnel rather than chlorine, is an insult to humanity.

Most military histories, when they talk of chemical and biological warfare, suggest that at several critical moments of conflict since 1915

1

the world has been on the edge of a chemical apocalypse and that it is only by a hair's breadth of good fortune that humanity has not, in an instance of molecular madness, cast itself into the abyss. A moment's rational reflection, however, will show that such was not the case at all. Chemical weapons have time and again proved themselves to be spectacularly ineffective and consistently unsuccessful in achieving militarily significant consequences. It is not, as is often assumed, the political reaction to civilization's overwhelming popular abhorrence of chemical weapons that has prevented their unconstrained use in modern warfare. It is, rather, the inherent uselessness of such weapons that has been the constraining factor. Used against a backward, un-civilized enemy such weapons might have some utility. The British, for example, had some success with gas as a border control weapon in the eastern dominions, and the Italians found the effects of mustard gas startlingly advantageous in Abyssinia, but against industrial and scien-tific equals its performance was dismal.

The first major instance of chemical warfare – the German use of chlorine gas in 1915 – came as a surprise to the Allies and caused great panic and many casualties, but within a few days *ad hoc* means of defence (rags soaked in bicarbonate to act as primitive gas masks), were devised. Thereafter the chemical battlefield became a game of ping-pong between opposing scientists striving to design increasingly more efficient gas masks to defend against increasingly more lethal gases. Occasionally the technical advances favoured the aggressor and cas-ualties increased, but the advantages were inevitably short-lived. Ultimately the balance was a fine one and the consequences tended towards cost and inconvenience rather than casualties. Although chemical and biological weapons tested under ideal laboratory condi-tions promised devastating effectiveness, their inadequacies under field conditions, and particularly the inadequacies of their delivery systems, soon became apparent. Shortcomings on the offensive side of the battle-field balance sheet were matched by similar failures in the defensive mechanisms, particularly in the design of gas masks and other pro-tective gear, and in the training of soldiers in their proper use. The majority of military men were at best suspicious of chemical weapons and most were vehemently opposed. The offensive failure justified their antipathy.

Although the first German chlorine attack achieved a modicum of success through the element of surprise – the Allies were utterly un-prepared despite compelling intelligence of German intent – subsequent attacks on the Western Front achieved rapidly diminishing returns because defensive measures, once the initial shock had been absorbed, were so easy to emplace. This illustrates the utter futility of chemical warfare. Undoubtedly the American Confederate Army were as shocked in 1862 as the Allies were in 1915, when the Union forces opened up on them with the revolutionary Gatling gun, spewing bullets at 350 rounds per minute. At the start of the First World War the startling efficacy of the Vickers machine gun as a killing machine was equally shocking, but the difference between machine guns and chemical weapons is that the guns could induce the same level of awe and generate the same death and destruction day after day, year after year.

Albert Vickers, in correspondence with his father in 1885, obviously realized the future value of the new Vickers-Maxim machine gun, when he wrote: 'We fired the new Maxim gun today and it is a most absolute success. I would not sell it out and out for less than a quarter of a million, and if our government had any brains, they would pay that price to keep it a secret.'

A gas mask stuffed with activated charcoal might well be effective in stopping elemental chlorine but no similar contraption has ever been devised for stopping elemental lead. After a short period of technical development, soldiers enshrouded in gas mask and cape could wade confidently through clouds of chlorine without fear for their lives, but wading through a hail of machine-gun bullets they could be confident only that they would be ripped to shreds in seconds. It is this defensive disparity that makes nonsense of the assertion by Fritz Haber, Nobel Laureate and head of the German gas warfare organization, that: 'In no future war will the military be able to ignore poison gas. It is a higher form of killing.'

In December 1915 Lloyd George estimated that the Vickers machine gun was responsible for 80 per cent of battlefield deaths despite the fact that there were only two guns to every 1,000 men. No similar claim could possibly have been made for poison gas at any time during the First World War. The best that could be said of gas was, in the words of the Official History of the First World War, that:

> while it was not a battle winning weapon, and certainly not a war winning one, there were a number of engagements on the European Fronts where the outcome would have been different had gas not been used .... Gas achieved but local success, nothing decisive; it made war uncomfortable, to no purpose.

Chemical and biological weapons are the creatures of a small number of misguided and arrogant, yet perversely influential, scientists supported, particularly during the interwar years, by fiercely competitive chemical conglomerates seeking to manipulate military and public paranoia for pecuniary gain. To understand the rather complex relationship between science, industry and the military establishment it is worth briefly examining the development of the modern chemical industry.

3

Until the beginning of the nineteenth century most scientific research tended to be intellectual exercises which were ends in themselves, unmotivated by the prospect of industrial application or economic benefit. The rapid growth in the textile industry from the late 1790s was the progenitor of the modern chemical industry and it was the demand for a reliable source of alkali, principally for the manufacture of soaps for the textile industry, that led to the first great discovery. This was the Leblanc process for producing soda ash (sodium carbonate) from salt which, like coal, was one of the few raw materials in abundant supply. The Leblanc process dominated the chemical industry for over sixty years but had certain drawbacks. Amongst these was the fact that the process produced vast quantities of hydrochloric acid gas that was initially seen as a useless by-product that was simply released into the atmosphere where it decimated vegetation in the countryside for miles around the factories.

Later, measures were taken to contain these lethal by-products but they were still largely useless and were simply casked up and dumped at sea. Early in the nineteenth century it was discovered that the waste hydrochloric acid could be oxidized with manganese dioxide to release elemental chlorine which could then be combined with slaked lime to produce bleaching powder. For both the textile and chemical industry this was a revolution. In the 1860s a cheaper and more efficient method of producing bleaching powder, known as the ammonia-soda process, was developed in Belgium by Ernest Solvay and the old Leblanc industry slowly fell into decline.

By 1900 yet another process had come to the fore to threaten the Solvay empire. In 1886 the electrolytic process for extracting aluminium from alumina had been discovered and during the following fifteen years the electrolytic process was successfully applied in the United States to the manufacture of caustic soda (sodium hydroxide) from salt. Caustic soda quickly became the world's principal source of alkali for the soap and other industries. Improvements were made to the electrolytic process by two simultaneous discoveries made by an American chemist, H.Y. Castner, and an Austrian, Carl Kellner. For some years Castner and Kellner tried independently to market their patents to the chemical industry. In the United Kingdom Ludwig Mond, one of the biggest chemical manufacturers, announced that he was not interested in the new electrolytic caustic soda process as it would probably be too expensive to operate, and anyway his existing Solvay plant was already producing two-thirds of the world's supply of soda ash and, significantly, two-thirds of the world's supply of chlorine.

In response to growing international competition opinions altered and by 1895 there existed a complex series of agreements under which a group of American and European firms licensed the electrolytic process and shared access to world markets. Sales of caustic soda were strictly controlled under these agreements but, again, it is significant that an unfettered trade in chlorine was allowed, principally because demand was still miniscule.

A new firm, the Castner-Kellner Alkali Company, was set up with an electrolytic works at West Point near Runcorn in Cheshire. Brunner, Mond and Company took a 25 per cent share in the new works. The by-products of electrolysis were hydrogen and, once again, vast quantities of chlorine gas. Initially, relatively small amounts of the chlorine were captured and converted into bleaching powder using lime as in the Leblanc process, but in the early years of the twentieth century scientists developed a way of compressing gaseous chlorine into its liquid state and storing it in pressurized cylinders. Due to the nature of the process the factory's output ratio of caustic soda and chlorine was fixed, and during the early working years of the factory the company found the balance of disposal of the two products impossible to maintain. World demand for caustic soda was virtually insatiable but, despite the increasing importance of organic chemistry, particularly in the field of dyestuffs, demand for chlorine remained low. Then in 1915 everything changed when, as recorded in the official history of Imperial Chemical Industries (the successor company to the Castner-Kellner Alkali Company): 'At the Second Battle of Ypres [22 April to 25 May 1915] chlorine became a weapon of war, and Castner-Kellner could shelve their problem of balance until peace came again.'

Having studied the evolution of the heavy alkali industry which resulted, inter alia, in the production of chlorine gas in volumes far in excess of those that the existing chemical trade could consume, we can now take a brief look at the second great pillar of the heavy chemicals industry, and at the man who revolutionized its development. The industry is that concerned with the production of nitrates, and the man is the enigmatic Fritz Haber.

During the nineteenth century the predominant use of nitrates was in the form of fertilizers and, as a result of the combined forces of a rapidly growing European population that had to be fed and the ongoing revolution in agriculture, the demand was enormous. At that time the world's principal sources of nitrates were the Chilean guano reserves which consisted, essentially, of mountains of bird droppings, a coastal strip some 220 miles long, 5 miles wide and in places hundreds of feet in depth. Although these deposits initially seemed limitless fear soon grew that with such rapid abstraction they might, in fact, be soon exhausted. Worse still was the fact that they were geographically isolated and thus strategically vulnerable. In the event of war, supplies might easily be blockaded. This latter possibility was a doubly depressing scenario because nitrate from guano had a second and equally important role to play. Until the First World War it formed the basis of virtually all modern explosives.

The fact that air consists of approximately 80 per cent nitrogen and that – as Sir William Crookes pointed out at a meeting of the British Association in Bristol in 1898, 'above every square mile of earth and sea there is a column of air containing 20,000,000 tons of nitrogen' – was a massive stimulus to scientists to find a way to capture this elemental bounty and turn it to commercial use. Throughout the last quarter of the nineteenth century they had sought ways of fixing nitrogen from the air to form nitrates, but the obstacles seemed insurmountable. High-pressure, high-temperature chemistry was required and it appeared that the required conditions could not be attained. However, in 1908 Fritz Haber, using only coal and water as raw materials, with a metallic catalyst, succeeded in producing ammonia from air by combining one atom of nitrogen with three of hydrogen. Although primarily an academic researcher at the Karlsruhe Technische Hochschule, Haber was retained as a consultant by the German chemical firm Badische Anilin-und Soda-Fabrik (BASF) and it was while working for that company that his high-pressure ammonia process was developed. It took some time to translate this discovery into a viable industrial process and much of the later work is attributable to Carl Bosch, BASF's pre-eminent development engineer, but the initial theoretical work is solely that of Haber. By 1911 BASF were sufficiently confident in the commercial viability of the process that they authorized the construction of a vast new plant at Oppau, near Mannheim, to produce 36,000 tons of ammonium sulphate annually. The Haber-Bosch process quickly became a cornerstone of the heavy chemical trade. As well as opening the door to a revolutionary, inexpensive source of nitrates and sulphates for agricultural use the new process also rendered Germany completely independent of foreign supplies of raw materials, particularly the nitrates required to make nitric acid for the production of explosives. Haber's discoveries and the subsequent joint developments by Haber and Bosch were only just being implemented on an industrial scale at the beginning of the First World War.

Ammonia produced by the Haber-Bosch process was exactly what was required to complement a second revolutionary chemical process, also developed in Germany by Ostwald and Brauer, to produce nitric acid by the oxidation of ammonia. The Haber-Bosch and Ostwald-Brauer processes were perfected in parallel and, between them, relieved Germany of reliance upon Chilean nitrate for the duration of the First World War.

At the outbreak of war Haber was in charge of the Kaiser Wilhelm Institute in Berlin, a position he had held since 1911, but in 1914 he placed his services at the disposal of the German government. Haber was an extraordinary, enigmatic and impenetrable man, utterly egotistical and fiercely principled, though destined, with a self-destructive inevitability, to renounce humanitarian principles in pursuit of a fanatical personal self-interest and a sinister, irrational form of national patriotism. Fritz Haber's apologists – principally scientific historians who would wish to see his towering achievements in the field of electro-chemistry brought to the fore but who would, with equal vigour, have a discreet veil drawn across his wartime works and his tragic personal relationships – have too frequently described him as a man who abhorred the futility and waste of war and whose driving ambition was to apply scientific principles to industry for the benefit of all mankind. Such, however, is far from the truth. Haber's personality, by coincidence similar in many ways to those of two other equally eminent scientists who were to play pivotal roles in the field of biological warfare in the Second World War, the Englishman Dr Paul Fildes and the Canadian Nobel Laureate Sir Frederick Banting, was deeply flawed. In the words of one biographer he was 'a man of intellectual brilliance, with a wide knowledge, overriding ambition and a certain lack of humanity. He was always seen as a scientist lording over his colleagues and collaborators, truly a *Geheimrat* par excellence.'

Perhaps the first indication of Haber's ambivalence was his decision in 1892, at the age of twenty-four, to renounce Judaism and convert to Christianity. This decision was taken not because of any deep-seated religious conviction but because he was aware that in Germany at that time the prospects of academic advancement for Jews were severely restricted. Thus relieved of the shackles of religious discrimination his reputation for intellectual brilliance grew to a stellar scale throughout the subsequent decade, and in 1905 he published his seminal work, *Thermodynamik Technischer Gasreaktionen* (Thermodynamics of Technical Gas Reactions).

A further indication of Haber's personality can be deduced from the tragic progress of his marriage to his first wife, Clara Immerwahr. Clara was the daughter of a respected Jewish family, possessed of immense intellect and, from the evidence of photographs of her taken during her days as a student, an extraordinarily beautiful young woman. Fighting against current conventions that tended to view women with intellectual ambitions as dangerous eccentrics she was eventually taken under the tutelage of Professor Richard Abegg, an early colleague of Fritz Haber. Through tenacity in the face of adversity she became the first woman to attain a PhD in chemistry, which she achieved at the University of Breslau in 1900.

Clara and Fritz Haber had been intimate friends since about 1887 and Haber had proposed marriage soon after their first meeting, but fell

7

foul of her family who were unsure of his future prospects. A second proposal in 1900 was met with hesitation but was eventually successful and they married in August of the following year. Shortly after their wedding Haber applied pressure upon Clara to abandon her promising career as a research chemist, working alongside her mentor Professor Abegg, in order to devote herself entirely to his own domestic arrangements and to the translation of his written works into English. She did so unwillingly and this early accession to Haber's will marked the beginning of an increasingly acrimonious union that was to end in tragedy.

Following the birth of their son Hermann in June 1902, Haber became increasingly remote from his wife and also from his colleagues. The latter, he suspected, harboured anti-Semitic feelings about him and believed that such sentiment was prejudicing his future career. Meanwhile, he was almost fanatically immersed in the problem of nitrogen fixation, becoming ever more arrogant and intolerant of criticism, thereby alienating more and more of his colleagues and collaborators. Clara, with the support of Richard Abegg, expressed a wish to resume her own academic research, but this ambition was firmly suppressed by her husband. In 1909, physically ill and deeply distressed, Clara wrote to Abegg: 'What Fritz has won in these eight years, that – and more – have I lost.' To make matters worse, there were suspicions that Haber was engaged in dangerous liaisons with a series of other women, suspicions that were eventually confirmed in 1915 when Haber was discovered in a compromising situation with Charlotte Nathan in the family home that was built to Haber's own design in the grounds of the Kaiser Wilhelm Institute.

In 1912 Fritz Haber, at the height of his career, was appointed head of the newly inaugurated Kaiser Wilhelm Institute in Berlin. At the start of the First World War the work of the institute was directed towards military research and, as we have seen, Haber, as a true German patriot, offered his personal expertise to the state. Initially his energies were devoted to petrochemical research, particularly into the discovery of alternative additives to replace toluene as anti-freeze in German motor fuel. German supplies of toluene had to be imported and, like Chilean guano, were vulnerable to the increasingly effective Allied naval blockade. Haber's work in this field, the successful replacement of imported toluene by home-produced xylene and naphthalene, was just one of his minor achievements in prolonging the First World War. The Haber-Bosch process was of much greater significance and was of immense importance to the German war economy in that, in the production of nitrates, it broke the blockade on imported raw materials for explosives, and in the production of sulphate fertilizers it boosted the output of German agriculture to overcome, partially at least, the blockade on foodstuffs. It has been estimated that if not for the Haber-Bosch process Germany would have exhausted her supply of military explosives within a year and that, even with German chemical plants using this process still only in a developmental phase, supplies of Haber-Bosch nitrates unnecessarily prolonged the war for at least a year and cost millions of lives. The importance of the synthetic ammonia process to the German High Command can be gauged from an entry in the diary of A.W. Tangye, a director of Brunner Mond who, with the connivance of the occupying powers, was able to ransack the office of the general manager of the Oppau works in 1919 as a state-sponsored act of industrial espionage. 'On the wall,' he recorded, 'I found a framed letter from the Kaiser, dated May 1914, an effusive letter of thanks for the successful production of this one missing military necessity for German expansion.' The ammonia process also, incidentally, made Haber a very wealthy man due to royalty arrangements he had made with BASF under the terms of which he received one pfennig for every kilo of nitrate produced.

Haber's most notorious contribution to the war effort, however, lay in the field of chemical weaponry. After some initial German successes the War settled into a grim, static battle of attrition fought from fixed lines of trenches and deeply dug-in artillery positions. This was not a situation that blockaded Germany could tolerate for long; enormous artillery exchanges were consuming her dwindling stockpile of explosives to no advantage, and those stockpiles, even with supplies of Haber-Bosch nitrates slowly coming on line, could not be replenished. What Germany needed was a faster, more dynamic, mobile war that her vastly better equipped and preponderant armed forces could win before she was defeated by the Allied sea blockade. The deadlock of the trenches threatened disaster. The wasteful dissipation of materiel in fruitless artillery exchanges was not so much a consequence of the inherent effectiveness of the trench as a defensive earthwork, but more of erroneous planning assumptions by all the belligerents at the very start of the War. It had been assumed that it would be a short conflict of open warfare with troops, mainly infantry, fighting for supremacy on the battlefield, and for this the ideal artillery weapon was the shrapnel shell which was a most effective man-killer. Shrapnel rounds required little explosive content – just a small amount of black powder to burst the shell above the enemy troops. This, perhaps, was just as well because, even in 1914 there was little military high explosive available. Although the British and German chemical industries had been turning out prodigious quantities of explosives, based upon Nobel's patents, for half a century these were all nitro-glycerine and nitrocellulose blasting powders of the dynamite type, ideal for mining, quarrying or civil engineering but quite unsuitable for military purposes. They were far too sensitive, far too powerful and detonated with far too fast a shock-wave to be of any use in artillery ammunition. Filled into a shell it was certain that if the shock of firing did not detonate it, and thus destroy the gun, then the shock of impact undoubtedly would. What was required of a high-explosive artillery shell was that its fuse should detonate the explosive contents a few milliseconds after it had pene-trated a fortification, or, in the case of naval or anti-tank rounds, after it had penetrated the armour plate, in order to do the maximum internal damage. The power of a shell that burst at the moment of impact would largely be dissipated in the open where its effects would be minimal.

The only military high explosives of a suitable type available at the start of the First World War were picric acid and TNT, both of which were essentially coal tar derivatives and for which manufacturing facilities existed on only a minimal scale. This lack of capacity was due almost solely to the strategic reliance on shrapnel. The problem for Great Britain was that the existing commercial explosives manufac-turers, particularly the Nobel Dynamite Company of Glasgow which controlled the market over half the globe, could not easily convert their plant to meet the military demand. Processes involved in the manu-facture of TNT were more akin to those of the dyestuff industry than those of dynamite and in this field the United Kingdom was at a distinct disadvantage. For decades the British clothing industry had chosen to buy its dyes from German manufacturers and by the early years of the twentieth century the residual British dyestuff manufacturers were in terminal decline. Meanwhile the German industry had achieved an unassailable world monopoly. Thus, when the demand for toluene-based high explosives for war arose in Germany she already had exist-ing plant easily converted from dye manufacture. This, together with the benefits of the Haber-Bosch and Ostwald and Brauer processes, and with Haber's independent work on the synthesis of toluene substitutes, gave Germany a potentially war-winning advantage. But there was a development gap. Although all the technologies were proven there would be an inevitable delay before they were synchronized and per-fected, and it was during this period that the War stagnated into dead-lock, creating a situation that, if it were not quickly tackled, might be fatal to the Germans.

It was soon realized that supplies of toluene, arising principally from gas works waste, were totally inadequate to meet the needs of TNT manufacture. In Great Britain, against powerful opposition from the Chiefs of Staff, Lord Moulton, Chairman of the Committee for Explo-sives Services, pressed successfully for the adoption by the Army of amatol, which was a mixture of TNT and ammonium nitrate. The nitrate on its own was not easily detonated, but mixed with only 20 per cent of its own weight of TNT it was a high explosive very little less powerful than TNT or any other high explosive currently available. Here again the Germans had the advantage: the Haber-Bosch plant at Oppau could produce ammonium nitrate from fresh air. In the United Kingdom research conducted by two Brunner, Mond chemists, H.E. Cocksedge and F.A. Freeth, resulted in the construction of a large-scale chemical plant at Swindon in Wiltshire producing ammonium nitrate by crystallization from solutions of sodium nitrate and ammonium sulphate. This plant, however, did not go online until September 1917. In the interim supplies of ammonium nitrate were obtained, much less efficiently, by treating sodium nitrate with calcium chloride in new factories erected by the Ministry of Munitions but operated by Brunner, Mond at Plumbley in Cheshire and at the Salt Union's Victoria Works at Northwich.

The problem of entrenchment was a source of increasing worry for all the belligerents by the beginning of 1915 and all sought independently to find a means of breaking the deadlock. Both France and Germany considered the use of irritant gases to clear the trenches but both were cautious of contravening the rather vaguely phrased proscriptions on chemical warfare framed at The Hague conferences some years earlier. Both sides drew nice distinctions between chemicals that might cause death and long-term suffering, and those that might cause temporary irritation, claiming some moral justification for using the latter. Researchers at Imperial College suggested that Britain should use mortars charged with ethyl iodoacetate to clear the German lines but this plan was rejected by a nervous war cabinet. The French, however, had fewer scruples and, in October 1914, used shrapnel shells loaded with ethyl bromoacetate against the Germans. This attack had little or no effect but offered an excuse for the Germans to retaliate in kind.

Some time earlier Haber had attended as an observer upon some experiments in Berlin conducted by Professor Nernst which involved the use of shrapnel shells in which the conventional lead balls had been intermixed with powdered ϕ-dianisidine chlorosulphate, a powerful respiratory irritant. Haber himself had at the same time been investigating the development of phosgene and arsenical grenades with little success. He was sceptical of the effectiveness of dianisidine-filled shells, codenamed Ni-Schrapnel, and, after some 3,000 105 mm rounds were fired into the French trenches at Neuve Chapelle on 27 October 1914 to no apparent effect, his scepticism appeared well founded. The French claimed to have been unaware that the novel weapon had been used against them and Ni-Schrapnel was never used again. Neither side found it difficult to justify the use of such weapons; how, they argued could the use of chemical agents routinely used by the French police to quell crowds of disorderly Parisian civilians contravene The Hague agreements when used against servicemen?

Although the Ni-Schrapnel experiment had been a failure, the first step had been taken beyond the boundary of morality. The second, and equally unsuccessful, German venture into chemical warfare was the *T-Stoff* shell designed by Dr Tappen, a chemist whose brother, by good fortune, was a field marshal in the German Army and through whose influence the idea was brought to the attention of the General Staff. Tappen's proposal was to adapt a conventional 150 mm high-explosive shell by removing two-thirds of the explosive content and replacing it with a lead canister containing a highly lachramatory mixture of aromatic hydrocarbons. A relatively high explosive content was required to burst the thick-walled shell and dissipate the volatile chemical contents in what it was hoped would be a concentrated and extensive lachrymatory cloud. Controlled experiments with the *T-Stoff* shell seemed sufficiently promising to warrant large-scale production and the weapon was first employed, with great optimism, against the Russian Army at Bolimow on 31 January 1915 where some 18,000 rounds were fired. Once again the results were depressingly disappointing. In the cold Eastern winter the supposedly volatile chemicals failed to evaporate and instead stood in sterile, inert pools where they did little harm. The dynamics of the bursting charges were disappointing too. Instead of being vaporized and spread over large areas the chemical contents of the shells were simply scattered in gobs near the point of impact. Two lessons were learned from Bolimow: first, that much basic scientific investigation was still required into the behaviour of chemical artillery shells; and second, that limited barrages were ineffective. What was needed was massive bombardments of highly accurate and sustained fire to produce meaningful concentrations of toxic vapour.

Despite the initial setbacks the concept of chemical warfare had aroused the interest of a small number of German staff officers – though most, as we shall see in a later chapter, were at best antipathetic to science on the battlefield in any form – and also, more importantly, the interests of the German chemical industry and its quasi-official advisors. In December 1914 Haber was appointed chief of the chemistry section in the War Department for Raw Materials and immediately applied himself single-mindedly to the task of mobilizing the German chemical industry. In this role he was, according to his son, Ludwig, 'an extremely energetic organizer, determined, and also quite unscrupulous'. A series of meetings was organized between members of the General Staff and the directors of Krupps, the munitions manufacturers and of a closely integrated group of German chemical manufacturers, including BASF, which would soon combine to form I.G. Farben, one of the world's greatest chemical companies. At one of these conferences a BASF representative suggested that in view of the prevalent, though temporary, shortage of high explosives, chemical agents should be used to destroy enemy soldiers rather than simply to flush them from the trenches in order that they may or may not subsequently be killed by conventional means.

Haber immediately seized upon this idea which, to his precise, methodical mind brought together all the disparate elements of Germany's problem-ridden war production, and concentrated them upon defeating the deadlock of the trenches that was threatening to kill Germany by slow attrition. He proposed the use of chlorine, not in the form of puny artillery shells or mortars, which he knew could not produce lethal concentrations of the gas and which had already proved their lack of worth, but in its raw, elemental form. Thousands of industrial cylinders of the stuff would instead be lugged to the front lines and released in massive frontal attacks using hundreds or even thousands of tons at one go.

To Haber, the logistical balance between military requirement and industrial output was perfect. Nitrates for high explosives were expensive and, until the new Haber-Bosch plants came on line, were in critically short supply. If firing continued at the current rate Germany's reserves would be exhausted within a few months but would have achieved nothing more than a few more craters in no-man's-land. The massive use of chlorine, heavier than air and flowing insidiously into the trenches of an unprepared enemy, would kill where bullets and shells could not. Gas, too, by rendering the trenches untenable, would force Allied infantrymen out into the open where German machine gunners and artillerymen might get better odds on killing them with their diminishing supplies of conventional ammunition. Gas, though, was never seen as a long-term alternative to high explosives. The role of chlorine was twofold: it acted as a temporary expedient until the new explosives factories could make up the shortfall; and it offered a possible means of breaking through a stabilized front. To the German government chlorine's greatest immediate asset was that it was available in spades. Electrolytic caustic works throughout Germany were turning out more than the country's industry could consume. Fritz Haber was immediately able to requisition 6,000 cylinders of compressed chlorine that the factories were almost desperate to get rid of. This was less than half of the surplus sloshing around in various German chemical works, and when orders were placed for a further 24,000 cylinders the firm was able to supply these with capacity to spare.

Once the concept was accepted by the General Staff, Haber's role was central to Germany's gas warfare programme. Working furiously he oversaw every aspect of the first offensive use of chlorine, organizing not just the manufacture and supply of raw materials, but also the transport and placement of the cylinders and even the final release of the gas. Clara Immerwahr was horrified and appalled by her husband's involvement in gas warfare, which she vilified as 'the perversion of science'. Haber's single-minded, blindly patriotic response was simply that 'a scientist belongs to his country in times of war and to all mankind in times of peace.' Her husband's involvement in gas warfare further widened the gulf that divided them, pushing Clara further into the abyss of clinical depression. Her burden was made heavier by the death of her close friend Otto Sackur, in December 1914, during one of Haber's experiments at the Kaiser Wilhelm Institute. Clara, who had introduced Sackur to Fritz Haber shortly before the War, said later that she felt responsible for his death. The accident that took his life was witnessed by the eminent physicist Lise Meitner who, writing to a colleague said:

> You will probably already have heard of the terrible misfortune at Haber's Institute that resulted in the death of Mr. Sackur and in which Mr. Juhr lost his right arm. It is a very sad, completely terrible thing! Poor Mrs. Sackur with her two small children and a third expected soon. One can only hope that Mr. Sackur died quickly, for he was terribly injured in the head, eyes and hands. He died only some hours after the accident and we must hope that he never regained consciousness. You can probably imagine how upset we all are about this tragedy as we were all nearby when it happened.

Ypres, April 1915

Throughout the latter part of January and early February 1915, many thousands of bulky, unmanageable cylinders of compressed chlorine gas were arriving on the Western Front and by the middle of February enough were dug in on the Ypres sector for Haber's first field trial to begin. Already, though, fundamental problems arose that had seemingly been completely overlooked by both the scientists and the military men. Belatedly it was realized that the prevailing winds on the Western Front blew to the east, offering limited windows of opportunity for the release of chlorine which was entirely dependent upon the wind to disperse it over the Allied trenches. During February's enforced delay more cylinders were emplaced and then, with the winds still unfavourable, on 25 March it was decided to establish a second battery further along the front where meteorological conditions might be more favourable. Arrangements were completed there by 11 April but the prevailing winds continued to blow stubbornly to the east.

The frenzied activity in the German lines appears to have gone virtually unnoticed by Allied intelligence, despite the fact that German prisoners of war had been captured in possession of respirators and had talked freely of the strange goings-on in their trenches. Throughout the enforced two-month delay conventional artillery bombardments continued and many of the forward cylinders were ruptured by shell fragments, yet the eerie, surreal and semi-iridescent green clouds that billowed from these direct hits and drifted in a haphazard and deadly manner across the German trenches seem to have aroused little or no interest.

Eventually, on 22 April, the wind turned to the north and at 5.00 pm Fritz Haber gave the order to release the gas. Meteorological conditions in the Ypres sector were still only marginal, however, and it was decided to discharge only the second emplacement, consisting of some 5,730 cylinders, dug-in along a 6 km front, held by the French, extending from Steenstraat, through Langemark towards Poelcappelle. Unfortunately the regular French army units guarding this front had just been relieved by two inexperienced Algerian battalions and seventeen companies of Territorials for whom this was the first experience on the front line. The Allied front broke up in rapid disarray leaving a 7 or 8 km opening into which the German's advanced no more than 200 yards. By this time dusk was descending and in line with their conventional practice they dug themselves in rather than take advantage of their somewhat unexpected strategic gain.

Interwar accounts, still repeated in the present day, give the impression of thousands of victorious, black-clad German troops wearing gas-proof masks and suits, looking for all the world like terrestrial frogmen, striding confidently through the murderous, swirling green fog, towering grimly over the few Allied soldiers who had neither retreated in panic nor died of asphyxiation, and whom they then picked-off at leisure. Such, however, is far from the truth. Poorly protected German infantrymen wearing no more than conventional uniform, disorientated in the green mist and their sight and movement greatly impaired by the most basic of respirators, picked their way nervously through the clouds of chlorine gas. There is plenty of evidence that the German field commanders were highly sceptical of the operation and viewed their involvement as little more than condescending to the whim of a group of eccentric scientists who had succeeded in catching the ear of Ludendorff. Because they had no expectations of success they had made no contingency plans to sustain any advantage that might be gained. This air of scepticism seemed to pervade the General Staff, too, for requests from a few of the more ardent proponents of gas warfare for extra ammunition to press home any territorial gains were refused.

Although the Germans appeared to have made a significant tactical blunder in not following up the first gas assault the operation was not unsuccessful. Some 1,600 prisoners had been taken and an unknown number killed or seriously injured. For several hours Allied commanders were unable to assimilate what had happened. Once the gravity of the situation became clear Canadian troops were moved in from the east in order to hold the line until the French forces could reorganize. The following day the Allied army launched a counter-attack to regain the lost ground but, to their misfortune, on 24 April the wind veered a few degrees to the east providing perfect conditions for the German gas men to release the remaining 18,000 cylinders against mainly Canadian troops. This time the chlorine was augmented by a heavy bombardment of *T-Stoff* shells, conventional artillery fire and a concerted infantry attack. The Canadians were not totally unprepared but casualty rates were still high. The two days of grace following the first attack on 23 April gave Allied commanders time to make no more than the most basic anti-gas preparations. Soldiers were given cotton wadding which they were to dip in buckets of bicarbonate of soda solution and then hold over their faces as primitive gas masks. Some infantrymen made their own from rags soaked in their own urine or from broken bottles filled with loosely compacted earth.

Widely divergent estimates of the casualties of the gas attacks at Ypres emerged over the next twenty years reflecting the current political perceptions of gas warfare. Lefevre, writing in 1921, claimed 5,000 deaths and some 15,000 to 20,000 serious injuries, a figure similar to those generally accepted in Germany at the time. By 1934, however, against a background of rising public antipathy to chemical warfare, the Germans withdrew this estimate, claiming that the true figure was probably no more than 1,000 dead and 3,000 injured. It was claimed that the immediate post-war German estimates were based upon Allied claims and that the Allies had deliberately inflated the true figures in order to discredit Germany. The most reliable statistics, though these are only partial, are those compiled contemporaneously by the gas clearing stations, which recorded 7,000 casualties, only 350 of whom subsequently died. A further 200 prisoners of war were treated for the effects of gas in German hospitals; of these twelve died. British government figures (estimates, not accurate body counts) suggest that a further 3,000 men may have lain dead and unaccounted for on the battlefield. The problem arises as to how to treat these battlefield deaths; were they due to gassing or the conventional hazards of war? To the victims, of course, it made very little difference.

There was one other collateral victim of these events. On the afternoon of 2 May, while Haber, still at the front, celebrated the success of the gas attacks at Ypres, servants at his home in the grounds of the Kaiser Wilhelm Institute heard two gunshots in the garden. Her young son, Hermann, later reported seeing Clara Immerwahr holding her husband's service revolver, which she had earlier taken from the desk in his study. Unused to handling firearms she first fired a practice shot into the air. The second shot missed her heart by a millimetre, though the wound was fatal and she died two hours later. The same servants swore to having seen a note in Clara's handwriting but nothing was ever produced. Haber did not attend the funeral.

Bolimow – May 1915

While preparations were under way for the first great gas experiment at Ypres the Germans were also making plans for the employment of chlorine on the Eastern Front in support of the advance upon Warsaw. By mid-May 1915, the Russian Army was aware of the gas attacks on the Western Front and, in anticipation of its use in the East, had begun to organize defensive measures, although these were inadequate and arrived too late. Ludendorff was aware that he did not have the advantage of surprise that had so aided the Germans at Ypres – surprise, the only real value of chemical warfare, had gone forever after its first use – but was convinced that the Russians were unprepared. In his memoirs he recorded that 'we had received a supply of gas and anticipated great tactical results from its use as the Russians were not yet fully protected.' It is interesting to note that the gas attacks on the Eastern and Western Fronts were planned simultaneously. Although the use of gas at Bolimow occurred some weeks after Ypres, its implementation was not dependent upon the success of the earlier exercise. If Ypres was just an experiment then it appears to have been one which the German High Command was extraordinarily confident would succeed.

The attack was launched against two stubborn infantry divisions of the Second Russian Army on a 12 km front near Skierniewice, southwest of Warsaw, on 31 May. The release of 264 tons of chlorine from 12,000 gas cylinders was followed up by a massive and sustained infantry assault, in sharp contrast to the hesitancy of the earlier one at Ypres. German confidence was ill founded, however, for as the respirator-clad infantrymen followed the tail of the dispersing chlorine cloud they were met by a heavy barrage from the Russian artillery which they were convinced had been silenced by the gas. The German advance thereupon lost its momentum, the commanders having assumed that the gas had been ineffective. Casualties amongst the Russians were, in fact, extensive, amounting to some 9,000 of whom 1,101 were fatalities. The failure of the Bolimow action was a matter of psychology. From its first inception the Germans had envisaged gas as a psychological weapon as much as one of physiological effect, a tool to frighten as much as to cause physical injury. The problem lay in the fact that the psychological effect lay primarily in surprise and by the time of the gassing at Bolimow the element of surprise had gone. Germany underestimated the tenacity of the Russian gunners, preferring instead, in the first instance, to lay the blame on the perceived ineffectiveness of the gas to which there was already an undercurrent of resentment and suspicion.

Psychology is a dangerously double-edged weapon and, where it relates to chemical weapons or any other novel form of warfare, it can easily react against the aggressor. The hierarchy of military command is and always has been intensely reactionary and conservative. Not only do soldiers, in the oft-quoted words of David Lloyd George, 'prepare not for the next war but for the last one or the last but one', but they also invariably exhibit a fierce resistance to new ideas or concepts generated outside the military establishment. This is perhaps not the blind stubbornness that it at first seems. In the heat of a battle involving many thousands of men, what is required above all else is simplicity; a simple command structure, a simple vocabulary of orders, a simple, easily learned procedural drill and simple weapons that produce predictable and repeatable results. Simplicity allows easy flexibility on a fluctuating battlefield and tends to minimize the adverse results when plans go wrong. Using the conventional tools of their trade – high-explosive shells, shrapnel and rifle bullets – tacticians and commanders can with some reliability assess how a future action might progress. The efficient use of these weapons is often the result of decades of training and experience in the careful control of dangerous energy. Soldiers like them because, under the most hazardous and perilous conditions, their familiarity imbues confidence. They are fearful, however, of new weapons which they do not fully control, which are not battle tested or which have been thrust upon them by whom they perceive as amateur outsiders. Chlorine failed in each of these criteria and it was these failures that ensured that it never gained the confidence of either the German or Allied officers. The absence of confidence was the psychological backlash of chemical warfare. No one wanted it or held any great expectations of its effectiveness, and this deep reluctance to believe in its efficacy ensured its failure.

Despite these setbacks chlorine continued to be used throughout the War. The largest of the 200 or so operations involving chlorine took place against French forces at Rheims in October 1915 when 550 tons were released from 25,000 cylinders. This would have appeared small beer in comparison with the planned assault by the British at the time of the German spring offensive in 1918. During the preceding weeks some 200,000 cylinders containing in excess of 5,800 tons of gas had been surreptitiously moved to the front on specially adapted railway wagons. This was calculated to be sufficient to wipe out not only a broad sector of the German front line but also the supply trenches and artillery positions well to the rear. Changes in the dynamics of the War caused the operation to be cancelled at the last moment.

The Problem with Chlorine

Chlorine gas released in bulk from cylinders presented a solution of sorts to the immediate problem of lack of saturation posed by early chemical artillery shells. Contemporary guns could not achieve a sustained rate of fire, nor could artillery shells carry a sufficient volume of chemical agent to generate a sufficient concentration of poison gas over the enemy trenches. Cylinders could generate the required concentration over a broad front but only at unacceptable logistic cost.

Most high-ranking officers were privately antipathetic to every aspect of gas warfare which they considered completely contrary to the established code of military ethics. This attitude is exemplified by Sir John French's comments following the Second Battle of Ypres in which, with reference to the German use of gas, he expressed 'the deepest regret and some surprise that an Army which hitherto has claimed to be the chief exponent of the chivalry of war should have stooped to employ such devices against brave and gallant foes'. More broadly there remained a pervasive military hostility to innovation, especially those of civilian scientific origin. There were practical difficulties too. Gas, particularly cylinder gas which was entirely dependent upon the vagaries of the wind for its dispersal, took the initiative away from military commanders and put it in the hands of the meteorologists. All other tactical imperatives became subsidiary to the weather conditions, which was an intolerable situation. Handling, storing, emplacing and operating the thousands of heavy cylinders became a logistical nightmare. Big and heavy and round, each cylinder was at best a two-man lift and once covered in slippery trench mud was almost unliftable. Thousands of men were taken from other duties to manoeuvre the cylinders to the front while hundreds of others, quickly trained in an alien technology, were required to connect the pipework and ultimately act as turncocks. Officers at the front were fearful of the cylinders stacked in their trenches where they got in the way and, more importantly, were highly vulnerable to accidental leakage or rupture by enemy fire. But if chlorine was to be used in quantities sufficient to achieve worthwhile results, there seemed no other way. The gas had to be released ahead of friendly troops and as close as possible to the enemy because the wind could not be expected to be co-operative over extended distances.

The fact that gas warfare in its earliest days tended to create a much higher proportion of injured but surviving casualties than conventional warfare caused its own logistical problems. Dead men could, in the short term at least, be left on the battlefield but there was a moral duty to recover and care for the injured. Thus every gas casualty carried to a medical centre took fighting men, the stretcher-bearers, from the battlefield and tied up many more in the medical services. Recuperation after gas injuries took many months and for all that time the wounded absorbed vital resources that could perhaps be more usefully disposed elsewhere. Anti-gas defences, as they became more sophisticated, imposed their own logistic burden. Decontamination centres required staff and materials that had to be taken to the front on transport that might be better used to carry ammunition or rations for the troops, and the mere act of decontaminating thousands of affected men removed them temporarily from useful duty. Most importantly of all, the adoption of anti-gas defensive gear hampered the individual's movement and sensory perception. Gas masks put an additional load upon the respiratory system, the tiny eyepieces limited peripheral vision, tended to mist up easily and caused mental disorientation. Early gas masks did not perform well and the later box respirators with their filter packs bouncing about on the wearer's back made movement difficult in confined spaces.

Overall, gas warfare exacerbated the problems that it was intended to solve. Instead of mobilizing a static battlefield, gas succeeded – due to its encumbrance of iron cylinders and ancillary pipework, its buried projectors and associated firing circuitry, its hampering gas masks, gas capes, anti-gas doors and drapes at every opening in the trenches, its decontamination centres and decontamination kit that had to be carried by each soldier on top of his already considerable personal burden – in bogging down the Western Front into an even more firmly entrenched, static and defensive quagmire.

Local commanders hated every aspect of it. Gas denied them the initiative they required. Day-to-day plans were impossible to prepare, timetables for infantry assault became dependent entirely upon the weather rather than more pressing military imperatives, the trenches were overflowing with sinister new-fangled apparatus filled with horribly hazardous materials with a penchant to leak and which no one fully understood. And when the moment for action finally arrived the wind seemed invariably to turn and the stuff all billowed back over their own men. Soon all interest was lost in following up the gas with a concerted infantry attack and the release of gas became a haphazard, random business, carried out in the hope of surprising a complacent enemy. The enemy, though, was rarely complacent and this was a minor victory in itself. Compelled to don gas masks almost continuously soldiers soon became heartily sick of them, demoralized and fatigued by stress.

It is difficult to understand why Germany initiated gas warfare on the Western Front in the way she did. Had she possessed a monopoly in the supply of chlorine then there would have been a strategic justification but, as we have seen, there was a worldwide surplus of chlorine and Britain was amongst the most prolific manufacturers. It was not a difficult technology to adopt; the Allies called for its use in retaliation early in May 1915 and by September sufficient supplies were available and sufficient troops trained in its use to enable them to launch a massive and successful gas attack at the Battle of Loos in September. Astonishingly, this attack seems to have taken the Germans by surprise even though front-line troops were issued with gas masks which indicates that retaliation was anticipated for some time. Heavy casualties were taken, mainly due to the fact that the German troops were poorly trained in the use of their respirators. It is probable that although lip-service had been paid to the possibility of an Allied gas attack there was a general feeling in Germany that Great Britain's chemical industry was not yet sufficiently motivated to meet the demands of war. It is difficult, too, to accept that the Germans did not take into account the meteorological conditions on the Western Front when developing their strategy. As a result of the increasing application of ballistic science to the art of gunnery, military meteorology was already making headway and, anyway, there was little skill required to observe that the wind almost invariably blew from the west. Following Germany's first qualified success the initiative turned to the Allies and thereafter the advantage of wind and weather remained firmly with them. While Germany had further minor successes against Russia, and the Austro-Hungarians caused massive casualties amongst the Italian Army on the Plateau of Dobero in June 1916, by far the greatest use of chlorine was made by the Allies for the rest of the War.

For chlorine to remain a viable weapon some other method less dependent on the weather was required to reliably deliver it in large quantities directly into the enemy trenches. Even as development work was under way on new, high-capacity chlorine projectiles it was generally accepted that for chemical warfare to hold its own on the battlefield chlorine would have to give way to more potent payloads of infinitely greater toxicity that could be delivered accurately by artillery shell. The first interim solution was introduced by the British at the Battle of Loos in September 1915. This device, the Stokes Mortar, consisted of a thin-walled projectile filled with approximately 8 lb weight of chemical agent. Its advantage was that the lightweight, easily handled weapon could maintain a high rate of fire of about twenty rounds per minute and had a range in excess of 1,000 yards. A battery of Stokes Mortars could easily produce an effective local concentration of toxic gas and was an ideal weapon for counter-battery work.

The next British development was the Livens Projector, an extraordinarily simple, effective and inexpensive weapon introduced in the winter of 1916/17, specifically designed to deliver all the advantages of the cylinder weapon while completely overcoming the weather dependency of the latter. In its crudest form the projector consisted of a simple, large diameter mortar tube fabricated from a couple of old oil drums set at an angle in the ground. An artillery shell propellant bag charge was thrown into the bottom of this tube and a complete gas cylinder was then dropped in on top of it. The cylinder was modified by the addition of a percussion fuse and small bursting charge, and the propellant charge was fired by means of an electric circuit. With a range of up to 2 km each projector could hurl a whole cylinder containing 15 kg of chlorine directly into the enemy trench where it burst on impact. Once the concept was proven Livens Projectors were manufactured in vast quantities and following their first large-scale deployment at the Battle of Arras in April 1917 they were used with stunning effectiveness in batteries of several thousand. The utility and versatility of the Livens Projectors was quickly appreciated and during the last two years of the War the apparatus underwent continued development. Special cylinders were manufactured, improved fuzes designed and the tubes were later adapted to fire incendiary and high-explosive rounds becoming, in effect, conventional large calibre trench mortars. Both the Livens Projector and the Stokes Mortar, by rendering gas warfare independent of the weather, returned the initiative to the infantry who were again able to dictate the timetable of battle.

Germany was slow to develop anything comparable although they did try adapting their 250 mm trench mortar, but it proved too unwieldy a weapon to be used effectively. A more practicable version was eventually employed on the Italian front in the autumn of 1917 and then against the British at Cambrai in December, but it was never deployed in large numbers and was not a significant element in the German arsenal. It is probable that the Germans were already, by the end of 1915, disillusioned by chlorine and the concept of massive gas-cloud attack, and were re-examining the use of artillery shells as the chief means of dissemination. It was clear, however, that for artillery to be successful it would require better designed shells filled with very much more toxic chemical agents.

Up until this time both Germany and the Allies had shown remarkably little interest in developing new projectiles to contain their toxic chemical payloads. Until the summer of 1915 German artillery fired only the dubiously effective, persistent irritant *T-Stoff* rounds. These were subsequently supplemented by projectiles filled with a mixture of chloromethyl and dimethyl chloroformates, code-named *K-Stoff* which, although at first officially classified as an irritant agent, was in fact highly volatile and twice as lethal as chlorine. Tactically, *K-Stoff* became increasingly used de facto as a lethal weapon, although its

22

potency was such that it was impossible to establish a truly lethal concentration with the limited capacity of current shell design. The next logical step was to fill projectiles with phosgene, a chemical with the same root as that used in the *K-Stoff* projectile, but many times more poisonous. The phosgene, or *K2-Stoff,* shell was the first of the truly lethal German artillery rounds. Early German chemical artillery was seriously hampered by the fact that projectile design had not advanced in line with the developments in shell filling.

The first phosgene projectiles were simply conventional, thick-walled high-explosive shells with half the explosive filling removed and replaced by a lead canister containing the toxic chemical. It was thought that the residual explosive content would be required to burst the shell and dissipate the contents but experience showed that this was counter productive. The large explosive charge ruptured the shell with such force that the contents were scattered over too wide an area to create lethal local concentrations, while the thick steel shells too severely limited the amount of chemical that each projectile could contain. The French were first to realize that a radical redesign was necessary and, in their Special Shell No. 5, had designed a thinner-walled phosgene shell which relied solely upon the gain of the fuze to burst it. The result was a smaller volume of air densely contaminated with poison rather than a large volume so thinly populated with poisonous particles as to pose no harm. Rather incompletely following the French example, the Germans had, by the end of 1916, dispensed with the high-explosive bursting charge but it was not until the summer of the following year that they realized the benefit of the thin-cased projectile. The new shells were not only thinner but also longer than their predecessors and of much greater capacity; that for the 77 mm field gun, for example, contained 1 kg of phosgene, twice the weight of the previous pattern.

Mustard Gas

By the winter of 1916/17 phosgene delivered by artillery was becoming the German chemical weapon of choice, but they were keenly aware of its shortcomings. Phosgene was not an exclusively military agent; it was a widely available intermediary used in many processes in the chemical trade and was taken up by the military, like chlorine, on account of its satisfactory toxicity and its ease of availability. Something better was required, however, and by September 1916 German scientists were hard at work developing it. The fruit of their research appeared on the battlefield in 1917 in the form of mustard gas, a viciously caustic percutaneous casualty agent that soon gained the reputation of the 'king of gasses'. Mustard gas is not a difficult substance to produce if manufactured on a large scale and the processes involved are common to those involved in other branches of the chemical industry. Existing plant in German dyestuff factories was easily and quickly converted to production of the king of gasses. Scientists in Germany had investigated a number of sulphur-containing organic chemicals and found two which exhibited satisfactory vesicant properties, dimethyl sulphate and bis 2-chloroethyl sulphide, or mustard gas. Dimethyl sulphate was only slightly less toxic than mustard gas and was much easier and cheaper to produce. However, the Germans chose mustard gas, presuming that the Allies had not yet considered developing such agents themselves, and reasoned that once attacked they would look with some promptness at producing the material themselves and reply in kind. At the time Germany had a world monopoly in the production of industrial dye-stuffs and the plants that produced these dyes were those that were most easily converted to the manufacture of mustard gas. Had they opted for dimethyl sulphate, the Germans argued, then it was likely the Allies would have blindly copied their example and built the relatively simple plant required to manufacture their own in a relatively short time. So instead they selected mustard gas on a similar basis – the Allies would copy it, but suitable factories did not exist in Britain or France, the plant was more complex and the manufacturing process more hazardous. It would be, they estimated, at least a year before the Allies would have adequate production facilities available. Meanwhile German dyestuff plants could be converted in just days or weeks.

Germany refrained from revealing its new weapon until a sufficient stockpile was available to launch a spectacular assault, then in July 1917 she began a massive ten-day bombardment which consumed 1,000,000 artillery rounds containing a total of 2,500 tons of mustard gas. Within three weeks mustard gas had produced more casualties than the entire gas shelling of the previous year.

German assessments of the Allied response had been correct in all but one particular. Britain had, in fact, examined mustard gas in the summer of 1916 but it was dismissed by the military authorities. Following the attacks of July 1917 there was feverish activity in France and Britain to develop a similar weapon but progress in the construction of mustard gas factories was slow. The first French supplies finally reached the battlefield in June 1918 and the British followed three months later. The main British production facility was located at Avonmouth near Bristol. Known locally as the 'Chittening Gas Works' the factory employed at its peak a workforce of some 1,100 personnel, mainly women, and produced approximately 20 tons of mustard gas per day. Working conditions in the factory were poor and its safety record notorious. During its operating life there were 1,400 serious injuries recorded and cases of minor burns and blistering exceeded 100 per cent of the workforce every three months. Although the area has seen substantial industrial redevelopment since the Second World War,

the Chittening factory was once in a remote countryside location surrounded by wasteland. Fields around the perimeter of the works were
so badly contaminated by effluent from the plant that barriers were
erected at a radius of one mile and notices posted warning local residents not to eat the wild blackberries that grew there. The Chittening
works produced one quarter of the mustard gas deployed by the Allies
during the First World War. The remainder was manufactured in an
equally hazardous factory in France.

Although advanced in the production of ever more lethal chemical
agents, Germany continued to lag behind in the development of suitable delivery systems. Their first mustard gas shells were similar to
those used for *K-Stoff*, using a low-power bursting charge. Similar
shells were used by all the belligerents and the initial battlefield results
were disappointing. Then it was realized that while a small bursting
charge was ideal for highly volatile agents like *K2-Stoff*, the effects were
far from satisfactory with the much less volatile mustard gas. A light
charge simply distributed widely scattered globules of liquid over a
wide area where they did very little harm. What was required was a
somewhat heavier charge that vaporized the gas, producing a cloud of
tiny droplets that remained suspended in the air for some time where
they were most likely to contaminate exposed flesh. Inaccurate fuzing
of the shells was another factor that reduced the initial effectiveness of
mustard gas artillery. Powder-train time fuzes, like those used to burst
shrapnel shells overhead of troops in trenches, were not sufficiently
accurate to ensure that chemical shells burst at the optimum time, just
before the point of impact. Percussion fuses invariably detonated milliseconds after the shell had buried itself in the ground. In these circumstances the usual result was, even with higher bursting charge shells,
that most of the mustard gas was contained within the shell's impact
crater where it could do little harm and was easily avoided. Later
patterns of German mustard gas shell included a large ejection charge
contained within the ogive of the head, designed so that after impact
the charge would throw the contents of the shell upwards out of the
crater.

Mustard gas had the potential to change the course of the War and, if
if it had not been shackled to an inappropriate delivery system and used
against an enemy that was Germany's technological equal, it would
undoubtedly have done so. Artillery shells were simply not an adequate
method of delivery; neither were contemporary ballistic theory nor
guns nor ammunition nor fuzes of sufficient precision to ensure the
required concentration of fire. It was quite impossible, given the two
limitations of calibre and rate of fire, for field ordnance of the day to
project a sufficient weight of mustard gas to be of any substantial
offensive purpose. Ammunition for small calibre field guns of, say,

77–105 mm could be fired at a reasonable rate but their individual agent capacity was insignificant. The largest calibre field pieces, while firing projectiles that might contain a respectable load of gas, could not maintain a sufficiently high rate of fire so the net result for both classes, in terms of weight of agent dispersed per minute, was much the same and in both cases far too low. Clearly the solution lay in adapting chemical weapons, the new science of warfare, to delivery via aircraft, the emerging new technology of warfare. Some attention was given to this in 1918 but, due to the typical, conservative inertia of the military mind and to the limitations of current aeronautical technology, no concrete progress was made. When the first practical steps were taken to wed mustard gas to aircraft they rather predictably first led into a blind alley and the marriage was not a happy one. Fixated upon the use of projectiles, military chemists and physicists jointly concluded that the future delivery system for mustard gas should be the aerial bomb. Given the minimal bomb load of contemporary aircraft this offered few advantages if any. Whilst it is true that the cases of aerial bombs need only be of thin sheet metal rather than the heavy castings required for artillery shell, thus producing a greatly improved ratio of filling to gross weight, the actual weight of gas that a flight of aircraft could carry was infinitesimal compared with the weight that might be discharged by a full artillery bombardment. The overriding advantages of the bomber aircraft over artillery were range and target selectivity but these were of little tactical or strategic value while bomb loads remained so severely limited. And, of course, the terminal results achieved by bombs were much the same as those of artillery shells – craters full of undispersed gas that could easily be avoided by an alert enemy. The first real breakthrough in the use of mustard gas, and the events which gave rise to widespread public fear and abhorrence of chemical warfare in the 1930s and induced such paranoia at the start of the Second World War, occurred during the Italian campaign in Ethiopia in 1935–6 and is described in the next chapter.

Counter-battery Gas Assault

By the summer of 1917, just months before the introduction of mustard gas, German and Allied tactics in the use of gas as an artillery weapon were approaching maturity. It was at last realized that mass attack was hazardous, expensive and largely fruitless but that carefully targeted counter-battery shoots immediately prior to and in support of infantry assaults could be highly effective. Counter-battery gas attacks like those used by the British at the Battle of Messines in June 1917, when 2,230 guns and howitzers firing mainly phosgene and irritant agent shells maintained a continuous thirty-minute barrage against the German gun positions, could largely neutralize the German offensive barrage leaving the way clear for advancing Allied infantry. The value of point bombardment with phosgene, and later mustard gas, was that a sufficient volume of gas could be laid to overwhelm the enemy gunners. Whilst it was necessary that fire should be reasonably concentrated upon the enemy batteries the same degree of pinpoint accuracy that was required for a direct hit with high explosives – and which was rarely achieved – was not necessarily needed due to the area effects of gas. The Germans adopted a similar technique but, despite their early advantages with mustard gas, were unable to maintain the intensity of attack as their initial stockpile was rapidly exhausted. Increasing pressure upon the German chemical industry, largely starved of raw materials, meant that her reserves of mustard gas could not be replenished until the spring of 1918. By that time the new British and French factories were in full production and supplies of mustard gas to the Allies thereafter continued to outstrip those of Germany which continued inexorably to diminish.

Mustard Gas in the Defensive and Offensive Role

Gas, as we have seen, was introduced primarily as a means of mobilizing a static battlefield, a role in which it largely failed. Until the introduction of mustard gas during the closing stages of the War, the low toxicity of the chemicals currently available, which required huge concentrations to be effective, and their unpredictable behaviour due to uncontrollable climatic conditions, imposed logistical and tactical burdens that prevented them from replacing or approaching equality with conventional weapons. Mustard gas had the potential to revolutionize this situation although it never did.

By the early part of 1918 a solid tactical policy existed within the German command for the offensive use of mustard gas. The enemy sector to be attacked would first be subjected to prolonged frontal bombardment with a mixed fire of non-persistent irritant and respiratory casualty chemical weapons including phosgene, bromobenzyl cyanide and a range of sternutators or 'sneezing gases'. This preliminary bombardment was intended to break up defending infantry formations, disable them where possible, disorientate them, reduce their moral and force them into respirators and all the other restrictive anti-gas paraphernalia. The use of non-persistent gas at this juncture was important because the region under attack would soon be overrun by German troops, by which time the chemical agents would have to have done their business and dispersed.

Simultaneously, concentrations of enemy troops and materiel on the flanks of the target sector would be heavily bombarded with highly persistent mustard gas in order to thoroughly contaminate men, machinery, material and equipment, clothing, boots and medical facilities that might otherwise be available for reserves. Even if no casualties were caused, the dislocation created by the task of decontamination would render the reserves useless. Other unoccupied flanks, particularly high ground that might later be used defensively by the enemy or through which a retreat might be routed, would be similarly contaminated in order to militarily sterilize it. The attack against the thoroughly weakened and demoralized enemy would then be pressed home using conventional weaponry. The finest example of this textbook policy occurred at the start of the German Somme offensive in March 1918, when for twelve days prior to the battle some 500,000 gas shells were fired into the Allied lines to contaminate and demoralize, followed by a further 2,000,000 shells during the battle proper.

A major limitation of this theoretically attractive tactic, however, was that the primary bombardment of the front lines with non-persistent chemicals was a clear indication of German intent. The immediate Allied response should have been to withdraw infantry from the front and lay a deep barrage of mustard gas over the same area, thus contaminating the ground and forming a chemical barrier which advancing German infantry would have to cross. Unfortunately the Allies were never fully able to implement such countermeasures, partly because there was never enough mustard gas available to achieve the required saturation and also because mustard gas, although being vastly more toxic than its chemical predecessors, was simply not a sufficiently powerful vesicant to form an impassable barrier of toxicity. Similar considerations limited the effectiveness of the German chemical offensives. Shortages of supplies made field commanders reluctant to waste ammunition on the contamination of unoccupied land where, whilst there might be future benefits, there seemed little immediate military advantage to be gained.

What became clear was that mustard gas, whatever the original intention of those who developed it for the battlefield, was essentially a defensive weapon or more precisely a weapon of area denial and territorial defence. In the offensive its action was too slow, it did not stop soldiers in their track but rather disabled them some hours or days later. What its proponents wanted but did not achieve was a cutaneous weapon of instant effect like the nerve gases of subsequent decades. Ultimately mustard gas, like its predecessors, did not help mobilize a static war but rather, if anything, once again bogged down a war that had, by the latter part of 1918, just shown the first shoots of mobility.

Casualties

The ability of the relatively simple chemical agents used during the First World War to cause casualties depended to a great extent upon three factors: surprise, ease of detectability, and the effectiveness of protective counter-measures. The element of surprise was largely lost after the first use of each agent because thereafter its use was expected even if it was not actually employed. Expectation of attack was a weapon in itself because it kept entire formations both on the front and in the rear support trenches perpetually in gas masks and other protective gear which severely hampered their efficiency as fighting units. Had the two major belligerents not been technologically and industrially equal this would have been of enormous advantage but, on the Western Front at least, there was a fine balance and the biter could easily become the bit. With both sides encumbered with respirators and gas capes, the front in 1918 degenerated once again to the stalemate that existed in 1914. Most agents used in large quantities were easily detected due to either their obvious physical attributes – massive green clouds in the case of chlorine – or to their pungent odour. Soldiers soon became aware that the absence of heavy high-explosive detonations after taking incoming fire was a likely indication that they were under bombardment with chemical weapons. The advantage, then, lay with the side that could most adequately protect its men and that, on balance, was held by the Allies.

Development of Gas Masks

The history of chemical warfare has been very much that of a contest between rival scientists who play with men for pieces. The object of the game has been to leapfrog the opponent in terms of scientific innovation but it is an inescapable characteristic of scientific progress that there can be no end-game to this process. No sooner are new substances introduced to the chemical battlefield than similarly clever contrivances are developed to counter or neutralize their effects. It is within the short interregnum between effect and counter-effect that casualties are caused.

The first chemical weapons, chlorine and phosgene, primarily affected the lungs, so if these were protected, men under attack were theoretically safe. By 23 April 1915, just one day after the first German discharge of chlorine, the first Allied countermeasures were in place. Buckets of sodium bicarbonate were rushed to the front and troops there were ordered to soak rags in this solution and hold them to their faces to filter out the chlorine. By 28 April captured German respirators had been hurriedly analysed and copies were already being made by countless housewives peddling furiously at their treadle sewing machines throughout Britain. Because of the hurried rate of manufacture and the inexperience of the workers, many of these early copies were sub-standard. Officers were soon loath to issue them and soldiers at the front had little confidence in them.

Meanwhile, a purely British design was under development and on 15 May, the War Office 'Black Veil' respirator was issued for use. It was a primitive but cheap affair, consisting of a long length of black veiling material into which was sewn a pocket to contain cotton-waste wadding soaked in a mixture of sodium thiosulphate and sodium bicarbonate. Glycerol was added to the mixture to render it more adhesive. The veil was simply wrapped around the head with the wadding over the nose and mouth. Although better than nothing the Black Veil provided a poor seal between face and filter and was regarded only as an interim solution.

The next Allied development was the 'Hypo Helmet', 2,500,000 of which were manufactured by the end of June 1915. The helmet consisted of a heavy flannel bag soaked in a similar bicarbonate and thiosulphate solution to that used in the Black Veil. It covered the entire head and could be tucked firmly into the collar to form a reasonably adequate seal. Two small cellulose eyepieces, supposedly transparent but in fact barely translucent, were attached to the front. Whilst the Hypo Helmet might be regarded as a victory for the Allies over chlorine, the eyepieces undoubtedly represented a minor victory for the Germans. Inside the helmets, barely able to discern night from day and with moving objects flitting across the field of view like grotesque shadows through the celluloid eyepieces, infantrymen had the sensation of being deprived of all sensation and blundered about the battlefield like zombies.

The Germans quickly discerned a weakness in the Hypo Helmet. Because it was not a tight fit against the face a volume of respiratory air was trapped inside it and it was this fact that was very effectively exploited. German artillerymen intermixed a proportion of chloro-formate tear gas shells amongst the chlorine, and the tear gas accumu-lated inside the hood, attacking the eyes causing extreme pain and irritation. Desperately seeking relief Allied soldiers tore off their helmets only to be struck down by the far more lethal clouds of gas that surrounded them. To counter this the Hypo Helmet was modified by the addition of tight-fitting goggles which protected the eyes well enough but rather accentuated the perception of sensory isolation.

During the summer of 1915 German and Allied chemical weapons policies began to diverge. Intent upon breaking the British gas mask, Germany investigated alternative agents that could not be neutralized by contemporary bicarbonate and hypochlorite respirator fillings. Simultaneously they rather neglected to develop their own respirator designs, a fact not overlooked by Allied intelligence. So, while German policy leaned towards the discovery of more lethal, respirator-breaking chemical agents, Allied policy was to develop tactics that involved larger and more prolonged bombardments of conventional gases in order to overwhelm the capacity of the inadequate German gas masks. The German solution was phosgene and, to a lesser extent, the use of cyanide-filled projectiles. Cyanide, because of its simple and stable chemical structure and low molecular weight, was a particularly effective mask breaker. As we have seen in the Introduction, however, cyanide possessed too many negative factors to make it a viable large-scale battlefield weapon.

It was unfortunate for Germany that just as she was considering the use of phosgene to overcome French and British masks, Britain was also experimenting with the same chemical agent. Before the Allies could introduce phosgene, however, it was necessary to develop a respirator that was proof against it to prevent Allied troops succumbing to their own toxins. Thus, almost by accident, by the winter of 1915 the Allies had designed, manufactured and issued over 9,000,000 new pattern respirators just in time to counter the first German phosgene attack in December. The new respirator, designated the 'P Helmet', was a modification of the earlier Hypo Helmet in which the flannel was replaced by an alkali-resistant material which was additionally impregnated with caustic soda and phenol. The addition of an external exhaust tube and valve improved the gas tightness of the helmet, but even then it was only barely adequate. Acting upon a Russian suggestion the chemical impregnation of the hood was supplemented with hexamethylene tetramine which marginally improved its effectiveness against phosgene. This latest incarnation, designated the 'P H Hood' ('H' for hexamethylene), entered service in mid-January 1916 and remained nominally in service until February 1918, although in practice it was quickly superseded.

It was soon apparent that German artillery was able to lay concentrations of phosgene sufficient to overwhelm the limited effectiveness of the P H Hood. What was required was a much larger quantity of sorbents than could be soaked into a textile hood in order that the wearer could remain active for long periods before the anti-gas agents were exhausted. From this requirement was born the 'Large Box Respirator'. Development of the Large Box Respirator marked a significant advance in respirator design for, although it had drawbacks, it allowed the user to carry a substantial supply of gas absorbent and neutralizing material, and also allowed for easy adaptation to meet previously unknown threats. The Large Box Respirator consisted of a reasonably close-fitting face-piece connected by means of a long flexible tube to a separate satchel, carried on the back, which contained the active chemical absorbents. The very large quantity of agent that could be contained in the satchel filter unit meant that the user could remain on duty for prolonged periods, enabling him to sit out safely prolonged chemical bombardment. Because the reagents in the filter pack were in powder form it was easy to add additional chemicals to cope with new German offensive agents. The most important of the new filter materials was activated animal charcoal (later coconut charcoal) which absorbed very effectively most of the toxic agents that could not be neutralized by existing filter materials. The disadvantage of the Large Box Respirator is implied by its name – it was *large*. The bulky haversack strapped to the soldier's back was a further burden to carry and an awkward impediment, particularly in confined trenches.

Within four months the Large Box Respirator had been largely replaced by a smaller, more efficient successor, named, with astonishing War Office logic, the 'Small Box Respirator'. With a more efficient mix of reagents and a higher proportion of charcoal than the previous model, the Small Box could efficiently dispose of virtually all the German toxic gases, posing a real threat to the balance of chemical superiority. The secret lay in the high proportion of charcoal which simply absorbed both diphosgene and chloropicrin, the most difficult of the German gases to deal with by chemical neutralization on account of their relatively inert chemical characteristics. Diphosgene had first been used by the Germans at Verdun in the summer of 1916 specifically to defeat the French XTX respirator which did not contain activated charcoal.

Germany, meanwhile, rather neglected respirator development while concentrating her effort on new toxins, arguably because she was confident that Britain did not possess the scientific resources to develop new weapons or the industrial resources to produce overwhelmingly large quantities of the existing types of chemical weapons. The immediate advantages of the British box type respirator were noticed, however, particularly the close-fitting mouthpiece and the increased capacity of the separate reagent container. The only real advance in German respirator design was an attempted compromise that did not really work. Rather than utilize a separate filter haversack the German design incorporated the filter chemicals in a canister mounted on the front of a rubberized face-piece, the intention being to avoid the inconvenience of a large backpack. The design was flawed in two important respects: the front mounted canisters were too heavy and tended to pull the mask away from the wearer's face, particularly under exertion; and, due to technical limitations, the canister, whilst an improvement over existing hood helmets, could not hold sufficient reagents to match the performance of the British box respirator.

Deficiencies in the German respirator enhanced the tactical advantage maintained by the British box respirators, an advantage that was maintained until the summer of 1917 when Germany introduced mustard gas. The simple consequence of the disparity between German and British respirators was that Allied soldiers could last out longer on the battlefield and this advantage allowed for great tactical flexibility.

Using high-accuracy, high-concentration weapons like the Livens Projector, Allied chemical weapons batteries could quickly saturate German respirators in a very short time. Later, however, Allied field commanders realized that high-density fire, which was a relatively expensive option, the success of which depended upon a number of factors beyond their immediate control, was not necessary. Equally effective results could be obtained by means of a prolonged low rate of fire so long as it was sustained. Under this type of attack, which was ideally undertaken by the Stokes Mortar, German soldiers were compelled to remain for long periods in their masks which soon became swamped.

Mustard Gas and the 'Blue Cross' Sternutators

Mustard gas completely wiped out the Allied lead in respirator design and once again changed the balance of chemical warfare. Because it was a vesicant agent, attacking the skin – particularly moist areas of flesh – rather than just the lungs, it more or less rendered gas masks irrelevant. Although the eyes, nose and mouth were very vulnerable to the effects of mustard gas, the inefficient methods of dissemination that dogged mustard gas throughout the First World War meant that concentrations of the vapour that were likely to do lasting damage to areas of the body some feet above ground level were rarely achieved. Where respirators were worn they might be of benefit as a shield but the effect was marginal. Mustard gas had a marked propensity to be absorbed by most materials, including battledress textiles and boot leather, and it was that characteristic that made it such an eminent area contamination weapon. There is little doubt, however, that mustard gas was originally introduced by the Germans as an offensive rather than a defensive weapon and that it was expected, before the limitations of contemporary dissemination systems became manifest, that the eyes and mouth would be its prime targets.

It was for this reason that Germany introduced mustard gas and the so-called 'Blue Cross' arsenical sternutatory agents simultaneously in July 1917. The sternutories, or 'sneezing agents', are little-known chemical weapons which, although they had great potential, were never used to full effect by the Germans. Diphenylcyanoarsine (DA) and diphenylchloroarsine (DC), the principal German sternutories, were officially classified as irritant agents, but such a nomenclature underestimates their awfulness as they induced intense pain and hysterical distress in the unfortunate victim. Unlike mustard gas, phosgene and the whole pharmacopeia of chemicals hitherto used in war, the arsenical sternutories were not gases or vapours but took instead the form of microscopically small grains of powder which were unaffected by the reagents in respirator filters and thus passed straight through.

The classic reaction to DA or DC exposure was to rip of the gas mask and, in a wild panic, to take great gulps of air. This suited the German battle plan perfectly for, from the very first mustard gas engagement, mustard gas was mixed with a small proportion of sternutatory shell fire. Exposed to the so-called 'sneezing gas' British troops tore off their respirators and, unknown to them because it was almost imperceptible, filled their lungs with mustard gas. In the first instance this would go unnoticed because many hours would elapse before the mustard gas took effect.

Whilst the theory was highly attractive the practical results were rather less satisfactory, due in part to the inadequate dissemination of mustard, as we have seen above, but mainly because the Allies had quite unknowingly already taken countermeasures. Although both Britain and the United States had independently yet simultaneously developed their own sturnutator, 10-chloro-5,10-dihydrophenarsazine, they were totally unaware of German developments in the same field despite the fact that a patent had been granted in Germany for a similar agent in 1914. In the United States the substance was named 'Adamsite' after Major Roger Adams who led the team that developed it at Illinois University in the early months of 1918. Oblivious to German interest in arsenicals, the Allies took no active countermeasures but, as a result of a coincidence similar to that which saved them from the worst of phosgene in 1915, they unwittingly developed an improvement to the box respirators that effectively countered them. Britain's good luck hinged upon the introduction of stannic chloride smoke, developed purely as a concealing smoke to visually obliterate from enemy view advancing Allied troops. Whilst not a war poison *per se*, stannic chloride produced nasty side effects if inhaled. Like the German arsenical sternutators, stannic chloride is a particulate substance and, in order to protect Allied soldiers, an additional layer of cellulose wadding was added to the box respirator filter packs to trap the particles. Quite inadvertently at first, the wadding also provided almost complete protection against the German sternutators.

Dealing with the vesicant effects of mustard gas, which seemed superficially a simple problem to resolve, in fact remained an intractable difficulty throughout the First World War. For a defending army the problem with mustard gas was its startling ability to permeate most materials including the leather uppers, if not the soles, of standard-issue army boots. It readily soaks through many layers of textile clothing and is easily absorbed by canvas and wood, rendering subsequent decontamination extraordinarily difficult and time consuming. Throughout the latter stages of the First World War, when mustard gas dominated the battlefield, there was little protection against its effects if applied in a concentrated fashion.

Three options were available: physical protection by means of impermeable clothing; protection of exposed skin by barrier creams; and post-attack decontamination. All were tried but none were particularly effective. The only impervious textile available was rubberized oilcloth which was too stiff, heavy and unwieldy for general use. Special oilcloth capes together with suits and leather gloves impregnated with linseed oil were provided for key personnel such as machine gunners but were not popular. Whilst the material effectively kept mustard gas out it was equally effective at blocking all ventilation, keeping vapour and bodily moisture in, and thus became suffocatingly claustrophobic after just a short period of use. Also, the capacious, airtight folds of the gas capes acted as gigantic bellows which tended to suck up vapour from ground contaminated with mustard gas that would otherwise have remained relatively inert.

Barrier cream was equally ineffective. The creams were not well formulated and, even under ideal conditions, would have offered only moderate protection. With insufficient training in the filth of the trenches it was inevitable that the creams would not be applied properly and those which did were soon rubbed off again. Least successful of all was decontamination which failed on two major counts. Theoretically, decontamination by the application of bleaching powder or permanganate to the affected areas should have been outstandingly effective, for both these agents almost instantaneously oxidize mustard gas to simple, inert compounds. Decontamination, however, failed utterly due to the insidious nature of mustard gas. Soldiers in the heat of battle were more often than not unaware that they had been contaminated; there was no immediate sensation and many hours or even days passed before the first symptoms appeared, by which time the opportunity for decontamination was long passed. The second shortcoming of decontamination, which applied to some extent to the use of barrier creams and, indeed, to protective measures in general, was that it loaded a further logistical burden upon the soldiery. Boxes of powder and cans of cream had to be carried wherever one went and, of course, in the heat of battle were the first things to be discarded when the choice was between them or extra ammunition.

Much of the defensive research undertaken at the Porton Down Chemical Research Establishment, of which we shall hear much more later, was concerned with mass protection rather than the safety of individual soldiers, and in this field success was more marked. A particular Porton success was the inclined anti-gas curtain which was used to segregate the trenches into gas-proof zones. These consisted of simple oilcloth sheets which could be quickly rolled down an inclined frame and sealed at the edges to form an airtight barrier. Similar gas curtains later became a common feature of most military and public buildings and air-raid shelters throughout the Second World War. More complex contrivances, like electrically driven fans to forcibly clear gas out of the trenches, were proposed but soon abandoned. There were a few other minor achievements particularly in the protection of beast and fowl. The Porton laboratories designed, for example, moderately effective respirators for horses and mules and, most successful of all, a very effective gas-proof cowl for crates of messenger pigeons.

Casualty Statistics

Although statistics of casualties for all wars, and for the First World War in particular, must be viewed with the greatest circumspection, there are obvious conclusions that can be drawn in relation to chemical weapons, even allowing for formidable inaccuracies and the haziest of estimates.

Table 1 clearly indicates the value of a new 'surprise' weapon when first used, but also shows the effectiveness of even the most minimal countermeasures. Despite the manifold increase in the volume of chlorine released against troops during the latter part of 1915 and early 1916, the number of casualties reported shows a decline of almost 60 per cent, while the casualty rate declined even more markedly. The relatively high ratio of fatalities to casualties amongst victims exposed to chlorine, even in the latter period, illustrates its potent toxicity under advantageous conditions and the perils of not taking precautions against it.

The figures for mustard gas, which show a huge number of casualties but relatively few fatalities, reinforces the view that it was very much a 'nuisance' weapon while shackled to the limitations of artillery delivery.

It is evident from Table 2 that, despite the popular conception of chemical weapons as the great horror of the First World War, and the continued abhorrence of chemical warfare perpetuated by the media and antipathetic pressure groups, such weapons were responsible for an insignificant proportion of the death toll of the First World War. For every man killed by chemical weapons of all types, 3,500 died as a result of artillery or small-arms fire, yet, while chemical weapons are

Table 1   Ratio of CW fatalities to total CW casualties

Period	Prime weapon	Casualties	Fatalities	Ratio (%)
1915	First chlorine attacks	10,000	3,000	30
1915–16	Chlorine in ascendance	4,207	1,013	24
1916–17	Diphosgene rising	8,806	532	6
From July 1917	Diphosgene in ascendance	18,134	1,859	10
	Mustard Gas	124,707	2,308	1.85

36

Table 2 CW casualties as a proportion of all battle casualties

Period	Total fatalities	Total CW fatalities
1915	304,406	3,007
1916	636,146	1,123
1917	727,022	1,796
1918	768,603	2,673

Table 3 Relative casualty rates of CW and conventional weapons for all combatants during the First World War

Agency	Total quantity	Casualties caused	Casualties per ton (CW)
Small Arms	50,000,000,000	10,000,000	
High Explosives	2,000,000 tons	10,000,000	5.0
Sternutators	6,000 tons	20,000	3.3
Lung irritant	90,000 tons	880,000	9.8
Mustard Gas	11,000 tons	400,000	36.4

Table 4 Quantities of chemical weapons expended in 1915–1918

Country	Total number of artillery rounds	Number of chemical rounds	Tonnage of chemicals fired by artillery	Total chemical tonnage inc. cylinder
Germany	485,000,000	33,000,000	48,200	52,000
British Empire	178,000,000	4,000,000	9,100	14,000
France	334,000,000	16,000,000	23,600	26,000
Others	392,000,000	13,000,000	17,300	20,000

universally vilified, to rip a man's body apart with bullets, explosives and shards of jagged iron is accepted with equanimity, and has achieved the status of an internationally ethical form of killing.

Fritz Haber – a Postscript

In 1914 Haber was under consideration for the Nobel Prize in chemistry but the War put a temporary end to this and it was not until 1918, under very different circumstances, that his name was once again put forward. At that time this was a contentious choice – Haber was one of the most reviled men in Europe and it seemed for a while that the man proposed as a Nobel laureate might simultaneously be indicted as a war criminal. The debate over the wisdom of Haber's nomination delayed the deliberations of the Nobel committee but in 1919 Haber was, in the face of much opposition, awarded the prize in chemistry 'for the synthesis of Ammonia from its elements'. Two years earlier, in October 1917, Fritz Haber had married Charlotte Nathan, the young woman, hardly half his age, with whom he had been intimately involved at the time of Clara Immerwhar's suicide. The marriage ended in acrimony ten years later.

In the years that followed Haber and his institute became involved in a number of controversial research and development programmes. Still dedicated to the German cause and a resolute patriot, Haber proposed in 1919, when the Allies were demanding war reparations equivalent to some 50,000 tons of gold, that this could be extracted from sea water along the German coast. Some years earlier the Swedish Nobel Laureate, Svante August Arrhenius, had estimated that all the oceans of the world contained some 8,000,000,000 tons of gold and Haber was confident in his ability to recover 50,000 tons of this for the benefit of the German state. Research continued for many years and pilot extraction plants were built, but the results were consistently disappointing. A reassessment of Arrhenius's original work showed that his samples were contaminated with minute quantities of gold from the laboratory reaction vessels he used and that the true gold content of sea water was actually less than 0.001 mg per ton, rather than the 5 mg estimated by Arrhenius. As a result of these findings the project was finally abandoned in 1928.

Meanwhile, in the early 1920s, Haber's institute was also working on the development of commercial insecticides and pesticides on behalf of I. G. Farben. Their most successful early development was a cyanide-based product bearing the trade-name Zyclon 'B', which was a mixture of cyanide combined with a stabilizer, a blue dye and a powerful warning odorant. Due to the high toxicity of the cyanide content the odorant was a statutory safety requirement insisted upon by the German government. Zyclon 'B' was manufactured under licence by two German companies, Degesch and Testa (Tesch and Stabenow) and shortly after the start of the Second World War both companies supplied their products to the German government for the control of lice and fleas in the concentration camps. In January 1940 the Nazis, by way of experiment, tested the efficacy of Zyclon 'B' on human subjects by gassing approximately 250 gypsy children at the Buchenwald concentration camp. Later, in September 1941, the experiments were repeated on a larger scale at Auschwitz. Thereafter orders were placed for much larger quantities of Zyclon 'B' with the warning agent removed; millions were subsequently to die by its action. After the War, two directors of Testa were tried by a British military court and executed for their part in supplying the chemical. Ironically, amongst the victims of Zyklon 'B' in the gas chambers of Auschwitz were several members of Haber's own family, including two whole generations, the children and grandchildren of his two sisters.

During the early decades of the twentieth century Western industrialists looked to the East to expand their markets. China, with her legendary isolationism, enormous, impoverished population and deeply entrenched traditions, was slow to develop and proved a difficult market to penetrate, but Japan was a radically different proposition. With a rapidly growing industrial base Japan was a magnet to speculative Western manufacturers who were quick to set up marketing agencies and, later, factories there. Amongst the first oriental pioneers were the chemical industries hawking fertilizers, alkalis and explosives, so it is no surprise to learn that by 1930 I.G. Farben had a strong foothold in Japan and that Fritz Haber was amongst its representatives who visited the country to extol the benefits of potential trading links with Germany. Haber's interest, however, went deeper than trade – he discerned a powerful commonality of interest between the two countries and used such influence as he could bring to bear in order to foster lasting cultural links between them. This culminated, in 1930, in the foundation of the Japan Institute, established to promote mutual understanding between the two countries, with headquarters in Berlin and Tokyo.

Within three years, however, and despite the nihilistic self-destruction of his reputation in the single-minded, forty-year patriotic pursuit of German nationalist supremacy, he had, in an astonishing volte-face, abandoned his homeland and transferred his allegiance to Great Britain and to the University of Cambridge. In 1933, in response to increased Nazi persecution of his Jewish colleagues, and despite the fact that thirty years previously he had renounced their faith in favour of personal advancement, he left Germany for ever. Less than a year later, ill, and seeking respite from the English winter, he died of a heart attack at Basel on 29 January 1934. The spectre of premature death hung heavily over the Habers. In 1946 his eldest son, Hermann, who had witnessed the suicide of his mother Clara thirty-one years earlier, and with his own will to live broken by the premature death of his wife from leukaemia, shot himself. Distraught, his eldest daughter took her own life also.

Chapter 2

The Interwar Years – Ethiopia and China

Contrary to the currently held common perception of public attitude to chemical warfare in the immediate aftermath of the First World War, there seems to have been little immediate public outcry against it or official moves to ban its future use following the armistice. Acceptance of gas warfare had crept insidiously beyond the pale of hollow moral indignation and, reflecting the hardened attitudes engendered by four years of increasingly brutal warfare, had become accepted as just another weapon in the arsenals of all the great and less great but aspiring nations of the world.

Mustard gas and other chemical weapons of both Russian and British origin were widely used during the Russian Civil War between 1919 and 1921. Gas was employed by General Deniken against Red Army forces in the forests around Archangel in 1919 and the Reds were reportedly preparing cylinder emplacements – using gas captured from the Germans during the earlier conflict – near Kakhova in the spring of 1920. Meanwhile the RAF was, with apparent impunity, utilizing mustard gas bombs in border control operations in the Middle East and along the North-West Frontier throughout the 1920s. These operations raised little international criticism and when queried the British government replied that, for example, at Datta Khel in Waziristan it was feared that White Russian gas might have fallen into the hands of dissidents there. There is evidence, too, that both Spain and France deployed mustard gas in Morocco. Although later denied by the French authorities it was widely believed that France had used gas around Fez in the summer of 1925 and there were somewhat more sustainable allegations of mustard gas bombs having been used by Spain against the Riffs earlier in the spring. It is also believed that chemical weapons used by Manchurian government forces were decisive in the defeat of Chinese insurgents led by Wu Pei-fu and Feng Yu-hsiang in the early 1930s. It is important to note that in all these operations poison gas was used successfully only against those opponents, ill-equipped insurgents and guerrillas, who had no means of protection and who were the only class of combatant against which it had any hope of success.

Two further interwar instances of chemical warfare were very different in character and deserve special attention. The first of these, the use of mustard gas and other chemicals by the Italian Army against Ethiopian troops in 1935–6, is interesting in that it illustrated the effectiveness against unprotected infantry concentrations of massive deployments of mustard gas sprayed from aircraft. The novel use of aircraft sprays by the Italians, the first large-scale use of chemical weaponry in this form, raised the spectre of terror attacks against civilian populations and thereby stirred public anxiety and roused, somewhat belatedly, the League of Nations into debating the future prohibition of chemical and biological weapons. The second major instance of use in the late 1930s was the use of a wide range of toxic chemicals including, inter alia, mustard gas, lewisite, chloropicrin, phosgene, diphosgene and hydrogen cyanide, by Japan against Chinese troops and civilians between July 1937 and May 1945. The noteworthy feature of the Japanese deployments is the precision with which they were undertaken and the fact that, based upon experiences in China, the Japanese Inspectorate of Military Education subsequently issued a series of pamphlets entitled *Lessons From the China Incident*, which include detailed appreciations of specific chemical weapons engagements.

Italian Action in Ethiopia – 1935 to 1936

Ethiopia's problems with the Italian government arose following the completion of the Suez Canal in 1869. The canal was of immense economic and strategic importance to countries bounding the Red Sea and immediately after the opening of the waterway all the major European powers took steps to consolidate their interests in the area. By the end of 1869 Britain and France had established themselves in Somaliland around the Bay of Assab and then, by agreement with Emperor Johannes IV, in 1885 occupied Massawa. Meanwhile, Italy advanced into the interior of the country.

European advancement into Ethiopia was aided by the continuing internal power struggle amongst rival tribal groups in the region which, inevitably, were turned to the colonial advantage of one or other Western power. Emperor Johannes IV of Ethiopia came to power in 1872 but his regime was under constant threat from Menelik, the dispossessed King of Shoa. Other threats to Johannes' power came from the Egyptians who threatened encroachment upon Ethiopia's northern plateau and from the Sudanese Mahdists in the west of the country. During the late 1880s Menelik regained much of his lost territories in Shoa, aided considerably by arms supplied by Italy. Johannes IV was killed at the Battle of Mettama in March 1889 in an action to stem the Muslim advance, and eight months later, on 6 November 1889, Menelik was crowned King of all Ethiopia. Meanwhile, under cover of the internal, factional power struggle, Italian troops occupied the territories of Kerin and Asmara and, in January 1890, proclaimed the Italian colony of Eritrea.

Disagreements over a vague and ambiguous treaty of co-operation between Menelik and the Italian government, ratified in May 1889, culminated in a land war between the two nations. Italian forces under General Oreste Baratieri were soundly defeated in February 1896, and in October a new treaty was signed that recognized Ethiopian independence. Internal conflicts continued throughout the final decade of the nineteenth century but were gradually resolved. Meanwhile, Menelik's skilful international diplomacy over a period of fifteen years up to 1908 resulted in a series of highly satisfactory treaties fixing Ethiopia's boundaries with the surrounding colonial lands of the Western powers.

The first signs of future troubles arose with the succession of Lij Yasu following the death of Menelik in 1913. Lij Yasu's sympathy at the start of the First World War with the Muslims and with the Central Powers allied with Turkey was viewed with alarm both within Ethiopia and by the Western allies. A revolutionary movement headed by Ethiopia's leading tribal chiefs and by the Christian Church in Ethiopia overthrew Lij Yasu and proclaimed Zauditu, daughter of Menelik, as Empress, with Haile Selassie as heir apparent. By the latter part of 1924 Selassie had brought internal peace to Ethiopia and was engaged on an extensive goodwill tour of Europe, Egypt and Palestine that did much to enhance his country's standing in the world. In the background, however, high-handed international diplomacy was conspiring to disrupt Ethiopian stability. A convoluted Anglo-Italian agreement of December 1925 placed western Ethiopia firmly within the Italian sphere of economic influence in return for which the United Kingdom demanded that Italy should use her dominant diplomatic position in the region to compel Ethiopia to construct a dam at Lake Taha in order to regulate the supply to Egypt and the Sudan. Appalled at this cavalier attitude to her national sovereignty, Ethiopia appealed to the League of Nations. To defuse the situation British pressure for the Taha dam was withdrawn and a treaty of friendship and arbitration agreed between Italy and Ethiopia. This treaty also included certain concessions regarding the free port of Assab in Eritrea and a road linking the port with Dessie in the Ethiopian interior.

Empress Zauditu died in 1930 and in November of that year Haile Selassie succeeded as Emperor. Relations with Italy, particularly concerning the Dessie road convention, immediately deteriorated while at the same time tension arose along Ethiopia's borders with Eritrea and Somaliland. An Anglo-Ethiopian Commission of Enquiry was set up to settle disputes regarding grazing rights and boundary demarcation at the point where Ethiopia met British and Italian Somalia, but while the commission met to resolve these differences there occurred a serious outbreak of violence near the armed Italian post at Walwal following long-running disputes about rights of access to wells there. At this stage Britain once again discreetly withdrew but Italy turned to military force. The Italian government demanded reparations which Ethiopia refused to accede to and instead appealed to the League of Nations to arbitrate. The League considered the case in September 1935, and concluded that neither party was to blame for initiating the conflict. Just a month later, on 3 October, in absolute and arrogant defiance of the League of Nations, Italy launched a full-scale assault from the frontiers of Eritrea and Italian Somaliland and within weeks was in occupation of Aduwa and Makale. The League immediately imposed economic sanctions against Italy but was unable to stop the fighting.

Although seemingly powerless to intervene, the international community took a keen interest in events in Ethiopia and, with military and political observers together with international Red Cross and ambulance units everywhere in the country, little that the Italians did went unnoticed. Unverified reports of the use of chlorine by Italian units appeared in the press during the second week of October 1935, less than ten days after fighting began. Some weeks later, towards the end of December, more reliable reports emerged that fleshed out the previously sketchy details of the Italian chemical weapons campaign. It appears that during the encirclement of Makele first tear gas and subsequently mustard gas bombs were deployed, the latter being described as 'torpedo shaped, about one metre long with a long nose that breaks off to release an inner container of 20 kilos of mustard gas'. Towards the end of the conflict, in the late spring of 1936, Haile Selassie escaped via Djibouti to Jerusalem and later made his way to Geneva where he made a personal appeal to the League of Nations. Explaining how Italy's initial assault using gas bombs was relatively ineffective, he went on to describe the later, devastating use of aircraft spray tanks by the Italian air force:

> Towards the end of 1935 Italian aircraft hurled upon my armies bombs of tear gas. Their effects were but slight. The soldiers learned to scatter. The Italian aircraft then resorted to mustard gas. Barrels of liquid were hurled upon armed groups, but this means also was ineffective. The liquid affected only a few soldiers, and barrels upon the ground were themselves a warning to troops and to the population of this danger.
>
> It was at this time when the operations for the encirclement of Makale were taking place that the Italian command followed the procedure which it is now my duty to denounce to the world. Special sprayers were installed on aircraft so that they could vaporize over vast areas of territory a fine death-dealing rain. Groups of nine, fifteen and eighteen aircraft followed one another so that the fog issuing from them formed a continuous cloud. It was thus that as from the end of January 1936 soldiers, women,

children, cattle, rivers, lakes and pastures were continually drenched with this deadly rain.

Soviet observers estimated that some 15,000 of the 50,000 Ethiopian casualties were caused by poison gas and further estimated that the Italians had expended over 700 tons of chemical weapons, 60 per cent of which were mustard gas. Italy initially denied that chemical weapons were being used but by the end of March, 1936 the evidence was irrefutable. Red Cross officials reported in excess of 100 casualties treated daily in the Korem, Alomata, Qubbo and Weldaya regions, all showing the characteristic lesions caused by mustard gas. It was confirmed that Korem was sprayed on four successive days during the first week of April in the manner described by Haile Selassie at Geneva and that many of the casualties were non-combatants. Faced with overwhelming evidence the Italian government admitted the use of gas but refuted suggestions that their actions were illegal, stating that 'as a reprisal against other illegal acts of war' their deployment did not contravene the Geneva Protocol. With an oblique reference to Britain's use of gas bombs in colonial policing operations on the North-West Frontier, and to the oft quoted references to her use of dum-dum bullets to stop ravaging natives who, fallacious common legend had it, could not be killed by ordinary bullets, Italy conjured up for international consumption images of Ethiopian soldiers as uncivilized savages who slaughtered or castrated prisoners. Ethiopians, they said, were guilty of 'torture and decapitation of prisoners; emasculation of the wounded and killed; savagery towards, and the killing of, non-combatants, the systematic use of dum-dum bullets'.

Ethiopian appeals to the League of Nations fell upon largely deaf ears despite the impassioned support of Britain's Foreign Secretary Sir Anthony Eden. Half-hearted requests were made that both sides of the conflict should observe the rules of war but the general international opinion, much biased by Italian propaganda, was that Ethiopia had been the author of her own downfall. Italy argued that the case put by the Ethiopian government was no more than a spurious attempt to rob her of her just fruits of victory, that the inhuman atrocities practiced by the Ethiopian army fully warranted chemical reprisals and that, anyway, many of the photographs of chemical injuries to Ethiopian troops produced as evidence to the League of Nations were, in fact, of self-inflicted gas casualties. In an attempt to discredit Eden's censures the Italian delegation to the League of Nations claimed that Ethiopia had purchased mustard gas bombs manufactured in British factories and, further, that the United Kingdom Board of Trade had issued export certificates for these bombs, thus colluding in Ethiopian chemical warfare activities.

Little was known at the time of the origin of Italy's chemical weaponry during the inter-war years, and even today details are sketchy. It is known that as a defensive response to the unrestricted use of poison gas during the First World War, a research and development programme was begun in Italy some time before the armistice and that this continued into the post-war years. By 1923 there was sufficient hardened military interest for the Army to establish a separate *Servizio Chimico Militaire*, with a *Centro Chimico Militaire* directly responsible to the Ministry of War, charged with co-ordinating chemical weapons research at a number of university laboratories.

All such claims of complicity against the United Kingdom were refuted and no concrete evidence was forthcoming. Prime Minister Stanley Baldwin completely refuted the allegations and went on, in April 1936, to condemn Italy's use of poison gas stating that:

> If these allegations are true – and I have every reason to believe that they are true – then the peril to the world I see is this: if a great European nation, in spite of having its signature to the Geneva Protocol against the use of such gases, employs them in Africa, what guarantee have we that they may not be used in Europe?

Similar anxieties stimulated across Europe and in the United States by events in Africa raised the profile of chemical warfare worldwide and soon its potentialities were being insidiously moulded by the vested interests of both government and industry. These developments will be discussed at greater depth later in this chapter but in the meantime we will examine the chemical warfare tactics employed by Italy during the Abyssinian campaign.

Italian Chemical Warfare Tactics

It has been suggested that mustard gas was deployed against the Ethiopian Army as a panic response by General Badoglio in the face of an imminent enemy incursion into Eritrea for which his forces were not fully prepared. In his memoirs, however, Badoglio insists that his army could have achieved an equally satisfactory outcome with the use of conventional weaponry and goes on to imply that the first use of chemical weapons, in the Tsakke Valley, was merely an experiment to test the effectiveness of gas against unprotected ethnic troops in the open.

Whatever their motivation, the initial Italian attempts at chemical warfare were not met with unqualified success, although certain lessons had been learned from the experiences of the First World War. The ineffectiveness of chemical artillery had already been accepted by the Italians and thus, from the very start of hostilities, the only means of dissemination employed was from the air, first by the use of aerial bombs, which proved disappointing, and later by means of aircraft spray tanks. We have noted already the comments of Haile Selassie to the League of Nations regarding his army's disdainful disregard of Italian mustard gas bombs; soldiers quickly realized that the bombs contaminated the ground within a 20 m radius of the point of impact and learned to simply avoid ground around bomb fragments, which were easily visible in the open terrain. Mustard gas bombs, like artillery shells, produced no appreciable aerosol effect so there was little risk of troops encountering unexpected clouds of drifting gas.

The Italians, quickly realizing the relative ineffectiveness of mustard gas bombs, immediately adopted a new tactic by fitting a small number of aircraft with spray tanks to disperse mustard gas in clouds above enemy troops. In the offensive role, just a few such aircraft flying parallel courses could easily saturate large enemy troop formations and huge tracts of land on all sides. Italian aircraft were capable of spraying many square miles of countryside with such speed and efficiency that Ethiopian soldiers, with little or no protective equipment and often barefooted, had no chance of escape and were compelled to retreat, with appalling consequences, over ground heavily contaminated with mustard gas. Evasive action against immediate attack was virtually impossible but, perhaps more sinisterly, aerial spraying gave no indication of previous contamination. On many occasions Ethiopian troops advanced unknowingly over land doused from the air in mustard gas hours or even days earlier but, because the symptoms of mustard gas do not appear until some hours after initial contact, they remained unaware of the traps they had fallen into until it was too late.

The Italians also deployed mustard gas with considerable effectiveness in a defensive role. Broad swathes of land on either side of the route of advancing Italian forces were repeatedly sprayed with mustard gas to protect the flanks of advancing columns, protect supply lines to the rear and prevent ambushes. This technique was of particular value in the highland regions where Ethiopian soldiers held the advantage of experience in mountain warfare. Liberal applications of mustard gas avoided the diversion of resources and the risks that would face inexperienced troops who would otherwise be required to picket the heights.

It was understood from the outset that, due essentially to its indiscriminate and delayed pathological effects, mustard gas would be unusable in close combat fighting and ineffective in stemming a concerted Ethiopian advance. The delayed effect, however, particularly when reinforced by persistent machine-gun fire and bombardment with high explosives, was a powerful psychological weapon that could fatally demoralize a retreating army and, as in the case of the repeated gassing of Korem, severely disable communications. Mustard gas was also used to great effect by spraying in the rear of Ethiopian forces, thereby disrupting and hindering the lines of supply.

The theoretical advantages of mustard gas as a territorial denial weapon had severe practical limitations. Spraying mountain tops or flanking ground to protect supply lines and deter ambush was all very well as long as the Ethiopians knew that the area was contaminated, but the delayed effect of mustard gas tended to negate its tactical value. Unknowingly occupying areas of contaminated ground from which to launch attacks, the Ethiopians might cause massive casualties upon their Italian enemies long before the symptoms of mustard gas poisoning appeared in their own ranks. As a purely tactical weapon, then, mustard gas was severely compromised, even against a technologically disadvantaged enemy. It worked effectively only if the enemy was aware of and intimidated by its power to harm and, secondly, only if they were aware of its deployment. If mustard gas is to be used successfully as an area denial weapon the attacking troops must be forced into awareness of the consequences of crossing the contaminated boundary. But this, due to the delayed effect of the gas, predicates a prolonged learning curve which the exigencies of war will often not allow. Once the lessons have been learned by the attacker it is necessary to ensure that he is aware, *or can be convinced into believing that,* contamination has actually taken place. Once this conditioned state of mind has been induced it is possible to play a prolonged game of Pavlovian cat-and-mouse. Soon the enemy will identify all small, low, slow-flying formations of aircraft as spray flights and will avoid those tracts of land beneath the flight path. The mere presence of the aircraft, whether loaded or not with toxic gas, will cast sufficient doubt in the minds of vulnerable ground force commanders. It is this scenario that, during the late 1930s, enabled many mustard gas protagonists and apologists to promote the use of poison gas as a humane form of warfare.

Aerial spraying of mustard gas was not wholly without risk to the attacker for, to be effective, the gas had to be released at an altitude of 300–500 feet. From greater heights the liquid particles were too finely divided and diluted to cause saturation, while at lower altitudes the risk was of wasteful and disastrously expensive over-saturation. At the optimum altitude for effective spraying, Italian aircraft were highly vulnerable to anti-aircraft fire. In a post-war assessment, probably biased in response to international criticism, General Badoglio asserted that chemical weapons were never intended to form a core element of the Italian arsenal but were employed progressively in the face of unexpectedly stiff Ethiopian resistance. Italy later claimed that with or without the use of chemical weapons the outcome of the war was never in doubt, but that 'the use of gas definitely shortened the war by nine months or perhaps more.'

The Sino-Japanese Conflict 1937–45

Italian chemical warfare activities in Ethiopia were not the only such events reported to the League of Nations in the late 1930s. Evidence of the deployment of chemical weapons against Chinese troops and civilians by the Japanese, gathered by Red Cross and League Health Organization observers, was presented to the League of Nations in October 1937, although the full extent of Japanese atrocities was not made clear until Soviet and American accounts filtered out towards the end of the Second World War. In July 1938 the initial Red Cross reports were substantiated by detailed accounts from a British surgeon at Nanchang General Hospital who described the injuries sustained by nineteen Chinese mustard gas casualties on the Yangtze front. The following month official Chinese government communiqués released to the world press told how two Chinese battalions in Juichang were wiped out in a massive Japanese gas assault. Throughout the period of conflict China cited 889 chemical warfare attacks perpetrated by Japanese troops against military and civilian personnel. Although many of the early events proved difficult to confirm, a major attack on the Yangtze front at Ichang in October 1941 was thoroughly examined by a team of United States investigators who subsequently verified 1,600 gas casualties of whom 600 were fatalities. Photographs of corpses showing classic symptoms of mustard gas exposure were released in Chunking in November 1941 and later published in the United States press. A post-war American military analysis of the Ichang incident describes it thus:

> In the Ichang action of October 1941 a heavy attack was launched by the Chinese to take the city and carry the heights beyond, where a defensive position could be organized. Chinese reinforcements had been moved into the area in late September and early October in preparation for the attack.
>
> The movement was observed by Japanese aircraft, so new defensive dispositions were made, but no sizeable Japanese reinforcements were moved up.
>
> Japanese artillery and mortar fire increased in intensity, and considerable amounts of tear gas and vomiting gas were reported to be mixed in with the H.E. firing. Between 5 and 8 October some additional mortar companies were reported and indications are that the bulk of the chemical munitions were fired by them. Harassing gases only were used prior to the Chinese attack which took place on 8 October.
>
> In the face of this heavy mortar and artillery fire of irritant agent and H.E. shell the Chinese re-occupied Ichang. Advancing further into the surrounding hills where the Japanese occupied a semi-circular ridge beyond the city, Chinese forces were heavily bombed and shelled with munitions containing a mustard/lewisite mixture, and suffered heavy casualties. The Japanese launched counter attacks from both flanks, great quantities of a persistent war gas were placed on the attackers and on the

low areas behind them. From 10 to 12 October aircraft dropped gas bombs all over the area.

The Chinese troops were either barefoot or wearing straw sandals, without gas masks or protective clothing, and they were severely gassed or burned. Their reserves were also gassed heavily and received many casualties, most of which proved fatal. Forced to abandon their attack the Chinese had to retreat through the low ground to avoid machine gun fire and thus crossed heavily concentrated gas barriers. Laboratory tests of samples of the gas and parts of shells and bombs showed the agent used to be a mixture of lewisite and mustard.

Against a similarly disadvantaged foe, the Japanese tactics show remarkable similarities to those employed by the Italians in Ethiopia. Whereas the Italians were more or less covert in their use of chemical weapons – at first denying their deployment, then justifying its use on the grounds of morality – the Japanese Army Inspectorate General of Military Education published accounts and appreciations of particular engagements in which chemical weapons had been deployed in the series of pamphlets entitled *Lessons From The China Incident,* already mentioned earlier in this chapter. It is worth noting, however, that the *Lessons* only refer to the use of harassing agents, the use of which the Japanese asserted did not contravene international convention or protocol. Japanese officers, interrogated in the course of post-war war-crimes investigations by the Russians and Americans, denied that casualty agents had been used although there is compelling evidence that such weapons had been deployed in considerable quantities. Nor were casualty agents used solely against Chinese troops, according to US investigators who discovered reliable evidence of atrocities in central Hopei where Japanese troops used gas to flush out or kill civilians who had taken refuge in caves. On 28 May 1942, in the village of Peihuan in Ting Hsien, some 300 Japanese soldiers surrounded a cavernous area in which they believed many Chinese were hiding. Gas was discharged into the tunnels, killing over 800 unarmed peasants.

Japanese chemical weapons research had been in hand since at least as early as the mid-1920s and by the mid-1930s the Chief of the Japanese Army General Staff authorized the transition from the experimental to operational level. Training in the use of chemical weapons began in 1934 and by the middle of the following year several industrial scale plants in Japan were producing mustard gas, lewisite and diphenylcyanoarsine, virtually all of which was filled into artillery shells, grenades, mortar rounds and pyrotechnic candles. Despite the highly successful and widely publicized use of aerial spraying by the Italians, Japan was slow to adopt this obviously superior mode of dissemination and relied, until very late in the war, solely upon ground weapons.

In October 1937 the Japanese chemical weapons service established research facilities in occupied Shanghai to investigate Chinese chemical weapons preparedness. Surprisingly, they found little or no evidence of chemical civil defence preparations nor of military passive defence measures. Upon the assumption that the first stage of research that would be undertaken by a nation contemplating arming itself with chemical weapons would be to investigate measures to protect itself from the effects of such weapons, the Japanese correctly concluded that China neither had chemical weapons of its own nor possessed the means of protecting itself from an aggressor so armed. Based upon this assumption deployment by the Japanese of chemical weapons, particularly lewisite and dichlorocyanoarsine, increased markedly through the winter of 1937/1938. Chinese troops remained devoid of protection until the United States entered the Pacific War after which limited numbers of American respirators were issued.

The repeated success of the early gas attacks against the ill-prepared Chinese Army greatly enhanced the kudos of the minority of chemical weapons protagonists in the Japanese military hierarchy and quickly led to their widespread acceptance throughout the Army where, as in Western Europe, there had previously been much reactionary scepticism. So universal was its acceptance that by the end of the war the Allies estimated that 25 per cent of all artillery shells fired by the Japanese were chemical filled and that, after a late embrace of aero-chemical warfare, some 30 per cent of aircraft munitions consisted of chemical bombs. Independent Soviet estimates concluded that in a number of pivotal battles up to one tenth of the casualties suffered by the Chinese were caused by chemical munitions.

Based upon interrogation of Japanese officers and evidence discovered in the *Lessons*, American intelligence staff put together an evaluation of the Japanese chemical weapons programme:

> Gas was said to have been employed in cases in which the Chinese were applying pressure at points where the Japanese wishes to conserve manpower. In general, large amounts were used on small fronts to support Japanese counter-attacks. The chemical operations were never widespread but, rather, were concentrated in certain areas and repeatedly used.
>
> In all those Chinese operations where gas was employed it was concentrated on the most important sections of the objective. Non-persistent gases were used on the offence and persistent ones on the defensive. Efforts were made to achieve surprise by firing chemical shells immediately after bombardment with high explosives, as well as by sudden gas attacks. Conventional smoke was used to hide gas clouds or to precede them.

Detailed contemporary accounts of certain Japanese offensive operations which included the use of chemical weapons appeared in the *Lessons*:

In the battle near Chu-Wuo waged by the 20th Division some 18,000 Special Smoke candles were accumulated for use over a length of 9 km in front of the enemy's strongly fortified positions. On 6th July 1939 we started screening by some 6,000–7,000 Special Smoke candles for about 5 km in front of the enemy's left wing. Under cover of this screen we were able to penetrate about 4 km into the enemy lines and the enemy could do nothing to check our advance.

Against an enemy poorly equipped with gas protective materials a small amount of Special Smoke let loose in the course of battle will cause fear and kill morale in the enemy rear echelon, which will often lead to retreat, thus enabling a comparatively small force to capture a strong position held by an enemy of superior strength.

In an attack upon the enemy's special firing posts, such as pill boxes, you will send the most daring and resourceful soldiers to sneak close to them and throw-in Special Smoke candles.

The enemy machine gun resistance was obstinate and could not be silenced even by concentrated shrapnel fire from our mountain and heavy artillery. Only with the aid of Special Smoke shells projected by our mortars was their fire overcome.

The Second Battalion of the First Regiment of the Hata Detachment attacked the enemy frontally, but our right flank was threatened by enemy artillery that continued firing from their position near Ta-Chao village. The detachment tried to overcome their artillery with ordinary shrapnel shells but without success as they were hidden in the woods. At this juncture our mortar company decided to use Special Smoke shells, and by firing ten such rounds succeeded in routing the enemy out of the woods into an open position near the village of Ta-Chao. As soon as the enemy came into an open field our mountain artillery annihilated them with ordinary shrapnel shells.

Japan produced in excess of 2,000 tons of dichlorocyanoarsine, its principal irritant agent, between 1934 and 1945, over two-thirds of which was manufactured and used before 1942. Although the agent was loaded into a wide range of weapons, those most favoured by the Japanese Army were mortar rounds and pyrotechnic candles, the latter proving to be a very effective and uniquely Japanese weapon which dispersed the irritant agent as a fine particle aerosol smoke from a device that resembled a large roman candle. As we have seen, Japanese officers responsible for chemical warfare attacks against the Chinese adamantly claimed during post-war interrogation that they used only humane, non-lethal irritant chemicals. Considerable doubt, however, is cast upon these claims by evidence contained within the *Lessons,* in which it is reported that 'when the Chinese soldiers came in contact with Special Smoke (dichlorocyanoarsine) some seriously affected persons bled through their noses and mouths and died from asphyxiation.' Other reports, contradicting Japanese intelligence that had previously confirmed that the Chinese possessed no chemical weapons, claimed that 'the Chinese fired phosgene and diphosgene shells against units of the Japanese Kwantung Defence Army at Ch'ing Hua Chen in September 1938. It was assumed that these were Japanese chemical artillery rounds captured by the Chinese in an earlier engagement.'

Chapter 3

Industry and International Disarmament

Common perception is that widespread publication of the chemical horrors of the First World War, coupled with similarly sensational press reports of events in Ethiopia – and to a lesser extent Japanese actions in China which were little reported and even less cared about in the West – reinforced the natural anathema of humanity to chemical warfare. Superficially it would seem that the civilized people of the world, their intuitive rejection of all forms of unnatural killing (i.e. not perpetrated by means of steel or lead or high explosives), given early recognition by The Hague agreement and the Washington Conference and, later, more solid substance by the as yet un-ratified League of Nations Geneva Protocol, turned their collective back on chemical warfare and carried their governments with them. It might seem as though there was a polarization between: on the one hand, the public, under emotive pressure from the press and manipulated by the paintings of Sergeant and the poetry of Sassoon and the like, that as a body rejected everything about chemical warfare; and on the other hand, the military establishment that welcomed with open arms this higher form of killing. Such, however, was far from the case as we shall see in the following chapter.

Once peace was established in 1919 more complex military, governmental and commercial influences came into play to mould public opinion vis-à-vis the future of chemical warfare. Except in the United States, where the fledgling Chemical Warfare Service – little more than a year old and fiercely fighting the corner of chemical warfare because on it depended the future careers of its officers – promoted chemical weapons in the face of united opposition from the reactionary conservatism of conventional artillerymen, the majority of soldiers from all the developed nations of the world were united in their rejection of such weapons. This was not on account of any high moral objection, but simply because their early experiences, reinforced by the examples of Ethiopia and China, proved pretty conclusively that chemicals were useless as strategic weapons and of only dubious tactical advantage, except for the suppression of savages. The overarching influence upon chemical warfare policy throughout the 1920s was the struggle for international supremacy between the chemical industries of Germany, Great Britain and the United States.

An objective analysis of public opinion regarding chemical weapons in the years immediately following the First World War shows quite clearly that the interest was minimal. Certainly, propaganda had aroused public opprobrium during the conflict but this was fairly fleeting, and the works of Siegfried Sassoon and others, briefly touched upon above, neither reached nor influenced a wide audience. It is only in more recent years that this material has become more broadly recognized, and even then there are questions to be asked about its true relevance. How many people who know, for example, that Sassoon wrote about gassed soldiers have actually read the verses, and just how many of those who know – probably because they have been told about it in some superficial television documentary – that George Singer Sergeant painted a picture entitled 'Gassed', know where the picture is or have actually seen it, even in reproduction? The true fact is that of all the literature and art that sprang from the First World War, the overwhelming majority concerns the horrors and degradation of conventional weaponry, the filth of the trenches, images of villages and farmland laid waste by artillery fire, and of tattered bodies impaled upon barbed wire and ripped apart by machine-gun fire. Public information was then and continues to be grossly distorted by propaganda. After four years of accumulated inhumanity, gas was, if it was anything of consequence at all to the majority of the population, and certainly to those who did not experience it first hand, just another one of those foul but inevitable things that happen in wartime and are best forgotten.

By 1919, depending upon one's reaction to propaganda or informed opinion, gas might be construed by the civilian observer as a humane weapon that actually reduced the slaughter on the battlefield, an inhumane terror weapon, or just another vile killing device like any other. An equally mixed opinion existed within the military community. Some saw gas as advantageous in certain tactical situations but most viewed it as a poor substitute for conventional weapons, a dangerous logistical burden and a magnet for retaliation. The received wisdom, after four years of war, was that gas in certain critical situations might possibly be a decisive weapon but was more likely to prove an expensive liability and, certainly in private, most military leaders were on balance antipathetic.

Beside the reactionary reluctance of the military establishment to immediately embrace new and untried technology imposed upon them by outsiders, particularly outsiders from the scientific community whom they tended often to regard as ethereal idealists, detached and shielded by abstruse formulae from the nuts and bolts, and the blood and guts of real warfare, there was another, surprisingly powerful, engine that powered their distrust of chemical warfare. This was simply that the whole concept of chemical warfare ran contrary to the established code of military ethics. This attitude was reflected in the comments of Sir John French in a reference to the German use of gas at the Second Battle of Ypres when he gave his view that 'As a soldier I cannot help expressing the deepest regret and some surprise that an army which hitherto has claimed to be the chief exponent of the chivalry of war should have stooped to employ such devices against brave and gallant foes.' Some years later, in May 1921, this theme of ethical decay was repeated by a renowned Cambridge professor of physics, a man, one might think, from the opposite camp, who in a debate about the legitimacy of chemical warfare, asked, 'What chivalry can a gasman show to a suffocated enemy? What personal prowess is there for a turncock?'

So, with public opinion largely indifferent, the intellectual intelligentsia determinedly opposed the military – except for a technocratic minority – dutifully lining up alongside them in opposition, and the politicians waiting patiently to see which side of the fence they should jump to further their own best interests, the advocates of chemical warfare faced an uphill struggle. In the United Kingdom the only true advocate was the failing chemical industry. In the United States this powerful industrial grouping was joined by the fledgling Chemical Warfare Service, whose brief glory days were threatened with an imminent and ignominious end.

Chemical Warfare and the British Dyestuffs Industry

In the United Kingdom, during the interwar years, the vacillating fortunes of the mustard gas generation of chemical warfare agents was intimately entwined with the development, or lack of development, of the country's organic chemical industry. For Britain and, indeed, the rest of the world, organic chemistry meant 'dyestuffs'. Despite the fact that the textile industry in Britain, though teetering on the brink of its slow decline, was one of the world's largest consumers of dyes, its dyestuffs manufacturing capacity was miniscule and its products poor in both range and quality. The dye industry, since its late-nineteenth-century inception, had been absolutely dominated by Germany. Of the 162,000 tons of dyes consumed worldwide in 1913, no less than 135,000 tons were manufactured in Germany; only 5,000 tons were made in Great Britain. In the same year Britain consumed 23,000 tons, the balance of 18,000 tons over her own production being imported from Germany. The situation in the United States was similar; in the same year America consumed 26,000 tons yet produced only 3,000 tons.

The strategic importance of this industry cannot be overstated. The processes employed in the manufacture of most modern synthetic dyes is so similar to those required to produce poisons such as mustard gas and its homologues that it would be difficult to slide a cigarette paper between them. It is only a slight exaggeration to say that it would require just a tweak here and an increase or decrease in temperature or pressure there and a plant that previously produced 'Bismarck Brown' dye could the next moment be decanting mustard gas. It was this ease of convertibility that allowed Germany to turn on the flow of mustard gas so quickly in 1917 and, conversely, it was the lack of existing dyestuffs plant in the United Kingdom, and thus the need for new factory construction, that delayed Allied retaliation.

The weakness of the British dye industry had rankled a few industrialists and certain members of government, particularly in the Board of Trade, since the end of the nineteenth century, but the problem seemed insoluble. German domination of the market was deep seated. Success in this field demanded great technical expertise which itself required a higher education system geared to the needs of science and industry. Whereas German universities precisely fulfilled these requirements, those in the United Kingdom were still mired in the Classics; the study of science or any subject that might be connected in any way with commerce was seen as somewhat second rate and derisory.

There were other prerequisites for a successful dyestuffs industry. Efficient production called for large plants and immense research budgets within the industry. Both these criteria were met in Germany where government policy was to encourage the formation of huge amalgamated companies, either by the establishment of trade-sharing agreements or by full integration, and German banks were prepared to make long-term loans to finance capital expansion and research. In Britain and the United States the opposite was true; rabidly free-trade governments actively discouraged any trade manipulation in the form of trusts or cartels, and, in the United Kingdom, banks were notoriously averse to funding any form of long-term capital works or research projects which did not offer immediate and tangible collateral value.

Another difficulty faced by the dyestuffs industry was that whereas the heavy chemical industry was a prime supplier and could dictate its terms of trade to its consumers, the dyestuff business was always treated as a service industry subservient to the textile industry. The years leading up to the start of the First World War saw the beginning of the great decline in the British textile trade and it was apparent that should the textile industry collapse it would carry the dyestuffs industry with it. Squeezed from all quarters, the textile firms were unwilling to support or invest in indigenous dye manufacturers that could only offer products that were both inferior to and more expensive than their

German competitors. In a period when free trade ruled supreme anyway it was inconceivable that the textile interests would support any parliamentary moves to apply tariff protection to help stimulate the home dyestuff trade.

A Board of Trade analysis prepared in 1913 estimated the value of the German dyestuffs industry, represented essentially by one organization that was shortly to become the immense Leverkusen works of I.G. Farbenindustrie, formerly Bayer, at some £50,000,000. Meanwhile the entire British industry consisted of eleven small coal-tar dye works, only two of which, those of Levinstein Ltd of Manchester and Read Holliday and Sons Ltd of Huddersfield, were of any significance and had a joint value rather less than £300,000.

Speaking retrospectively, two men of supreme importance in the pre-war dyestuffs industry gave candid analysis of the ills besetting their businesses. In November 1938, A.G. Green, at the second Ivan Levinstein Memorial Lecture at the Manchester Chemical Club, commenting upon the lack of technical and scientific higher education in the United Kingdom, stated that in his opinion 'Insufficient attention was given to the details of dyestuff manufacture to secure the highest yields and purest products, which brought British dyestuffs into disrepute in comparison with Germany.' Some ten years later Herbert Levinstein, son of Ivan Levinstein, the founder of the firm that carried his name, commenting on his father's difficulties in financing expansion, wrote:

> The application of knowledge requires finance and the capacity on the part of those who control finance to judge the value of a scientific discovery. The main cost of industrial research is not in the laboratory but in the application to the larger scale. Who in England was going to find money for this? In Germany, the banks would and did find it. We suffered and have always suffered from a lack of 'educated' money.

At the very start of the First World War, long before the concept of chemical warfare was even a gleam in the scientific eye, the shortcomings of the British dye industry were abruptly brought to the attention of the government. Cut off from German supplies the War Office could not even obtain sufficient khaki dye to colour its soldiers' uniforms. The reaction was quick and, for the British establishment, surprisingly efficient. The passing of the Munitions of War Act paved the way for the Ministry of Munitions under the leadership of Lloyd George, its main task being to shake up and reorganize British industry, particularly the chemicals industry, in order to meet the demands of war. Habits of competitive private enterprise were swept away and cross-interest power groups established at the head of affairs of business, in politics and in government departments. The Committee on Chemical Production was formed under the chairmanship of Walter

Runciman, President of the Board of Trade. Included among its members were no less than nine academic scientists together with Herbert Levinstein and Milton Sharp, leader of the Bradford Dyers' Association, representing the main textile weavers. Under the committee's new regime, efficiency was forced upon the dye producers. Levinstein's, who had never previously held a government contract, turned out 600,000 lb of khaki dye by May 1915, enough to clothe 9 million men. Improved working practices were also fostered amongst the smaller dye companies – British Alizarin, for example, from its works in Silverton, increased production from 3,603 tons in 1914 to 5,055 tons in 1915. Jointly, within the first six months of war, the British dyestuffs manufacturers were able to fulfil the entire UK demand, over three-quarters of which had previously been imported from Germany.

Whilst this arrangement was adequate to cope with the immediate problems at the start of hostilities it failed to look forward to the new requirements of the post-war peacetime economy. Indeed, some of the decisions taken in 1914–15 were to be of grave detriment to the future of Britain's organic chemicals industry. The origin of the later difficulties lay in the appointment of Lord Moulton PC FRS as chairman of the Ministry of Munitions Explosives Committee. By 1914 Moulton was a scientist of the highest reputation, but his expertise lay not only in the field of science, for he was also one of Britain's most eminent lawyers, particularly in the field of patent law. Contemporary accounts described him as 'a figure of overpowering eminence, with a long career of multiple brilliance behind him'. Moulton's problem was that he defined his responsibility on the Explosives Committee in terms solely of directing the chemical industry towards the provision of nitrated explosives for the War Office. He seemed totally unconcerned about the role that the nation's dyestuffs industry might play in the development of new weapons of war – particularly chemical weapons – and any consideration of the long-term future of the industry was pushed firmly into the background. Just as the Bradford Dyers' Association had viewed the dye manufacturers as no more than hand-servants of the textile industry, Moulton saw them as no more than servants of the artillerymen.

Oversight of the dye businesses was delegated to James Falconer who, it must be said in his favour, drew up sound plans for the dye industry both for the War and for the peace that was to follow, but lacked the dynamism or power to overcome the resistance of the dye men and bring his plans to fruition. Falconer's plan was to form a new national company to be known as British Dyes, financed jointly by the Treasury and the users, which would buy up all the existing manufacturers, guarantee to take all their products and pay for enlargement of their capital plant and for an enhanced research base.

The Treasury looked favourably upon the scheme and it attracted a certain amount of support from some of the textile manufacturers, although the majority were sceptical that in the long term Germany, with her immense technological lead, would still dominate the market. Amongst the scheme's proponents, somewhat surprisingly, was George Douglas, managing director of the Bradford Dyers' Association, whose opinion was that, to guarantee wartime output and future survival of the industry:

> There should be a big undertaking, financed largely by the textile trade on the lines of, say, the Leverkusen works of the Bayer Company. Let it buy up as many as possible of the existing firms, especially Read Holliday, as Mr Turner of that firm is the man most qualified to act as managing director. Let there be a government supervising committee and a Board of the new company including industrial men experienced in big equipment; one man, at any rate, of the type and experience of Sir W. H. Lever.

The scheme appears to have fallen apart from the start. For the most part, commercial rivalry and self-advancement seems to have transcended national interest, and those companies that were not wholly antagonistic were greatly concerned about the necessity, implicit in the plan, to continue to take all the output of British Dyes after the War. To the conservative textile magnates it looked, in an age of virtually unrestricted free trade, too much like protectionism via the back door. Eventually, after extraordinarily protracted negotiations, the second largest of the dye houses, Read Holliday and Sons Ltd, and a couple of very minor operations, were brought into the scheme at enormously inflated cost. By an inexplicable oversight the dominant player in the industry, Levinstein and Co., were excluded from the merger negotiations and remained outside the guaranteed purchasing agreement. Thus, the new Board of Trade inspired British Dyes Co. was essentially the old Read Holliday propped up by government and textile industry funding. What made this situation even more farcical was that by 1917, under the policy prescribed by Lord Moulton, Read Holliday's works had been converted almost entirely to the production of conventional nitrate explosives so, when the requirement for mustard gas arose that year, the firm, whose plant had hitherto been ideally suited to its production, was in no position to participate in its manufacture. Similarly, at the time of the armistice, it was not in a position to fill the temporary vacuum in the dye trade created by the absence of German imports. This was all absolutely contrary to the fundamental purpose for which British Dyes had been established.

The Board of Trade, the War Office, the textile industry and, not the least, Levinstein and Co. were all appalled by the manner in which the British Dyes affair had degenerated. Piqued by being excluded,

Levinstein went on a buying spree, first snatching a small but important synthetic indigo plant at Ellesmere Port from beneath the nose of British Dyes, which it quickly converted in 1916 to the production of the anaesthetic Novocain, then, a few months later it acquired Claus and Company of Manchester, another independent dye firm of moderate importance. By the end of the War the only dye maker of any consequence not owned by British Dyes or Levinstein and Co. was British Alizarin.

Detached from the quagmire of British Dyes, Levinstein and Co. was the only manufacturer competent to meet the demand for mustard gas when it arose. Notwithstanding the urgent military demands upon its resources, Levinstein kept an eye firmly on the future dyestuffs business and in 1917 the firm requested a grant of £1,000,000 from the Treasury to fund capital works in order to meet competition from post-war Germany. This was something of a snub to the Board of Trade because it was exactly what British Dyes had been set up to do with a spectacular lack of success.

In June 1918, Sir Albert Stanley, a British-born entrepreneur with wide experience of American business practices, and who had earlier replaced Runciman at the Board of Trade, demanded the compulsory amalgamation of the ailing British Dyes Company and Levinstein's. Stanley, who had been responsible for the spectacularly successful reorganization of London Underground in 1907, saw such an amalgamation as the only chance of survival for the now strategically important British dyestuffs industry. In November a government White Paper outlining Stanley's plans proposed a series of grants-in-aid for new manufacturing facilities, the modernization of existing plant and for research. Stanley got his way and in July 1919 a new public-private corporation, an alien concept in those free-trade, free-enterprise days, was formed under the name of the British Dyestuffs Corporation. W.G. Reader, historian of Imperial Chemical Industries Ltd, described the birth of British Dyestuffs Corporation thus:

> In Germany, defeated but not shattered, the largest dyestuffs businesses in the world were preparing to come back into the market. In the USA, where during the war a new dyestuffs industry had been called into existence, great coalitions were taking shape. This was the competition which the BDC would be called upon to face.

The corporation, like its predecessor, British Dyes, was a disaster but its further history need not divert us much. Briefly, the Board of the new corporation consisted of Herbert Levinstein of Levinstein and Co., Sir Joseph Turner, formerly of Read Holliday, and a government representative. The problem was that Levinstein and Turner loathed one another. Both were absolutely determined that the factories they formerly ran would play the dominant role in the new corporation. Millions of pounds of government money which was intended to finance the rationalization and modernization of old plant, the construction of new efficient factories and the formation of a centralized research unit were instead siphoned off into wasteful duplication of facilities at all the plants, irrespective of its efficiency or cost effectiveness. The money just disappeared into unnecessary new buildings, duplicated and badly integrated research facilities, competitive marketing arrangements, petty jealousies and competition for government funds.

Even with substantial government support it was obvious to all informed analysts that the British Dyestuffs Corporation had no hope of making any perceivable inroad into the German dye monopoly. Germany might be beaten, but her factories were intact and her scientific intellectual assets were still secure. Germany's difficulties must not be underestimated: her worldwide trading links were shattered, social disorder was rampant, the economy was on the point of collapse and every raw material was in short supply and, as part of a more or less covert strategic plan, which will be described below, her dyestuffs industry was targeted for reparations. The inescapable fact, however, was that all the world wanted to buy German dyes.

In the United Kingdom the government invoked the 1876 Customs Consolidation Act in order to put up tariff barriers against German dye imports, but the textile manufacturers employed every ruse short of brazen smuggling to avoid the restrictions. Whereas, for example, numerous breweries in Britain were forced into bankruptcy because Englishmen, after the War, boycotted en masse any beer that bore a vaguely Teutonic name, even if it was brewed in Burton upon Trent, the textile manufacturers' goodwill towards Germany remained high. In the contest between perceived patriotism and profit, profit won by several lengths. The British Dye Corporation expected to be cushioned from competition for ten years by the customs embargo but even in that time and without the internal squabbling that dragged it to its knees within the first year, it would have been impossible for the corporation to have gained the necessary skills and expertise to develop the thousands of individual colour nuances, each with multiple formulations to suit the hundreds of different materials, that were already in the German inventory.

The corporation, still struggling with the factional infighting between the Levinstein and Turner camps as well as external pressure from the government shareholding which wanted the business run in the national rather than private shareholders' interest, suffered a further severe setback from an unexpected quarter. In December 1919, Mr Justice Sankey ruled that the government's protectionist proclamation under the 1876 Act was unlawful so, overnight, the dye-makers tariff firewall disappeared. Failure followed upon failure and in utter desperation, in December 1920, the government appointed Sir William Alexander to the Board to sort things out. After some acrimony, Levinstein and Turner retired but the problems were yet still far from resolved. For a while it seemed that the only solution was some sort of market-sharing agreement with I.G. Farbenindustrie, but negotiations were protracted and ultimately unsuccessful. Then, in 1925, British Dyestuff Corporation was swallowed up in the largest corporate amalgamation in British history when it joined Brunner, Mond, the ex-Nobel industries Explosives Trades group, and United Alkali to form Imperial Chemical Industries.

British Dyestuffs and Chemical Warfare

Why was the government so keen to support the British dyestuffs business, even to the extent of becoming a minority shareholder in a private company within the trade, and attempting to subvert the prevailing free-trade tariff policy of the time to artificially shield the industry? The answer is that by 1917 the dyestuff industry was intimately entwined in the production of chemical warfare agents, particularly mustard gas, and was determined to take the greatest strategic advantage of that involvement. For some twenty years the industry manipulated government and public opinion, skilfully raising or lowering the threshold of fear about future chemical warfare, moderating or intensifying its programme of propaganda according to its perception of the common mood. Its task was made easy by the institutional secrecy of the British establishment, and also by the desperate lack of scientific education within its ranks. Neither the military nor the government were prepared to speak openly about chemical warfare effects or policy; few people in government, even in the highest office, were capable of understanding the fundamental facts or principles and, like the general public, were therefore prey to every item of disinformation, propaganda and rumour. The innate antipathy of the military, already alluded to, expressed itself in positive disinterest and misunderstanding. Put simply, the chemists told government that mustard gas was the weapon that was going to win the next war; mustard gas was made by the dye industry therefore government must, as a strategic necessity, support the dye industry. Immediately after the armistice they went further – not only must the British branch of the trade be protected, but the Allies must ensure that the German industry be destroyed, either by military restriction on output, tariff barriers or, most satisfactorily, by looting her trade secrets and intellectual property by way of reparations. If mustard gas from dyestuffs was the pivot around which the next war was to revolve, then Germany must be denied such an industry to destroy her war-making potential.

Prominent industrial chemists from both sides of the Atlantic pressed home the same message. Numerous articles appeared in *The Times* penned by Dr Herbert Levinstein under the sensational headlines 'Dyes the Key of War', followed by 'Military Value of the Dye Industry' and 'Dyes as the Key to Gas Warfare'. Similar views were being voiced in the United States, an article in the most influential of the country's chemical industry journals reading: 'Bestir yourselves, chemists of America! The country glories in the services you have already rendered in peace and war. Opportunity for further service now presents itself. Whether we wish it or not, gas will determine peace or decide victory in future war. The nation must be fully prepared!'

On a similar, if more restrained vein, S.A.H. Whetmore, spokesman for the British Dyestuffs Corporation, wrote: 'We, the British, are going to have a dyestuffs industry, not because we want it as a woman wants a new hat, but because we believe our safety as a nation depends on the organic chemical industry.' In the United States the campaign launched by the chemical industry was even more strident. The huge DuPont company, the largest chemical manufacturer in America, put aside a budget of $370,000 to broadcast its message. Speaking tours were organized, representatives of the company appeared at all local and national conventions; special meetings of prominent Chambers of Commerce and Rotary Clubs were organized at which the chemists pressed home their arguments, and over 1,000 DuPont-sponsored headline editorials appeared in the press.

The barrage of pro-gas propaganda continued from all quarters of the industry. The true motivation for their demands was let slip, however, in a widely broadcast speech by a vice president of the Dow Chemical Company in 1919 when he told his audience that:

> Chemical warfare is the most effective weapon of all time, the most humane ever introduced into war by man. Our land armies for future struggles will be officered entirely by trained chemists ... We need a protecting tariff. In this war after the war our battle cry must be 'To hell with all German imports! Down with everything opposed to American Industries!'

The motive for linking chemical warfare and dyestuffs in the United States was particularly powerful. Prior to 1914 the American industry had been miniscule, less significant even than that of Great Britain. During the latter years of the War, however, great strides had been made, a new industry had been born, factories and plant erected and huge investments made. Although the outbreak of peace saw no appreciable increase in the worldwide demand for dyes, production capacity, particularly in the United States, had increased dramatically and it was not a market from which aggressive American entrepreneurs would willingly withdraw.

The Versailles Peace Treaty forbade Germany from ever again making or acquiring chemical weapons, but chemical interests in Britain, France and the United States stressed the perils of 'convertibility', suggesting that as long as Germany possessed a dye industry it would be impossible to differentiate between its military and civil potential. The newly formed Chemical Foundation of the United States was most vociferous in its demands for the total destruction of the German chemical industry. The Foundation's ulterior motive was made quite clear in an open address to President Wilson in which he was asked to 'be mindful of the $500,000,000 invested in the United States dye industry and in the textile, paint, varnish and other industries dependent upon the American dye industry'. Wilson, however, was one of the few willing to express scepticism of the prevailing view, stating that in his opinion exaggerating the fear of 'convertibility' was a dishonest, unethical subversion of military negotiation to achieve an unjustifiable economic end. Nevertheless, throughout the years 1919–25 the chemical interests relentlessly magnified the future peril that would face the United States if it did not maintain a dominant chemical industry, cynically conjuring up fear for commercial gain.

It was important in both the United States and Great Britain that the chemical industry's programme of propaganda should closely reflect the popular national mood; too high a profile, for example, might create the impression of warmongering while feigned disinterest might imply corporate indifference to national security. Public perception and the consequent pressures upon the propagandists differed markedly on opposite sides of the Atlantic. In the United States the industrialists were powerfully supported by the fledgling Chemical Warfare Service which had come to rapid prominence during the short time that the American Army saw service in the European theatre and was now threatened with equally rapid extinction. In order to bolster its own credibility the Chemical Warfare Service had to generate a generous mythology of its own achievements which inevitably required the gradual release of military information, some true but much of it somewhat massaged, on a scale that surprised the American public which was accustomed to military secrecy.

Overall the record of the Chemical Service was not glowing so the myth-creating process proved an uphill struggle. The principal reason for the difference in perception of chemical warfare, both historically and in terms of the future threat, was that British soldiers were exposed to chemical weapons as early as the spring of 1915 and grew up with the threat, whereas American troops, when they arrived in France in

1917 were thrown into the conflict just at the time when the mustard gas war was at its fiercest. By the time peace finally descended upon Europe British troops had learned to cope with chemical weapons and the public were inured to news about them; to the British, gas was just another item in a long and ghastly inventory of carnage and had long lost any particular significance. The Americans were completely unprepared, either materially or psychologically, for chemical warfare and suffered terrifying early losses, the gravity of which Washington was slow to appreciate. We have already seen that America was ill provided in terms of offensive chemical capability but her gas defence, operational organization and equipment dispersal was even more chaotic. The various elements of the gas warfare organization were distributed amongst a number of army departments which together lacked unity, orchestration, urgency or enthusiasm to come to grips with the situation. Gas masks – what there were of them – for example, were provided by the Medical Department; munitions, filled with mustard gas scrounged from the French or British, were dealt with by the Ordnance Department; and field operations were overseen by the Corps of Engineers. Under such circumstances casualties were inevitably severe; back home, the news was grim and chemical weapons maintained a high profile in the public mind. A unified Chemical Weapons Service was not established until July 1918 and was not much respected in military circles. Understrength at 20,000 men and unappreciated, the service was quickly wound down. Just six months after the end of the War it was reduced to a complement of 800 men and was an early candidate for extinction.

The General Staff was initially sceptical of the utility of a Chemical Warfare Service in peacetime but, as a result of skilful joint manipulation of the media by the service's commanding officer, Brigadier Amos Fries, a vehement proponent of chemical warfare, and the chemical industry, Washington eventually agreed to the continued existence of an autonomous Chemical Warfare Service under the terms of the new National Defense Act.

Thereafter, with its future assured the CWS began the process of enhancing its wartime reputation, driving home the danger the world faced from the proliferation of chemical weapons and the vital need for a powerful and effective American deterrent chemical capability. Recent sensational but much exaggerated claims for America's own so-called super-weapon, lewisite, helped further the cause of the CWS. It had long been understood that the easiest way to convince an uncertain public about the need, in peacetime, for powerful armed forces was to exaggerate the external threat to the homeland, and this, with the aid of the inflated reputation of lewisite, was what the CWS proceeded to do. With the United States buffered from any potential enemies by thousands of miles of ocean to the east and west it was difficult for the CWS to convince the population that it was at serious risk from any aggressor, but much stress was laid upon the fact that lewisite was ideally suited to air delivery by bombs or spray, a claim that was given added urgency by an expert involved in its development whose opinion, published in the US press, was that 'a dozen lewisite air bombs of the greatest size in use during 1918 might with a favourable wind have eliminated the population of Berlin.'

In conclusion, then, the situation in 1920 was that in the United Kingdom there was an overall, war-weary public indifference to chemical warfare, and within the military there was a scepticism that verged upon suspicion. The only active protagonist was the chemical industry which wanted to break Germany's monopoly in dyes and other organic chemicals by a combination of suppression, sanctions and tariffs, fuelling their demands with propaganda intended to rouse fears of the 'convertibility' of Germany's peacetime dye plants. These efforts largely failed; the judiciary, in the form of Mr Justice Sankey refused to sanction tariff protection; government hesitated about continuing financial support for the obviously struggling dye industry; the textile trade similarly refused to support it, using instead every ruse to circumvent restrictions and buy German dyes; and, finally, there was little enthusiasm in the military or in government for further research into chemical weapons.

Meanwhile, in the United States, the prevailing atmosphere in 1920 was somewhat more confused. With casualties at a shockingly high level still very much in the public mind, and with open arguments in the press between conservative elements in the Army and avidly pro-gas Chemical Warfare Service, the future of gas warfare was high on the public agenda. Whilst memories of the horrors of 1917–18 might serve to turn the masses resolutely against chemical weapons, the contra-argument that a strong deterrent gas organization was the only guarantee against surprise attack only served to confound. In the United States, too, the vociferous chemical industry, much more aggressive in its anti-German propaganda than the British, did little to quell the confusion.

Washington and Geneva, 1921–5

The principal risk associated with trying to mobilize public opinion for the sake of military or commercial interest, especially if the distinction between the two is as blurred as it was in the immediate post-war years, is that of pushing a little too hard. The result then is that instead of public opinion being insidiously led by vested interest the masses suddenly say 'enough is enough!' The proponents of the cause in question then find themselves faced with a vociferous opposition that, once organized, might quickly scupper their ambitions. This is what happened in the early 1920s. The constant wailing and railing of the pro-gas, anti-German militarists and vested industrial interests seemed increasingly at odds with the growing international embracement of the pacifist cause. Just prior to the Washington Conference in 1921 American chemists changed their stance, stressing the humaneness of gas rather than its superiority as a war-winning weapon, but it was really too late, they had grossly overplayed their hand.

The American press now turned against Fries' Chemical Warfare Service and the chemicals industry in a torrent of searing editorials. The following report in the *New York Evening Mail* is typical of the reaction to the chemical proponent's justification of gas as a humane weapon:

> What is this 'humane' method of warfare of which the chemists speak? Is it the spreading of gas that will torture and poison honourable and gallant men not only through their lungs but through their skins, that will reach far behind the fighting lines and send women and children to horrible death, that will kill all vegetation and secure the starvation of peoples for years after war ceases? If this be a chemist's idea of humane warfare, God deliver the world from its chemists! Evidently it is not a soldier's idea of warfare, or General Pershing would have indorsed it. And be it remembered, the soldier fights on the field, not in the laboratory.

And from the *New York World*:

> That poison gas warfare is 'humane' in character may come as a surprise to the thousands of 'doughboys' who have not yet recovered from the effects of gas during the World War. Yet that is the contention of Brigadier-General Fries, Chief of the Chemical Warfare Service of the United States Army. His opinion, moreover, is upheld by a resolution by the American Institute of Chemical Engineers, and by American Army officers in general.

Although letters to the editor of the *New York Times* overwhelmingly supported the newspaper's stance, there were sporadic representations from supporters of the Fries philosophy. Typical of these pro-gas letters was one from Professor Zanetti of Columbia University who, during the First World War, served as a Lieutenant Colonel in the Gas Warfare Service. Zanetti wrote:

> No right-minded person can seriously entertain the idea that any weapon of war, let alone chemical warfare, should not, if possible, be set aside. To dwell on the horror of chemical warfare and characterize it as a 'viper weapon' is a platitude. The manufacture of a new gas, discovered in some obscure laboratory, could go on in some remote chemical factory for years; enormous stocks could be accumulated and stored and, if necessary, harmlessly labelled, until the moment came to use it. Who can guard

against such a contingency? Would we dare in the light of past experience to expose our men to a slaughter similar to that suffered by the French and British at Ypres and run the risk of its consequence? The knowledge that both sides are fully equipped and ready at a moment's notice to retaliate in kind would make more toward preventing a chemical war than – as experience has shown – any treaty, no matter how clear and definite.

Fries and his supporters, including Senator George Chamberlain of Oregon, behind whom were marshalled the chemical industry interests, were, however, very much in the minority. Opposition to the gas warfare programme coalesced around the highly influential figure of General John Joseph Pershing, Commander-in-Chief of the American Expeditionary Force in the First World War and, following the War, Army Chief of Staff. Pershing adamantly refused even to consider the use of chemical weapons, and wrote:

It is inconceivable that the United States will initiate the use of gases and by no means certain that it will use them even in retaliation. Aside from this, it is quite unlikely that the prospective enemy will invite retaliatory measures by using gases in any form. Should he do so, however, the action to be taken will be decided when the time comes.

In a stinging criticism of the pro-gas stance of Brigadier Fries and his followers, the *Philadelphia Evening Bulletin* wrote: 'General Pershing, on the other hand, recommends that poison gas be abandoned in warfare. Here is practical military knowledge against civilian chemical theory.' In the same vein, it was the opinion of the *New York Evening Mail* that: 'The stand of such a distinguished professional soldier as Pershing should have a tremendous effect upon public opinion everywhere.' Meanwhile an editorial in the *Louisville Courier-Journal* warning caution of the dubious chemical deterrent theories put forward by Brigadier Fries, commented that:

It is the business of the Chemical Warfare Service chief to develop the use of poison gas, and nothing is more natural than that he should be partial to its use, but his view is narrowed by his occupation.

There never will be a method of warfare so terrible that men will refuse to engage in it. Flirting with death is inherent in human nature. The invention of firearms was, perhaps, just as radical an improvement in the art of killing as was the introduction of poison gas. Firearms might have been called 'intolerable'. But they did not put a dampener on war, any more than did the use of the war chariot or the long-bow or the metal sword. Compared with the trireme, the modern battle-ship is a horrible engine, but its appearance did not spell the cessation of naval warfare.

General Fries overlooks the fact that as soon as an 'intolerable' instrument of death appears, the immediate sequel is the invention of protection against it. Armour counteracted swords and the battle-axe, just as the gas-mask was almost coeval with gas.

There is a way, however, to prevent nations from using chemical poisons in warfare; the creation of a militant public opinion against the practise, and the agreement of nations to refrain from their use. If dum-dum bullets were eschewed by both sides in the last war, why is it not possible to ban gases?

By 1921, on the eve of the Washington Treaty negotiations, American public opinion was overwhelmingly opposed to chemical warfare. The results of a national public opinion survey released in December of that year revealed that of those polled, 366,975 Americans favoured prohibition of poison gas, while a mere nineteen favoured its retention, but only with severe restrictions imposed upon its use.

In the United Kingdom, where alarm was already growing in reaction to the machinations of the American chemical industry, there was mounting concern about the amount of covert research work on chemical weapons being undertaken in British universities at public expense. The research that was under way was, in fact, very modest in its ambition and probably would have passed without comment had it not been for some rather seedy recent newspaper revelations. Unfortunately the upsurge in pacifism began just as the Royal Commission on Awards to Wartime Inventors issued its report, which led to the airing of bitter and acrimonious recriminations in the press between various groups of scientists competitively claiming credit for inventing some of the vilest weapons employed in the late conflict.

Washington Naval Conference, 1921–2
An agreed American and, to some extent, international policy regarding the legitimacy of chemical weapons evolved, to the surprise of many participants, at the Washington Arms conference. The conference was convened essentially to moderate the naval arms race in the Pacific where the United States found itself vulnerable to the growing strength of the Japanese Navy. The race to build and equip more and better warships and submarines was proving prohibitively expensive for the United States and she hoped, by reaching an international diplomatic agreement that included Japan, to relieve the pressure on the Pacific fleet. It was at first expected that the conference would discuss only naval, submarine and air power but, at the last moment, US President Harding and Secretary of State Charles Evans Hughes forced chemical weapons onto the agenda.

Unfortunately, at the start of the discussions about chemical weapons in January 1922, the War Department was represented by General Fries whose rabidly pro-gas stance was at odds with both the American national sentiment and the general international consensus reached just two years earlier at Versailles. Fries was supported by

Secretary of State Hughes and also by the British and French members of a sub-committee appointed to review the chemical weapons question. No one was surprised by the final report of the sub-committee, which was chaired by the president of the American Chemical Society, when it concluded that the United States should be prepared to use chemical weapons and that the 'only limitation practicable' was to prohibit the use of gas against cities and non-combatants.

Aghast at the sub-committee's conclusion, President Harding passed their findings to a newly formed Advisory Committee which he had previously established to guide and promote what he realized would be a highly controversial treaty to final ratification. Harding's view was far more pragmatic, long term and humanitarian than the narrow, militaristic outlook of Fries and his followers, and to ensure a more balanced view he took steps to ensure that the Advisory Committee was heavily weighted with men whose anti-gas stance closely mirrored his own. Prominent on the panel were General John Joseph Pershing, Jonathan Mayhew Wainright, Assistant Secretary of War since March 1921, Rear Admiral Thomas Rogers and Secretary of Commerce Herbert Hoover. The Advisory Committee's findings were the absolute antithesis of those of the Fries sub-committee. Appealing to the collective conscience of the United States, the committee stated that they were:

> of the opinion that the conscience of the American people has been profoundly shocked by the savage use of scientific discoveries for destruction rather than construction. The American representatives would not be doing their duty in expressing the conscience of the American people were they to fail in insisting upon the total abolition of chemical warfare.

Harding appears to have sensed something beyond the mere tangible and scientifically calculable in the growing international revulsion to chemical warfare. He realized that the revulsion stemmed not just from the absolute inhumanity of chemical weapons which, by their very nature have only one purpose, to maim or kill human beings – whereas high explosives, it could be argued, destroy material assets in the first instance and people collaterally – but that a great moral trust had been broken by the Germans when they first deployed chlorine in 1915. To Harding and many like-minded people, it seemed as though a whole order of society had collapsed; the entire basis of trust upon which all international contracts and convention, protocols, practices and procedures survived had been swept away. The Germans, like Pandora, had released upon the world all the diseases, sorrows, vices and crimes that afflict poor humanity and there was no way they could be cajoled back into the box. The anti-gas faction knew that talk of usage with restraint was nonsense and it was for this reason that Harding

70

demanded not just a convention for the control of chemical weapons but their total abolition.

Acting on President Harding's explicit instructions the American delegation introduced the following additional clause to the proposed agreement:

> The use in war of asphyxiating, poisonous or other gases and all analogous liquids, materials or devices, having been justly condemned by the general opinion of the civilized world and a prohibition of such use having been declared in treaties to which a majority of the civilized nations are parties [...] this prohibition shall now be universally accepted as a part of international law binding alike the conscience and practice of nations, the Signatory Powers declare their assent to such prohibition, agree to be bound thereby between themselves and invite all other civilized nations to adhere thereto.

The American chemical warfare amendment was universally accepted and became Article V of the *Treaty Between the United States of America, the British Empire, France, Italy and Japan Relating to the Use of Submarines and Noxious Gases in Wartime*, signed by all parties on 6 February 1922.

Although the Chemical Warfare Service decisively lost the war for chemical weapons – the CWS budget, for example, was immediately cut by 50 per cent to $1,500,000 in the fiscal year 1922 – the chemical industry won minor battles. Tariff barriers were imposed against German dyestuff imports but, as in Great Britain, demand from textile and paint manufacturers largely nullified their effect.

Geneva Conference, 1925

America's decisive disavowal of chemical weapons in 1922 did much for her international prestige in the years that followed and, similarly, the American stance enhanced the credibility of other nations that followed the same line. President Coolidge, who succeeded Harding in 1923, held views on chemical warfare similar to, if not even more resolute than those of his predecessor. Coolidge sought to strengthen international recognition of US chemical weapons policy at the forthcoming Geneva Conference for the Control of the International Trade in Arms, Munitions, and Implements of War. The Geneva Conference was in many ways an unsatisfactory meeting. The original terms of reference of the Conference included only the control of trade in conventional weapons; the further amendments to include discussion of chemical weapons, as proposed by the American and French delegations, and biological weapons, as proposed by the Polish representatives, served only to muddy the final outcome and offer scope for unsatisfactory compromise on the central issues.

71

In the United States, pressure for the addition of chemical weapons to the Geneva agenda was imposed upon the State Department by a powerful group assembled by President Coolidge that included Pershing and Hoover, both of whom had earlier served on Harding's anti-gas Advisory Committee at the Washington Conference. The US delegation wanted the prohibition on the use of chemical weapons agreed at the Washington Conference extended to encompass not just use but also the manufacture and export of chemical weapons or of chemical intermediaries essential to the manufacture of such weapons. To this end, and at the suggestion of the French delegation to the conference, it was agreed that the following amendment should be inserted into the agreement as a separate protocol:

> The High Contracting Parties therefore agree absolutely to prohibit the export from their territory of any such asphyxiating, poisonous or other gases and all analogous liquids, intended or designed for use in connection with operations of war.

While chemical weapons were dropped from the trade provisions of the final Geneva Treaty, in 1925 the delegates approved the separate Gas Protocol reaffirming the complete prohibition on chemical warfare. The protocol was subsequently ratified by all the major powers except Japan and the United States. Ratification, however, for a number of signatories including the USSR, France and Great Britain, was conditional; the agreement would not be regarded as binding on them if their enemies, or the allies of their enemies, failed to respect the prohibitions of the protocol. Thus the protocol absolutely failed in its attempt to prevent the manufacture and proliferation of chemical weapons becoming instead a 'no first use policy' which by its nature predicated the assembly of large stockpiles of deterrent weapons.

Senate opposition to the protocol prevented its ratification by the United States where the War and Navy departments, while not strong proponents of chemical preparedness, nonetheless objected to being excluded from US deliberations at Geneva and put forward strong resistance. Working in concert with chemical industry lobbyists and the pro-gas American Legion to conduct a national publicity blitz they succeeded in preventing ratification. The Senate seemed, somewhat in contradiction of public opinion, to be backing away from the 1922 consensus. Referring to the Washington conference, the chairman of the Senate Military Affairs Committee commented during a speech opposing ratification of the Geneva Protocol:

> I think it fair to say that in 1922 there was much of hysteria and much of misinformation concerning chemical warfare. I was not at all surprised at the time that the public very generally – not only in this country but in many other countries – believed that something should be done to prohibit

72

the use of gas in warfare. The effects of that weapon had not been studied at the time to such an extent as to permit information about it to reach the public. There were many misconceptions as to the effects and as to the character of warfare involved in its use.

The truth was, however, that few members of the American administration or of any government worldwide possessed any technical knowledge of chemical warfare and this applied to the majority of the representatives at the Geneva Conference also. Very few countries were involved in active, viable chemical warfare programmes that could provide worthwhile data upon which any political or military assertion could be justified. Even in the United States, where the research facilities and the funding were potentially available should there be the political will to proceed with chemical rearmament, no such funding was forthcoming and little research was undertaken.

The continued lack of focus on chemical weapons in the United States War Department continued despite the Senate defeat of the protocol. Herbert Hoover, who became president in 1929 and had helped develop this position on the Advisory Committee in 1921, made clear that he was not going to change this stance. Hoover's instructions to the US delegation to the World Disarmament Conference in 1932 were that they should ensure that the American tradition of strong international leadership against the use of chemical weapons was maintained.

In the United Kingdom the chemical warfare programme was virtually moribund. Most of the information employed to justify arguments on both sides of the debate was hypothetical puff and hyperbole. Such public debate as there had been tended to split the public into two camps: the left-wing pacifists, who equated chemical weapons with the worst horror of war; and a hard-right wing that viewed preparations for chemical warfare as the correct response to the terrors of communism and fascism. The minority right-wing view in the United States was bolstered by the advantage of geography: America's physical isolation, separated from potential enemies by thousands of miles of ocean and thus less vulnerable to a chemical weapon attack, made the possession of chemical weapons a positive military asset that went beyond the utility of a mere deterrent.

Broadly, however, the world followed the pacifist line of the League of Nations. While the Geneva Protocol was tacitly adhered to by all the nations of the world – until Italy transgressed in Ethiopia in 1936 – whether they formally ratified it or not, it was a deeply flawed agreement. It was an inherently weak resolution calling only for abstention subject to reciprocity with no quantitative agreed force levels, no machinery for verification and no sanctions against transgressors. Consideration of chemical warfare and, indeed, of war in broader terms, slipped gradually below the horizon of public consciousness in the 1920s as the world eased into a period of pacifism and military retrenchment. The Treaty of Locarno, with its prospect of a rolling programme of peace for ten years promised an easy future and, with the USSR tied up with its own internal domestic problems and the United States backing quietly off the world stage into apparent isolationism, the problems of arms limitation were reduced almost to irrelevance. One feature of the Geneva chemical weapons protocol that is often overlooked, as one is distracted from the main theme of the negotiations by the fretting over convertibility and verification, is the absolute ease with which agreement was reached on the main issue. Everyone condemned chemical weapons and all were prepared, albeit with conditions, to agree to their prohibition. The unanimity and willingness seems astonishing until one considers the simple fact that it is very easy indeed to make great international gestures by negotiating away something one really does not want anyway. And the fact was that no major military establishment, except perhaps a vocal minority within the United States War Department, was seriously committed to a belief in chemical weapons.

Rearmament, 1934–9

The post-Locarno euphoria soon gave way to doubts, fears and suspicion as Hitler came to power in 1933, the ten-year rule was suspended and the Standing Committee of the Disarmament Conference at Geneva was adjourned indefinitely. In the United States Franklin Roosevelt assumed power just as the War Department established its own formal policy calling for the acceptance of chemical warfare. Roosevelt, however, maintained his predecessor's prohibition, discouraging by the withholding of funds any preparation for large-scale adoption of chemical weapons. Following the breakdown of the Geneva Conference, at which the United States only narrowly succeeded in forcing through a British scheme which would allow limited chemical warfare preparations for defensive purposes only, a serious schism opened between the US Department of State and the War Department. The State Department insisted that the United States must be bound by the policy of defensive preparation. The War Department, however, argued that following the collapse of the Geneva Conference the United States was no longer 'a party to any treaty, now in force, that prohibits or restricts the use in warfare of toxic or non-toxic gases', and immediately convened a Joint Board that called for a comprehensive chemical warfare programme, both defensive and offensive.

United States Policy, 1941–5

Roosevelt remained absolutely intransigent in his opposition to War Department demands right up to the Second World War, despite intense pressure from the War Department and the national press in 1943–4 when American forces were engulfed in ferocious battles with the Japanese in the Pacific Islands. Japanese troops had developed a strategy of using tunnels and caves from which to launch surprise attacks on American troops trying to take the islands and then retreating into the tunnels or using them as a means of escape. Because Japanese soldiers would never willingly surrender it was too dangerous for the Americans to flush them out of the tunnels. Conventional weapons were of little use although flamethrowers were used to some good effect. Both the War Department and local commanders on the ground demanded that chemical weapons should be made available for the task and, locally, detailed war plans had been prepared for their deployment. Roosevelt, however, remained adamant. A year earlier, when he was cornered into agreeing with Prime Minister Winston Churchill that the Allies should respond in kind with overwhelming force should Germany use chemical weapons against Russia, he had still tempered his consent with an affirmation of his belief in the essential humanity of his enemies, when he wrote:

> I have been loath to believe that any nation, even our present enemies, could or would be willing to loose upon mankind such terrible and inhumane weapons. Use of such weapons has been outlawed by the general opinion of civilized mankind. This country has not used them, and I hope that we never will be compelled to use them. I state categorically that we shall under no circumstances resort to the use of such weapons unless they are first used by our enemies.

By early 1944 the President and the American intelligence services must have been aware of the routine use of both chemical and biological warfare agents by the Japanese in northern China, which would have provided adequate justification for Allied retaliation in kind, yet Roosevelt continued to veto deployment. His resolve was severely tested early in 1945 as news of American casualty rates on the island of Iwo Jima filtered home. During the February assault over 6,800 Americans lost their lives and a further 20,000 suffered serious injuries, representing, in total, one third of all Marine Corps casualties in the War. Large sections of the press and public opinion swung decisively in favour of using chemical weapons in order to save American lives. Between September 1944 and June 1945 polls indicated that the percentage of the population in favour of using gas against the Japanese rose from 23 per cent to 40 per cent. Newspaper headlines demanded 'We Should Gas Japan' and, most famously of all, with reference to the arguably limited success of napalm in flushing Japanese troops from the caves: 'You Can Cook 'em Better With Gas!' Roosevelt's policy was resolute: the United States' unambiguous and unbreakable policy was that it would not, under any circumstances of provocation, be the first to use chemical weapons. So firm was the Roosevelt policy that after his death in April 1945 proponents of chemical warfare were unable to muster enough momentum within the War Department even to bring the issue before President Truman.

British Policy, 1934–9

Although the growing political and military tensions that rippled out from central Europe during the early 1930s imposed broadly similar pressures on British and American foreign and domestic policies, there existed in Great Britain a subtle sense of real threat that was less obviously felt in the United States. Britain's problems were twofold: firstly, she was intimately entwined in a network of complex, overlapping diplomatic agreements with all the great and lesser European powers that, in 1939, were to lead her inexorably to war; and, secondly, although an island, she was protected from potential enemies by only 30 miles of calm sea. The latter fact was of immense significance. Developments in aircraft technology and, particularly, the growing power of the German Air Force led analysts to predict that the next war would be fought in the air. At the same time there was a growing awareness that the combination of bomber aircraft and chemical weapons produced a strategic weapon of such importance that no advanced nation could afford to deny itself. Terrifying predictions of the consequences of aero-chemical attacks on European cities appeared in the press. 'A single bomb,' it was said, 'dropped in Piccadilly Circus, in the middle of London, would kill every man, woman and child in central London from Regents Park to the Thames.' Another, subsequently much-derided report claimed that 'forty tons of one of the new chemical warfare agents would destroy the whole population of London.' The basis for this nonsense was a sloppy report from a London newspaper in 1928 that tried to compare London smog with the likely concentration of a poison-gas attack. Though most of the articles appearing in the press were no more than hysterical scaremongering, the theme was taken up by many respected organizations that subsequently seemed to give them an ill-deserved credibility. At its Rome conference in 1929, for example, the International Committee of the Red Cross predicted 'uncontrollable civil casualties in an aero-chemical war'.

At the same time, spurious reports were appearing in the press referring to large-scale, surreptitious chemical weapons research programmes secretly under way in Germany and the covert construction of a network of pilot production facilities. There were vaguely substantiated rumours, too, that Germany and the Soviet Union were secretly collaborating on chemical and biological warfare experiments. As we shall see in the following chapter, there was a limited amount of German-Russian joint chemical and biological warfare research under way in Russia, but this was exclusively defensive in character.

Probably the most alarming so-called intelligence report to come to public attention in the United Kingdom concerning German intentions was that published by Henry Wickham Steed in *The Nineteenth Century and Beyond* in July 1934, and subsequently repeated more widely in the national press. Wickham Steed's revelations were concerned more precisely with Germany's alleged biological warfare programme but, coming at a time when chemical warfare matters were once again attaining a high profile in the public mind, the transference from one scientific discipline to another in the perception of the scientifically illiterate masses was inevitable. The early 1930s was a time when popular public perception of the power of science, though tempered with a very shallow understanding, was at its peak. It was a time when the outward façade of science blended almost seamlessly with the visual arts in the art-deco movement. For the first time the concept of design was applied to industrial plant – the control room at Battersea Power Station, for example, was designed as much to be seen as to perform its function. In the cinema, films like Fritz Lang's *Metropolis* exemplified the fusion of art and science and also presented a sinister, exaggerated impression of the scientist's power to tinker with the secrets of life itself. It was also the time when the 'boffin' first made his appearance in the popular media – the archetypal scientist clad in a white lab coat, with bizarre hair and bumbling delivery, dubious in personal hygiene and perpetually engulfed in clouds of acrid tobacco smoke billowing from a foul briar pipe clamped between his teeth as he contemplated eerie, glowing, discharge tubes, bubbling retorts or notebooks dense with obtuse formulae. Bombarded from the new world about him, from the picture palace and the popular press, by such images of sinister science, there is little wonder that the average man in the street was so gullible and easily influenced when those with a vested interest, whether government, military or industrial, found value in frightening him with the fear of chemical weapons.

According to Wickham Steed, German military scientists had carried out clandestine experiments on the London tube system and on the Paris Metro to test the efficacy of using the underground railway systems to disseminate deadly bacteria. His allegations seemed to have had little immediate impact on the security services that treated them with considerable scepticism, but the effect on public opinion was sensational and this, in turn, exercised a profound subsequent effect upon government policy. When asked for clarification the British government made the classic security-service response that they could 'neither confirm nor deny the truth of Mr Wickham Steed's allegations'.

Subsequent research has proved beyond little doubt that there was no foundation to his assertion.

It must be remembered, however, that Wickham Steed was not a disinterested observer but had, in fact, worked for much of his life as a professional propagandist and held very strong anti-German views. He had served as editor of *The London Times* until 1922, when he left following a very public rift with Lord Northcliffe over the paper's reporting of events in Palestine. During the First World War, Wickham Steed had worked, at the invitation of Lord Northcliffe, as co-chairman of the Advisory Committee of the Austro-Hungarian section of the Enemy Propaganda Department. Wickham Steed's interpretation of the role of propaganda at that time, a philosophy which was obviously employed some twenty years later in his own privately sponsored diatribes against Hitler's Germany, was that:

> Propaganda must be two-edged. It must cut through obstacles on the home front while it cleaves the mental armour of the enemy on the outer front. Next to the work of physical fighting, no work is more urgent than this, it must fit policy as the sabre fits the scabbard.

Whether his assertions about German preparations are solely his own fabrication – 'to cut through obstacles on the home front' – or whether they were based upon hard evidence, culled either from legitimate or fabricated documentation, is a question as yet unanswered. In more recent years, however, it has come to light that Wickham Steed's prime source was the refugee anti-Nazi German activist Helmuth Simons. This combination of axe-grinding dissidence with a penchant for propaganda does not make a fertile field for the propagation of rational truth.

The Wickham Steed allegation was just one of a whole host of indicators, each in itself of minor significance, that were inflated and exaggerated by the hawkish, anti-appeasement factions within the British establishment in order to construct a convincing picture of Germany's evil intent. Similar things were happening in Germany, too, where public opinion was far from in universal favour of the increasingly right-wing government policy. In 1927 the War Materials Law was passed, national legislation which ratified and enforced the provisions of the Treaty of Versailles. This law was widely and routinely breached on a small scale but such contraventions were pointedly ignored by the government in power. Opposition political groups within Germany, particularly the Social Democrats, sought to publicize each breach they uncovered as widely as possible in order to further their cause of curtailing the influence of the Army in the German policy-making process. Those who questioned Germany's adherence to the Versailles Treaty – as well as the hard-pressed German Communist

Party, which used the event to bolster their attacks upon German industrialists – felt vindicated in May 1928 when an enormous explosion in a storage tank at a factory in Hamburg operated by Dr Stoltzenberg released a large volume of phosgene into the atmosphere. Although casualties were relatively light with just a small number of fatalities, the explosion initiated an international outcry. Stoltzenberg, whose factory had already been accused of shipping prohibited chemical agents to the Soviet Union and whose name was tentatively linked to some of the alleged chemical weapons research there, protested that phosgene was a legitimate chemical intermediary product widely used in a number of industrial processes. While this assertion was undeniable, the explosion, and the reporting of the subsequent compensation claims, once again highlighted the question of convertibility in the organic chemical industry.

ARP and the Road to War

By 1935 there was a general acceptance that another world war was inevitable: rumours of rearmament and preparation were rife; the instability of Germany, both politically and economically, was obvious to all; Spain was in turmoil; Italy was flexing its muscles in Africa; Britain distrusted everyone while fretting about India and the end of the Empire; and America twitched nervously about Japan's expansionist ambitions in the Pacific. Meanwhile, in every major city in Europe, groups of men appeared in unfamiliar uniforms and Civil Defence exercises occurred with increasing regularity.

From the perspective of the British government the overriding threat in the coming war was aerial bombardment by conventional high-explosive bombs. Pessimistic mis-assessments of the strength of the Luftwaffe led the Air Ministry to believe that on the day war with Germany was declared the skies over London would blacken with German bombers, the capital and the seat of Government would be utterly and instantly destroyed, the morale of the people would evaporate, the nation would descend into immediate, irreversible anarchy and it would be the end of England.

Public perception of the probable progress of the next war was very different though. Conventional warfare seemed somehow too mundane, the greater part of the population had first-hand or vivid second-hand experience of the First World War and was more or less inured to the horrors of death or mutilation by high explosives and shrapnel. It would be hard to frighten or intimidate the populace with dire warnings about a hazard with which they were already too familiar. The threat of sudden and horrible death through the invisible agency of chemical weapons, though, was a different matter and one that was seized upon by the Home Office. For years the media had whipped up

Britain's easily influenced masses into a frenzy of fear about chemical warfare. Grossly exaggerated accounts of genocidal extermination were lapped up by an eager nation, fascinated by, and bizarrely desperate to be petrified by, the unknown.

The disparity between the British government's own rational analysis of the likely progress of the coming war and that of the general public posed a dangerous problem for the Home Office. It was feared that the city dwelling public, convinced by media propaganda that they would be immediately targeted in a mass gas attack when war broke out, would panic and thus neglect to take precautions against the real danger which was, of course, from high-explosive bombs. At the same time, government perceived a marked reluctance on the part of the public to assimilate the risks of conventional bombing or to learn to take countermeasures for their own protection. It was imperative that the population, particularly the urban population of great cities like London, should for their own safety be trained in effective air-raid precaution practices, but while they were distracted by the chimera of gas warfare this would prove to be an intractable problem. The solution was a sophisticated process of psychological mass manipulation that required great precision in its application if it was to succeed. The first stage was to exaggerate further the threat from poison gas; the second to show that government scientists were in control of the threat; and that merely by taking a few simple measures the public could easily protect themselves. Once people fell into the habit of taking anti-gas precautions and adopted a mindset of effective self-preservation it would then be relatively simple to transfer those modes of behaviour to the real threat of fire and explosion.

A concerted Air Raid Precautions (ARP) scheme first appeared on the government agenda in July 1935 and the first wardens were appointed in April 1937. From its inception ARP and Civil Defence were synonymous with anti-gas training. Virtually all of the first ARP manuals and other publications were concerned with protecting the public from gas attack, despite the fact that there was a solid body of evidence that the strategic bombing of cities with chemical weapons was not an attractive military option to the Germans. Of these publications, the earliest, entitled *Anti-Gas Precautions and First Aid for Air Raid Casualties*, was issued in July 1935 and was quickly followed by a pair of booklets dealing with the gas protection of shipping, ports and factories. *Air Raid Precautions Handbook No. 1 – Personal Protection Against Gas*, published in 1937, had been provisionally entitled *The Protection of Your Home Against Air Raids*, the late change in title emphasizing the current government policy of enhancing public awareness of chemical attack.

All the available evidence conclusively proved that gas was far less effective than high explosives against large targets and also that percutaneous agents like mustard gas produced consistently lower casualties than high explosives. Evidence from Ethiopia, already examined above, indicated that while mustard gas might be effective against natives in open country the results would be significantly lower in a city offering physical cover for an educated population already aware of the nature of the threat. Gas, while having an unquestionable demoralizing effect upon the workforce, had no capacity to destroy factories and machinery and its anti-personnel effects were easily nullified by simple precautions. Thus it was very much an inferior weapon strategically to an aggressor and Civil Defence anti-gas measures would render it even more so.

The overt concentration by the Home Office and later the Ministry of Home Security upon the chemical warfare aspect of Civil Defence had the desired effect of taking the initiative away from the press while heightening public anxiety. Government intervention in the gas warfare debate served to focus the public mind. The fact that government was now not just talking in vague terms about an avoidable future conflict but was actually putting substantive defensive measures in place for a gas war that was suddenly seen as imminent concentrated the mind wonderfully.

The next stage was to demonstrate to the public that the government was in control of the situation and was developing all the required protective measures. ARP recruitment was stepped up, very obvious ARP exercises were staged and very visible experiments conducted in London parks using smoke bombs to demonstrate the dispersal of gas clouds. In Southampton, as part of a Civil Defence exercise, the city centre was sprayed from the air with an extract of molasses to simulate a mustard gas attack. Home Office Civil Defence officers ran lectures in community halls and works canteens calculated to deflate the previously hyped-up climate of fear by reassuring everyone that if they followed government advice then the dangers from chemical attack could be minimized. By the end of 1937 over 200,000 volunteers were trained in anti-gas measures, every policeman in Britain had been instructed on the subject and 20,000 doctors and nurses had received training on the treatment of gas casualties.

Proof of the British government's competence in dealing with the chemical threat was reinforced by an extensive programme that included the compulsory provision of gas decontamination centres in large public buildings and the issue of millions of gas masks. Production of gas masks started in November 1936 and within six months over 5,000,000 were held in Home Office stores with further shipments arriving at the rate of 500,000 per week. Some 30,000,000 of these were issued in September 1938 at the time of the Munich crisis. The deflation of international tension that followed did not stem the flow of respirators from the factories and by May 1939 the stockpile of available gas masks significantly outnumbered the population of Great Britain. The gas mask programme, whilst an unquestionable propaganda success, attracted much criticism from individuals and organizations that did not realize its true significance.

Writing as early as 1944, J.M. Spaight, a former Principal Assistant Secretary at the Air Ministry, questioned the excessive emphasis placed upon the gas threat in the immediate pre-war years:

> We were particularly concerned with the danger from gas. We had warnings from many sources that our cities would be flooded with toxic vapours the moment hostilities began. It is evident, in retrospect, that the Government of the time took this particular menace far more seriously than any other. The precautions taken to meet it were much more thorough and elaborate than those which were considered necessary for active defence. The provision of anti-aircraft guns and searchlights left, in comparison, much to be desired. There was a general obsession with the gas menace in the years 1937–39. In the House of Lords, for instance, on 13 December 1937, Lord Swinton, the Secretary of State for Air, in moving the second reading of the Air Raid Precautions Bill, devoted all the earlier part of his speech to the measures that were being taken to protect people against gas attack. They were most comprehensive.
>
> In the subsequent debate there was one discordant note only in the general acceptance of the necessity for the measures proposed. It was struck by Lord Trenchard. He suggested that rather too much attention was being paid to the gas menace. The greatest danger, in his opinion, came from high explosive and incendiary bombs.

Much criticism of the minutiae of the government's Air Raid Precautions scheme came from a vocal coterie of left-wing activists that coalesced around the Cambridge Scientists Anti-War Group. Prominent amongst the opponents of government policy was the renowned scientist, the Eton and Oxford educated son of an equally famous father, J.B.S. Haldane, whose book *ARP,* published in 1938, provides the most complete criticism of contemporary policy. Without understanding that whether or not such provisions would function adequately was largely irrelevant to the government's ulterior scheme, Haldane roundly condemned almost every aspect of the ARP organization. Hastily constructed, ad hoc gas-proof rooms in domestic buildings, he said, would not work and, more importantly from the left-wing point of view, could not be afforded by the working classes in the East End of London where the heaviest raids were predicted. Civilian issue gas masks were also targeted for criticism. Haldane and his followers demonstrated the supposed ineffectiveness of the respirators by blowing cigarette smoke through the filters which, they said, showed that such filters would be unable to prevent the passage of particulate organoarsenical poisons. Despite the fact that such poisons would be useless in the strategic role against cities and, if used at all, would be employed only in the tactical battlefield role, supplementary particulate filter elements were later added to the civilian respirators to appease the critics.

Haldane and his left-wing colleagues argued publicly that the real threat was, as the government already privately accepted, from high-explosive and incendiary bombs and that the emphasis on poison gas was a gross misdirection of resources. They argued that what were needed were not gas masks and decontamination centres but deep air-raid shelters and an effective fire service. This was all very well, but, as we have seen, government was convinced that even if they could afford to provide universal deep shelters for city dwellers – which they could not – and if the political will existed to provide them – which it did not – then the public response would be one, at best, of apathy or, more likely, active antipathy. However, the somewhat devious underlying policy of generating real fear through the threat of mass extermination by poison gas and then rationalizing the threat by means of demon-strating the effectiveness of simple protective measures, successfully conditioned the public to accept the real necessity for taking air-raid precautions seriously. Once the bombing began it was a simple task to translate this response to the threat from high-explosive and incendiary bombs.

Chapter 4

Interwar Research – Europe, Japan and the USA

The strictly enforced provisions of the Treaty of Versailles in conjunction with the economic consequences of the punitive reparations payments demanded by the Allies at the end of the First World War effectively denuded Germany of much of her munitions-making capacity, both conventional and chemical. Her chemical industry in particular was, as we have seen in previous chapters of this book, particularly targeted for motives that went rather beyond the immediate needs of international security. All her offensive research was terminated with the closure of the Kaiser Wilhelm Institute in 1919, although a limited amount of protective research was allowed to continue at the Berlin Reichswehr Hauptgasschultzlager.

Covert offensive research, still masquerading as protective experimentation, increased gradually as the influence of the Allied Control Commission declined after 1924, but continued to be of only limited significance due partly to a lack of funding, reflecting the parlous state of the German economy, but more importantly from the distinct, lingering disinclination of the German military leadership to embrace the concept of chemical warfare. The Reichswehr establishment, which had transferred from Berlin to Hanover in 1924, was by 1926 supplemented by a second Hauptgasschultzlager at Spandau which purported to be involved only in the maintenance of gas masks, but in fact was a cover for the recently formed Central Chemical Research Laboratory. While the Spandau laboratory's prime concern was with the development of mustard gas detectors and analysers, additional undercover research was progressing at the Chatlottenburg laboratory, at Wurzburg University, and several other academic laboratories, into the development of new toxic agents with military potential.

The 'Tomka' Project
A secret agreement allowing joint military research and field testing, in contravention of the Treaty of Versailles, existed between Germany and the Soviet Union from 1922. Generally known as the 'Tomka' project, an important component of the agreement, ratified in 1927,

concerned chemical warfare investigations into the toxicology of mustard gas under extreme field conditions at a secret site at Shikhani, approximately 15 miles from Volsk. For this purpose the field-testing facilities at Shikhani, established in 1928, were perfect, for the seasonal temperatures fluctuated between –45 degrees and +45 degrees. Other, arguably legitimate, work undertaken under the 'Tomka' umbrella included post-exposure therapeutics, sampling and quantitative analysis of mustard gas, and the development of rubberized protective clothing.

To run in parallel with the primary research undertaken at Shikhani the Germans agreed to co-operate in the construction of a factory complex at Trotsk, near Samarsa, to be operated by a nominally independent joint company to manufacture chemical warfare agents. Work here began in 1922 but progressed hesitantly and was only completed in 1928. The whole period of German-Soviet co-operation was marked by a distinct atmosphere of mutual distrust. The Germans built their own barracks and welfare facilities at Shikhani, supplied all their own equipment, financed all aspects of their own infrastructure and research programme and maintained independent accounts. The Soviets, meanwhile, insisted upon two of their own staff members of equal rank shadowing the work of each German scientist. When they withdrew in 1933 the Germans dismantled and removed all their equipment and destroyed any structures and facilities that could not be physically transported away.

The German contingent at Shikhani consisted of a senior commanding officer and two administrators who directed a scientific staff of three chemists, one toxicologist, one meteorologist and one physician. These were supported by a small technical staff of one engineer, two pyrotechnicians and five laboratory assistants. Field testing was undertaken by three Luftwaffe pilots and eight service engineers. The much larger Soviet staff was under the command of Y.M. Fishman, head of the chemical weapons branch of the Red Army and an utterly committed proponent of chemical warfare.

German Research Establishments

There can be little doubt that chemical weapons research in Germany throughout the mid-1930s was exclusively defensive in nature, such research being actively encouraged by the Reichswehr, particularly after the Soviet proving ground at Shikhani became available. The higher military authorities in Germany remained stolidly indifferent to the acquisition of an offensive chemical capability until at least 1934 when, under pressure from the Waffenampt, an overt programme of rearmament was instituted and chemical weapons research accelerated. Only a year earlier, however, in 1933, the Army Truppenamt, in a five-year plan that would establish procurement targets up until 1938, concluded that the acquisition of an offensive capability would not be worthwhile even as a precaution against possible enemy initiation. This decision was based largely upon the assumption that France, Great Britain and the Soviet Union had gained an unassailable fifteen-year lead in the field of chemical weapons research and that even the most concerted effort to gain ground would be a fruitless and wasteful diversion of resources. Flawed intelligence garnered by the notoriously inept German intelligence services during the years of faltering co-operation with the Soviets at Shikhani had grossly exaggerated the Soviet chemical arsenal, while similar inflated estimates of French and British capabilities provided further incentives for despondency.

Just as in the United Kingdom the RAF took a rather more proactive lead than the land or sea services in embracing the perceived benefits of chemical weapons, air force interests in Germany took the lead in pro-moting the advantages of a powerful offensive chemical arm. Within the Waffenampt a separate chemical warfare department, Waff Prufwesen 9, was formed in 1934, ostensibly to test anti-gas equipment but in fact to develop all aspects of chemical warfare. Waff Prufwesen 9 rapidly took control of the Heeresversuchzlaboratorien at Spandau, developed the Heeresversuchsstelle proving ground on Luneburg Heath, where work begun under the 'Tomka' project was resumed on a larger scale, and erected a pilot plant for the production of gas weapons at Munsterlager. A little later, a $120 \, km^2$ proving ground was laid out near Raubkammer.

Two years later, in 1936, the Army established its own indepen-dent Chemical Troops and Gas Inspectorate within the Army General Office and completed a new gas defence training establishment at Celle, near Hanover, in 1938.

Under a decree of 1935 all discoveries in academic or industrial laboratories of new chemical agents that might have warlike applica-tions were to be reported to the chemical weapons research centre at Spandau for evaluation. The most far-reaching consequence of this decree, the accidental discovery and subsequent development of organo-phosphorous nerve gases, following upon the work of Dr Schrader in the Wuppertal-Elberfeld laboratories of I.G. Farben, is detailed in Chapter 7. Thereafter an increasing volume of work relat-ing to chemical warfare was done in German industrial laboratories, particularly those of I.G. Farben at Leverkusen where much funda-mental research was undertaken into the nature of activated charcoal for respirators and the synthesis of fluoroacetic acid, the halogen fluorides and the nerve gas precursors.

German Manufacturing Facilities
Although a certain amount of pilot production was undertaken in state-owned facilities, the prospective scale of manufacture meant that in

Germany, as in the United Kingdom, the mass production of chemical warfare agents could only be undertaken with the co-operation of the largest of the industrial chemical firms. In the chapter that follows we will look in some detail at the factories built and operated in the United Kingdom by Imperial Chemical Industries on behalf of the Ministry of Supply, but here we will more briefly examine the strikingly parallel organization that evolved in Germany.

Responsibility for the manufacture of offensive chemical agents, principally mustard gas, inevitably devolved upon I.G. Farben and its associate companies. By the winter of 1938 Germany's first mustard gas plant at Huls was producing some 600 tons of vesicant per month, increasing to its maximum capacity of 1,400 tons per month by the following February. Pre-war factories at Hannover-Seelze and Ludwigshaven were producing approximately 200 tons of chloroacetophenone per month while other plants at Ammendorf and Strassfurth, the latter completed in 1938, manufactured arsinol, an additive used to depress the freezing point of mustard gas, at the rate of 600 tons per month. The Ludwigshaven works was extended in 1940 by the addition of a 290-ton per month phosgene plant.

Towards the end of 1938 two new I.G. Farben subsidiary companies were created to oversee the construction and operation of a series of formidable new factories that came on line in 1941–2. The new plants, at Gendorf, Urdingen, Ludwigshaven, Wolfen and Dyhernfurth near Breslau, were designed and built by Luranil-Baugesellschaft and operated on behalf of the German Army by Anorgana GmbH. By far the most important of these factories was the Gendorf works, the monthly output of which peaked at 4,000 tons. Other plants operated by Anorgana produced mainly phosgene, adamsite and chlorosacetophenone at the rates of a few hundred tons per month. In 1941 a small nitrogen mustard facility was added to the existing arsinol plant at Ammendorf. The spectacularly sinister group of factories at Dyhernfurth, erected during the closing years of the War, were involved in the manufacture of nerve agents and will be examined in a little more detail in Chapter 7. It is illustrative of the controversial 'convertibility' issue that so exercised the minds of delegates to the Geneva Conference that a factory erected at Hahnenberg-Leese in 1940 as a standby reserve arsinol plant – in case the main production centres at Ammendorf and Strassfurth were destroyed – never, in fact, entered production and was instead adapted for the manufacture of saccharine and other artificial sweeteners.

At the start of the War, Germany's stockpile of chemical warfare agents amounted to approximately 12,000 tons, some 80 per cent of which was mustard gas, almost all retained in bulk storage rather than filled into weapons.

The United States

We have seen already the tension that existed between the United States War Department, the Chemical Warfare Service and the Administration regarding chemical warfare policy throughout the interwar years. We have seen, too, the manner in which elements within the chemical industry sought to manipulate this tension and the larger international security anxieties to its own pecuniary interests. Although the great American chemical houses were swift to promote the military advantages of a strong organic chemical industry – reliant largely upon appropriated German technology and intellectual assets, with the implication that they could only fulfil the nation's chemical warfare needs if thus endowed – when push came to shove, in both world wars, they demonstrated a marked reluctance to deliver the promised goods in full or even part.

Following the United States' late entry into the First World War in 1917, just at the height of the chemical conflict, the US administration sought in vain to galvanize the chemical industry into developing and delivering much-needed supplies of chemical warfare agents. The unwillingness of the industry may be put down partly to the commercial unattractiveness of the proposals that were put to them, but the major deterrent factor was that the necessary plant and expertise simply did not exist. The US situation mirrored exactly that which pertained in the United Kingdom – mustard gas was sprung upon the Allies as a complete surprise for which they were absolutely unprepared. Although the manufacturing process was not, in comparison, for example, with the recently developed high-pressure nitrogen processes, a particularly complex one, it was a novelty which had not previously been addressed. Significantly, there was a similar reluctance to commit amongst the established British manufacturers and ultimately it was one of the firms conspicuously left out of the government-sponsored amalgamations of 1915 that was the only manufacturer to produce mustard gas in substantial volumes.

Unable to interest industry, the United States Army Ordnance Department constructed its own manufacturing and filling facilities at Edgewood Arsenal late in 1917. The finished complex consisted of four separate manufacturing plants producing chlorine, as a raw material for other agents rather than as a weapon in its elemental form, chloropicrin, phosgene and mustard gas. Four shell-filling plants were also erected although only two were completed before the armistice. By June 1918, when the collective plants at Edgewood were taken over by the newly formed Chemical Warfare Service, they were producing colossal amounts of chemical warfare agents of all types including lewisite, mustard gas, bromobenzyl cyanide, chloropicrin, phosgene and diphenylchloroarsine. At the end of the War the Edgewood complex was producing four times more toxic agents than the entire German chemical industry, and double the output of France and the United Kingdom combined.

Mass production ceased immediately after the armistice although Edgewood's days were far from numbered. The site became the headquarters of the United States Chemical Warfare Service, extensive new research laboratories were established and both new and existing plant were operated to produce a wide range of toxic agents on a pilot scale for experimental purposes. The potential of Edgewood Arsenal figured significantly in General Fries' campaign for an offensive chemical weapons policy. The CWS *Annual Report* of 1920, which was in essence a statement of Fries' personal ambition, stated that an enemy would be dissuaded from starting a war with the United States or its allies, should the United States adopt a 'first use' chemical weapons policy, 'knowing that the United States with its incomparable natural resources and highly developed manufacturing possibilities will be able to manufacture and deliver on the field of battle a greater quantity of chemicals than any other single nation, or indeed any other group of nations'.

Developments at Edgewood were determined largely by the prevailing Presidential attitude regarding America's international treaty obligations, and Fries' policies were consistently rejected throughout the 1920s. Despite Roosevelt's disapproval which was, if anything, somewhat more entrenched than that of his predecessors, there was, however, a perceptible shift in attitude in the early 1930s. The War Department had, by 1933, adopted the view that chemical warfare preparations should be both defensive and offensive in nature, with a ready capability for retaliation in kind. With increased Congressional support for the Chemical Warfare Service, authority was given for the partial refurbishment of the Edgewood Arsenal, although mainstream military disinterest and a crippling lack of funds due to the economic depression meant that concrete progress was slow. On paper, though hardly in practice, the attitude of the War Department had hardened further by the end of the following year when the Joint Board announced that:

> The United States will make all necessary preparations for the use of chemical weapons from the outbreak of war. The use of chemical warfare, including the use of toxic agents, from the inception of hostilities is authorized, subject to such restrictions or prohibitions as may be contained in any duly ratified international convention or conventions, which at that time may be binding upon the United States and the enemy's state or states.

It was not until the end of 1937 that the First World War mustard gas plant, manufacturing cheap but impure and rather unstable vesicant by the Levinstein process, and the existing phosgene plant, were back in limited production. Thereafter, however, little more rehabilitation was undertaken until the United States entered the Second World War. A second phosgene plant was opened at Edgewood in the winter of 1941, the chloroacetophenone plant was extended and the mustard gas plant was brought up to full capacity. Rather late in the War, in 1945, a new, small-scale, distilled mustard gas factory was constructed prior to the completion of a similar but larger facility at Rocky Mountain Arsenal.

To meet the growing demands of the Chemical Warfare Service three further chemical weapons production facilities were built. The first of these, at Huntsville, Alabama, was completed in August 1941 at a cost of $63,400,000. The complex of factory and storage sites was spread over an area of 33,000 acres and employed a peak staff of 6,707, some 90 per cent of whom were low-grade civilian workers. Huntsville Arsenal produced a wide range of toxic chemical weapons together with incendiary weapons, marker smokes and masking smoke. The first plant to open, manufacturing incendiary bombs, began production in February 1942 but came to a premature end three months later, in April 1942, when the entire works was destroyed in a catastrophic fire.

Huntsville produced its own chlorine from two plants with a combined daily output of 90 tons of liquid chlorine and approximately 100 tons of caustic soda. Production started in May 1942 and continued uninterrupted until July 1945. Mustard gas was manufactured in six separate plants, all of which ceased production in May 1943 when it became evident, as in the United Kingdom, that the stability of the vast stockpiles that were building up could not be guaranteed. As the Pacific War entered its final phase and it was thought likely that an invasion of the Japanese mainland might be inevitable, preparations were made for the resumption of mustard gas production at Huntsville. In June 1945 three of the six plants were reactivated and five batches of the intermediary product sulphur monochloride were manufactured before the Japanese surrendered.

Huntsville also manufactured lewisite and phosgene, the two other staples of the chemical warfare industry. Six lewisite plants were planned but of these only four were operational before production ceased in October 1943. Phosgene was something of a late starter, the single plant starting up in February 1944 and closing down only eleven months later. The agent produced by this plant was filled into 500 lb and 1,000 lb bombs, all of which were, immediately after the War, broken down on site and the recovered contents sold into the commercial sector at a modest profit.

Two separate mustard gas filling lines were authorized at Huntsville in July 1941, one to fill artillery shells (mainly 105 mm M60s), and one to fill aerial bombs. A third plant, commissioned immediately after

Pearl Harbor, was altered during construction to fill oil incendiary bombs. All mustard gas filling ceased in March 1944 although No. 2 plant was briefly reactivated in October 1944 to fill M70 bombs. It was reactivated again, somewhat sinisterly, in August 1945 in order to fill a further 5,556 M70 bombs.

The third major chemical weapons plant was at Rocky Mountain Arsenal, Colorado, where construction of the 20,000-acre site started in June 1942. Production of Levinstein mustard gas and lewisite began approximately nine months later in the spring of 1943. Following the success of the experimental distilled mustard gas plant at Edgewood in 1944 a large-scale factory was erected at Rocky Mountain which produced 4,100 tons of very pure mustard gas before manufacture abruptly ceased in 1945.

Pine Bluff Arsenal in Arkansas also contributed to the US chemical weapons stockpile. Work on the 15,000-acre complex, originally established for the production of thermite- and magnesium-based incendiary weapons, began in November 1941. It was decided, however, to extend the range of materials developed and in 1942 two new production units were opened for the manufacture of mustard gas and lewisite. The following year, building upon pilot plant experience at Edgewood Arsenal, a new plant was erected at Pine Bluff for the manufacture of nitrogen-mustard. Development of this fast-acting form of mustard gas, in which the sulphur atoms of conventional mustard gas are replaced by atoms of nitrogen (i.e. two CH2-CH2-Cl chains linked by a single nitrogen atom) was begun in Germany two years earlier and was developed there with some enthusiasm. British research was halted abruptly following an explosion at the pilot production plant. Pine Bluff produced about 100 tons of nitrogen mustard but it never became a mainstream chemical warfare agent due principally to questions about its long-term stability in storage. As a vesicant it produced debilitating blisters almost instantaneously, unlike sulphur mustard which took many hours before symptoms developed, but its overall effects were somewhat less severe.

Private industry, as we have seen, was particularly reluctant to engage in the manufacture of chemical warfare agents. Three firms, Monsanto, DuPont and the American Cyanamid Company provided small quantities of chemicals which, in their natural state, were staple peacetime products yet which straddled the boundary between run-of-the-mill chemical compounds and offensive toxic horrors. Monsanto supplied phosgene from its Duck River plant in Colombia, Tennessee; American Cyanamid shipped quantities of cyanogen chloride from its Warners plant in New York and from Owl plant in Azusa, California; while both American Cyanamid and DuPont jointly supplied approximately 560 tons of hydrogen cyanide, a ubiquitous peacetime product, from several of their factories.

At the end of the First World War the United States possessed a stockpile of approximately 8,000 tons of poison gas, mainly mustard gas and phosgene, all of which was either recovered for industrial use or dumped at sea. Between 1937 and her entry into the War, she produced a small, mixed inventory of no more than 500 tons of chemical warfare agents, over half of which consisted of Levinstein mustard gas of dubious purity. Between 1942 and 1945 the stockpile had increased phenomenally to 134,500 tons, most of which had been manufactured before October 1943.

Japanese Research and Manufacture

Although American chemical warfare policy, under the Fries principle, was to maintain a sufficiently preponderant mass of chemical weapons to dissuade any potential enemy, anywhere in the world, from contemplating initiating a war against the United States, it is patently obvious that, given the paucity of its arsenal – no more than 500 tons – prior to the declaration of war with Japan, that this was a policy unfulfilled. It was the prospect of a war with Japan, a nation whose value systems and alien code of military ethics were, to American eyes, largely unknown, that catalysed American chemical weapons production, rather than the distant and largely irrelevant threats posed by Germany. Post-war intelligence analysis proved that American apprehension with regard to Japanese chemical warfare capability was largely groundless but, given the reports emanating from China since 1937, such fears were far from irrational.

Amongst the major Second World War combatants, Japan was unique in that it had no first-hand experience of chemical warfare upon which to formulate a national policy. Similarly it was, with the exception of the United States, the only country sufficiently distant from its enemies to be effectively immune from the likelihood of immediate attack upon its homeland. Japan's geographical and psychological isolation from the experiences of the First World War profoundly affected public and military attitudes to chemical warfare in disparate ways. Without the personal experience of chemical warfare that haunted every community, if not every family, in the Western world, Japanese public opinion was unaffected by the wave of popular revulsion that spread across Europe and North America during the 1920s. On the other hand, the high profile that was assured to chemical warfare by both its opponents and proponents in the West rendered chemical warfare an inevitable subject of intense interest in Japanese military circles. The absence of moderating historical baggage may explain the apparent lack of inhibition on Japanese employment of both chemical and biological weapons against China during the Sino-Japanese War. Contrarily, lack of awareness of its potentially catastrophic consequences if used against a poorly protected civilian population may explain Japan's pitifully poor anti-gas civil defence measures.

The high level post-war international debate over chemical warfare stimulated much interest in the Japanese Army and Navy. Anything, they thought, that could create so much intense controversy must have some military value. Consequently, in August 1919, the Japanese Army established a scientific research department that included within its remit the study of chemical warfare. The Japanese Navy initiated independent investigations into the potential of poison gas in 1923 but did not embark upon a comprehensive research programme until 1931.

By 1925 the Army was sufficiently confident of the military value of chemical weapons to found a separate chemical warfare department. Responsibility for primary research was delegated to the Army Ordnance Bureau's Scientific Research Station, which moved from Itabashi to Yodobashiku, Tokyo, in 1922 when it assumed the chemical warfare role. Renamed the Sixth Military Laboratory in 1935, the research facilities were manned, by the end of the War, by a staff of 100 military scientists and a support staff of some 600 civilians. A Manchurian outstation was built at Chichihara with a staff of 300 and proving grounds were established in Manchuria, Formosa and on the home islands.

Although, as in the United States, the commercial sector in Japan had for many years maintained substantial production facilities for phosgene and, to a lesser extent, chloropicrin, very little of this was acquired for military purposes and, indeed, the Japanese largely discounted phosgene as a war gas. The army concentrated its interest on mustard gas, diphenylcyanoarsine and lewisite as its principal war gases, and tinkered also with hydrogen cyanide and chloroacetophenone. Production of all five agents was concentrated in the Army's own factories at Tadanoumi Arsenal at Hiroshima-ken, where the first experimental batch of mustard gas was made in 1928. Full-scale production of all three major chemical warfare agents did not start until 1934. American intelligence reports compiled in 1946 from captured Japanese records indicate that prior to the declaration of war with the United States, Tadanoumi Arsenal produced a total of 3,082 tons of mustard gas and lewisite, 1,067 tons of diphenylcyanoarsine, 40 tons of chloroaceto-phenone and a small quantity of cyanide. Between 1942 and 1945 production amounted to rather less than 1,000 tons of mustard gas, 431 tons of lewisite, 770 tons of diphenychloroarsine and insignificant amounts of the two minor agents. These quantities included gases supplied to the Japanese Air Force. Although the Air Force had initiated chemical weapons research in the Third Air Technical Laboratory at Tachikawa Air Base in 1931 it never went on to develop its own manufacturing facilities.

Chemical warfare research undertaken by the Japanese Navy began within the Naval Technical Institute at Tsukijij near Tokyo in 1923 but was transferred to the Naval Powder Factory at Hiratsuka, Kanagawa-ken, in 1931. Pilot production of some 30 tons of mustard gas began in 1923 but, although a large-scale production plant was commissioned at the Naval Powder Factory, which subsequently became incorporated into the Sagami Naval Yard in 1943, the total output by the end of the War was less than 500 tons. The factory at Sagami also produced approximately 100 tons each of chloroacetophenone and diphenylcyanoarsine between 1931 and 1945.

The relatively small quantities of chemical warfare materiel produced by Japan is indicative of the distinct lack of enthusiasm that existed in the higher ranks of the military for this form of warfare. It was accepted that in certain circumstances such weapons might demonstrate a limited tactical advantage, an advantage that was demonstrated in a number of engagements with the Chinese Army, but there was little faith in its strategic value or in its value against a well-prepared, more sophisticated enemy.

France

By the end of the First World War military laboratories in most European countries were engaged to a greater or lesser degree in chemical weapons research, either with a view to developing civil defence measures because they felt threatened by its possession by its neighbours, or as a promising new weapon for their own defence. By 1936 German war preparations were in train and she looked in trepidation at the states of readiness of her future enemies. Fuelled by an inexact assessment of France's gas warfare capabilities during the recent war and by pessimistic intelligence reports of current developments in that country, the German High Command considered France, along with the Soviet Union, as dangerous adversaries in the field of chemical warfare. A report from Dr Rudolph Hanslian, a German expert in chemical warfare, suggested that as many as thirty factories in France, all but six of them in the private sector, were actively involved in the production of war gases, and that research in any number of academic institutions had continued unabated since the First World War. Whilst Hanslian's report was much exaggerated he was correct in that France was deeply concerned about both the defensive and offensive aspects of chemical warfare, as far as the offensive aspect could be contained within the mantle of deterrence. That France should be so concerned should have been the cause of no surprise considering that the soil of France, along with that of Belgium, had borne the brunt of Germany's gas offensive and stood to fall on the debit side of the account again in the next war. Where France's fears lay was plain to see. The huge but fatally flawed chain of buried fortifications that comprised the Maginot Line uncompromisingly pointed at Germany and the internal arrangements of the Maginot Line, which was built in 1927 and planned many years earlier, clearly illustrates the French fixation with Germany's potential to wage chemical war. Complex air conditioning and ventilation systems provided fresh air to the entire complex which was spread across many levels, most of which were deep underground. All the inlet shafts through which external air was drawn were fitted with special filters to trap poison gas and particulate poisons, and measures were taken to ensure that a slight positive pressure was maintained within the entire complex at all times to prevent the accidental inward leakage of contaminated air. Exactly the same principles of positive pressure plenums were followed in the proliferation of bunkers built throughout the cold war to protect against the ingress of chemical, biological or nuclear contamination.

Chapter 5

Interwar Research in the United Kingdom

The United Kingdom was completely unprepared for chemical warfare in 1915. No research, manufacturing or laboratory facilities suitable for the study of chemical warfare agents existed, so when the first German attacks occurred in the spring of 1915 it was necessary to hurriedly set up ad hoc analytical stations on the battlefield to exactly determine the nature of the threat that faced the Allied forces. Later, a few existing French academic laboratories were pressed into service but, as the use of chemical weapons intensified, it soon became apparent that a proper research facility was required in the United Kingdom where all aspects of gas warfare could be scientifically studied. It was realized that as well as conventional laboratories such a facility would require large tracts of land upon which to carry out field trials of offensive agents, dissemination apparatus and defensive equipment. The necessity of providing extensive safety zones to prevent accidental contamination of civilians or surrounding land somewhat limited the scope of the War Office team charged with locating a suitable site but eventually, after rejecting a proposed site on Cannock Chase after a few initial trials, the War Department Experimental Ground was established at Porton Down in the early spring of 1916.

In the early decades of the twentieth century Salisbury Plain was a wild, sparsely inhabited area yet not too remote from London, the south coast naval dockyards and a number of important War Office sites in southern England. Huge tracts of land on the plain had already been taken over by the War Office for training purposes so it was a logical move to utilize further areas for gas experimentation. At first it was assumed that only minimal field facilities would be required; just a large enough area of countryside to simulate a typical European battle front across which the dispersal of cylinder gas could be observed. To this end, a few dozen cylinders of chlorine – later supplemented by cylinders of hydrogen sulphide – were transported onto the plain in March 1916 and stored under light military guard in a small copse later known as Gas Wood. By 30 March a couple of temporary wooden huts had been erected, one to serve as a store, the other as offices for the small Royal Engineers detachment that would oversee operations there. The first experiments were scheduled to begin early in April but were

96

delayed for some weeks due to adverse weather conditions. Six civilian mines rescue personnel, the only men at that time experienced in the use of respirators, were brought down from Hednesford in the mining district of Derbyshire to collect samples from the gas clouds while protected by their industrial respirators. The samples, collected simply by removing the bungs from a number of previously evacuated Winchester quart bottles, were analysed in an open-air laboratory established in Gas Wood. Later, on 26 May, the previous chlorine experiments were repeated on a larger scale using hydrogen sulphide. Some 120 cylinders of hydrogen sulphide were spaced at one-yard intervals in a shallow trench to make a front rather more than 100 yards in length, downwind of which concentric arcs of caged rats were laid out to a range of approximately a quarter of a mile. It was found that more than half the rats at a range of 300 yards from the release point died. The concentration of gas in the atmosphere was calculated from samples taken by the mines rescue men and from this data the lethal human dose could be extrapolated. This early experiment high-lighted a major shortcoming of hydrogen sulphide, which it was hoped would prove a superior killing agent to chlorine, in that the gas was rather too light and thus prone to rise in currents of air. Subsequently, a denser mixture of hydrogen sulphide and chloropicrin, code-named 'Green Star', demonstrated sufficiently promising qualities for large quantities to be shipped to France for operational use. Routine inspection of the battlefield stockpiles revealed that some three quarters of the cylinders were dangerously corroded and the whole exercise was subsequently abandoned.

Meanwhile, under pressure from the Chemical Advisory Committee of the Trench Warfare Research Department the War Office agreed to greatly extend the scope of the Porton establishment and to create permanent facilities there. Large-scale works began under the guidance of the officer in charge of works, Lieutenant Murray RE, in January 1917. Gradually, as increasing numbers of men were drafted to Porton, the original pair of temporary huts developed into a full-scale military establishment with a final muster of 916 officers and men, 500 civilian workmen and 33 women of Queen Mary's Army Auxiliary Corps employed as typists and clerks. Permanent laboratories were built along with sixty-four barrack huts for the men, medical and welfare facilities including a cinema, concert hall and dining rooms. An electricity generating plant was installed early in 1918. Special facilities were built for a photographic unit and meteorological staff, carpenters and black-smiths shops were provided to service the general needs of the camp and specialist machine shops were built for the teams of precision engineers employed to fabricate or adapt experimental projectiles and artillery for the chemical role. The arrival of the Anti-Gas Department of the Royal Army Medical College in 1917 strengthened the work of the station's physiological unit in the fields of individual and collective protection, principally as a result of a series of investigations conducted under the control of Captain H. Hartley who later went on to become Controller of the Chemical Warfare Department of the War Office at the end of the War.

As the focus of chemical warfare turned from cylinders to artillery delivery the workloads of both the engineering division at Porton and of the Royal Artillery Experimental Battery increased enormously and more land was acquired for an extended artillery range. To facilitate movement of fuel, materials and men around the extensive camp site and ranges, a 2-foot gauge railway was opened in 1918. The line, which eventually reached to over 8 miles in length, extended from interchange sidings at the London & South Western Railway main line station at Porton to the main camp site with a complex network of sidings to serve the various stores, machine shops and coal yards. Further extensions served ammunition magazines at Gas Wood and beyond. Rolling stock consisted of a mixed inventory of freight and passenger vehicles, the latter being used regularly by civilian employees who travelled to work daily from Salisbury via the LSWR line to Porton station where they transferred to the War Office narrow-gauge system. Until replaced by a small fleet of diesel locomotives shortly before its closure in 1951 the Porton railway was operated by five steam saddle-tank engines, supplemented by a small petrol-paraffin locomotive.

Staffing at Porton throughout the First World War and beyond illustrates the degree to which eminent men from all the scientific disciplines were involved, with varying degrees of willingness, in the unpleasant world of chemical warfare. A quick scan of the muster rolls might give the superficial impression that the work of the station was firmly in the hands of military scientists with only one civilian, Joseph Bancroft, on the payroll, but this would fail to give a true picture of the integration of academic and military science, even in the popularly repugnant field of chemical warfare. The first camp commandant at Porton, for example, was A.W. Crossley FRS, previously Professor of Organic Chemistry at King's College, London. The genesis of Crossley's involvement in chemical warfare lay with his position as Secretary of the Chemical Sub-committee of the Royal Society War Committee. In November 1915, he was given the rank of Lieutenant Colonel and despatched to France as Liaison Officer for Chemical Warfare, returning in June 1916 to take up the position of Commandant and Superintendent of Experiments at Porton. Under his dynamic leadership the range and depth of research at Porton progressed prodigiously and by the time of the armistice the station had issued 7,769 reports on every conceivable aspect of offensive and defensive chemical warfare. Immediately after peace was declared Crossley was offered the Daniell Professorship of Chemistry at Kings College, a position he took up following his demobilization in October 1919.

The armistice saw an immediate cessation of chemical weapons manufacturing in the United Kingdom but research continued for some years at a level only a little reduced from its wartime rate. In October 1917 responsibility relating to gas and anti-gas research had been transferred from the War Office to the Ministry of Munitions which incorporated the Chemical Warfare Committee and some functions of the Trench Warfare Research Department into its existing design and research department. With the rundown of the Ministry of Munitions following the end of the War, the administration of chemical warfare matters passed back to the War Office as a responsibility of the Master-General of the Ordnance. Although, by 1921, the War Office was expressing reservations about the continued existence of the Chemical Defence Experimental Station at Porton, the Chemical Warfare Advisory Committee had, just a year earlier, signalled its intention to 'develop to the utmost extent the offensive and defensive aspects of chemical weapons'. Initially some sixty leading academic and industrial scientists were invited to participate in the work of the committee in conjunction with a large group of members drawn from the military. Over time the committee stabilized at twenty-five permanent members and approximately ninety associates and consultants. Throughout this period, during which the Advisory Committee worked in parallel with a Chemical Warfare Sub-committee of the Imperial Defence Committee, both bodies were subject to antipathy from the public and Parliament. Such research ran contrary to the prevailing public mood, and Parliament, in a period of economic retrenchment, questioned both its cost and relevance.

Despite the 1921 remit to 'develop ... the offensive and defensive aspects of chemical weapons' a subtle change in emphasis arose in the committee's public assessments of its work during the late 1920s in an attempt to more closely align itself to the national mood. Right up until 1936 it laid great stress upon the fact that its work to date had been solely in the field of chemical defence. There was some disquiet when, as we have already seen, it was revealed in 1932 that government-subsidized weapons research was under way at Oxford, Cambridge and London Universities, the implication being that the intensity of the development programme was such that the existing laboratory at Porton was unable to cope. It was also revealed that industry had been recruited to assist in respirator research and, more sinisterly, there were suggestions that industrial scale plants had been erected for the manufacture of chemical warfare agents. Information had been released in

1923 concerning the ailing United Alkali Company, soon to become a minor player in the great ICI combination, which was manufacturing chloroacetophenone (CN) under a government contract at the initial rate of 100 kg per month. By 1927 output had increased to 2,000 kg per month but the War Office insisted that all of this was required for field testing respirators. ICI, however, admitted that considerable quantities were also loaded into riot-control weapons.

Questions were asked, too, about the status of the chemical defence manufacturing establishment at Sutton Oak in Lancashire. Sutton Oak, like the CDRE at Porton and the headquarters of the Chemical Defence Research Department in London – which controlled and also financed the university research programmes – came under the nominal control of the War Office via the Master-General of the Ordnance, but offered its facilities to all three services. Sutton Oak had operated as a gas production factory during the War and for a few years afterwards, but in 1925 it was reconstituted as the Sutton Oak Research Establishment, its function essentially that of an experimental pilot production plant for agents developed at Porton. In the same year the recently redesignated Chemical Defence Experimental Station, Porton – in a period of pacifism, its new name reflecting its supposedly peaceful, purely defensive purpose – was, for purposes of efficiency, reorganized into six discrete departments: Meteorology, Technical, Physical, Physiological, Chemistry and Design.

The future direction of research at Porton was set out in May 1919 by the Holland Committee, under the chairmanship of Lieutenant General Sir Arthur Holland. The committee's report, issued in 1920, recommended that work at Porton should continue as before until the League of Nations ruled on the legitimacy of chemical warfare. More importantly, however, from the point of view of raising the standard of research undertaken there, Holland stressed that, whereas most of the wartime work was reactive in nature, what was required was a programme of fundamental proactive research. The committee realized that to achieve this would require the recruitment of the best minds from the academic establishment, stressing in its report that 'nothing short of £2,000 per year could be relied upon to induce a man of the first rank to accept the post of Director of Research at Porton.' Though it is inconceivable that the lure of money was by itself an adequate incentive to attract such men to the murky world of chemical warfare, particularly when such activity was held in such low public esteem, Porton continued throughout the interwar years to attract the most eminent of Britain's scientists, including amongst its stellar luminaries Professor F.A. Lindeman – later Lord Cherwell, Churchill's controversial and widely disliked wartime scientific advisor – Lord Rayleigh,

Lord Rutherford, Lovatt Evans, Professor R.A. Peters, J.S. Haldane and Sir William Bragg.

Five defined lines of development emerged from the Holland report which determined the direction of the station for the next fifteen years. Four were overtly defensive: the development of efficient personal respirators and cutaneous protection; the collective protection of Admiralty warships; meteorological studies (which had been woefully overlooked during the Great War); and the retrospective treatment of the casualties of chemical warfare. The fifth sphere of activity, the development of improved weapons and delivery systems, especially aerial bombs, was more ambiguous. Although the necessity for developments in this field was argued to be wholly defensive in nature – in that the only way to counter enemy weapons was to anticipate their own advances in weapons design and then build those weapons in order to test defensive systems – there is no doubt that the chemical arsenal with which Great Britain entered the Second World War was far more sophisticated than that which existed at the time of the armistice.

Shortly before the start of the Second World War responsibility for the Porton establishment and its pilot plant at Sutton Oak was transferred from the War Office to the Ministry of Supply, and legitimate offensive work resumed. Much of Porton's wartime chemical offensive work was done in association with Imperial Chemical Industries, the giant of the British chemical industry that managed all the Ministry of Supply poison gas factories on an agency basis. Typical of the relationship between the various establishments involved in chemical warfare is the process by which new head-filling machines were developed for use in the Ministry of Supply factory at Rhydymwyn in north Wales. A requirement for modified filling equipment was identified at the factory and notified, via ICI and the Ministry of Supply, to Porton where the engineering staff designed and built a prototype machine. This was then transferred to the pilot plant at Sutton Oak for evaluation, subsequently modified to meet specific operational needs and then put into serial production for installation at Rhydymwyn.

Although major advances were made in the design of poison gas delivery systems, progress on the development of new agents was disappointingly slow. Modifications to the physical composition of mustard gas – in order, for example, to reduce the size of droplets released by the airborne Spray Curtain Installation (SCI) or to adjust its freezing point to make it more suitable for release from high-altitude bombers or for use in humid, tropical areas – were made, but the prime inventory of Britain's chemical warfare arsenal in 1942 was mustard gas, just as it had been a quarter of a century earlier. Pilot production plants were erected at Sutton Oak based upon the results of Porton research for the production of a number of mustard derivatives or mustard-like compounds, including diphenyl cyanoarsine, sesqui-mustard, and three nitrogen mustards, but none entered quantity production.

Porton made many other, less contentious, contributions to the war effort, particularly in the development of concealing smoke screens, coloured marker smokes and marker pots. There is, however, a power-ful if superficial impression that Porton's chemical work – until the frightening discovery of Germany's immense advances in the develop-ment of organo-phosphorous nerve gases – was overshadowed after 1940 by Britain's brief, frantic and ultimately fairly fruitless flirtation with biological warfare.

Chapter 6

United Kingdom Mustard Gas Factories

Porton and Sutton Oak had for some years been working towards a satisfactory production technique for the large-scale manufacture of mustard gas in various forms for a range of different applications. Coincidentally, just when, in the early summer of 1936, the Cabinet took the decision to fully embrace the concept of chemical warfare, Sutton Oak issued Monograph CW652, the final specification for basic mustard gas, codenamed 'Pyro'. The government immediately turned to Imperial Chemical Industries Ltd, the huge chemical combine formed in 1926 to compete in international markets with Germany's formidable I.G. Farbenindustrie, to translate the theoretical, pilot plant procedures into an efficient industrial process.

The question of how the enormous new plants required to produce chemical weapons would be financed was a thorny issue. During the First World War manufacturers of munitions, particularly in the United States, had charged what appeared to be exorbitantly inflated prices for their produce, but the economic rationale used to justify these costs was sound enough. The companies were asked to erect plant at their own expense to make products solely for the government and for which demand would cease abruptly at the end of the War. It was imperative, then, that the capital cost of the factories should be paid off as quickly as possible from revenue by charging very high prices for the products made in them. Nevertheless, there was a common feeling that through-out the First World War the industrialists indulged in rampant profit-eering at the expense of the taxpayer and this was a situation that, in the later 1930s, the British government sought desperately to avoid in the war that was on the horizon. The solution, not just in the limited sphere of chemical warfare but throughout the whole armament supply industry, was the 'agency' system. Under this arrangement private companies built and ran factories for the government and the Treasury met the bills. Strict limits were set upon both the capital and operating costs, which were calculated to ensure that profits should be severely limited in order to avoid all question of profiteering, but that the companies would not be subject to any post-war losses. Companies involved in these schemes received a management, or 'agency' fee. In the case of the works overseen by ICI this amounted to approximately

1.2 per cent of the capital cost of construction of the new works and a day-to-day operational management fee varying between 0.5 to 1.5 per cent of the capital value of the plant, depending upon the size of the factory. ICI's official historian, W.J. Reader, makes the point that:

> ... the small return accepted on agency work during the war was no mere formal token of patriotic goodwill. The work was on such a scale that if it had been paid for at anything approaching commercial rates the income from it would have made an important, instead of negligible, contribution to ICI's revenue.

At the end of the War it was intended that the agency factories would revert to government control and whilst that was the case with some, including the works erected by ICI at Rhydymwyn, others were acquired by the company on favourable terms which to some extent redressed the balance of wartime financial control.

Six agency factories were built by ICI for the manufacture of toxic gases and intermediary products, details of which are given in Table 5.

Table 5 ICI chemical weapons factories

	Start date
Mustard gas factories	
Randle	April 1937
Springfield	January 1940
Valley Works (Rhydymwyn)	January 1941
Intermediate product factories	
Rocksavage	September 1939
Wade	April 1940
Hillhouse	June 1941

Randle Works

The original design brief for the first mustard gas agency factory was surprisingly modest. The Ministry of Supply required a factory with a rated output of only 40 tons per week of Pyro together with on-site storage capacity for 500 tons of finished product. The storage facility was to take the form of 100 buried tanks or 'pots', each of 5 tons capacity, widely dispersed over an area of ground remote from the main factory site in order to minimize the risk of destruction in what was then still considered the unlikely event of attack by enemy aircraft. The 'pots' consisted of enamelled cast-iron tanks sunk into concrete wells. Pots 1 to 32 were buried at the east end of the site, numbers 43 to 100 at the west end with the remaining ten pots (numbers 33 to 42) in the centre of the factory where they served as buffer storage.

Few definite conditions were imposed upon ICI regarding the location or design of the factory except that it should be built at a site beyond the anticipated range of German bombers, which at that time meant at least 20 miles north or west of the London metropolitan area, and that it should be built with a view to economy in capital cost. A number of potential sites were identified by the ICI design team, all in relatively close proximity to the company's existing factories in the Runcorn area. Following negotiations with the War Office throughout January and February 1937 it was agreed that a site immediately adjoining the ICI Kemet works should be developed for poison gas production. The location met most of the War Office and Ministry of Supply criteria. It was beyond the notional danger limit from German bombing – although the wisdom of placing it on the Manchester Ship Canal, within a few minutes flying distance of the docks of Liverpool and Manchester, and at the centre of Britain's industrial heartland, all of which were prime potential targets, particularly after Liverpool became the main transhipment port for American war materials, was debateable – it was close to a number of other ICI factories which would produce adequate quantities of the necessary raw materials, and it had convenient rail access via Acton Grange. The site was also well provided with process-cooling water from the ship canal, had ample power supplies from the Mersey Electricity Company and it allowed what was, at the time, safe discharge of toxic effluents into the Mersey estuary. Luckily, too, the prevailing winds tended to blow polluted air from the factory out across the Mersey mudflats towards a sparsely populated area.

Agreement to proceed with the scheme was made with the exchange of letters some weeks before the first survey of the site was prepared in early March. On 30 January 1937 the Director of Army Contracts wrote to the Board of ICI:

> I am directed to refer to the discussions which have taken place between representatives of the Department and of your company and to Mr Rogers' letter of January 15 addressed to Vice Admiral Sir Harold Brown in connection with the erection of chemical plants by your company for the War Office. The Department is desirous that the plant for the production of 40 tons per week of HS (Pyro) and the storage and filling capacity included in your estimate of £239,000 (excluding fee) on the site of the Manchester Ship Canal near your Kemet Works should be erected as soon as possible.

At that time it was believed that the plan outlined was final and that no further extensions were envisaged. Whilst ICI's agency status effectively regulated their administration fees, it did little to protect against the inflation of costs on the part of firms subcontracted by ICI. Finance arrangements for the project were extraordinary and appear to presage the notorious 'costs-plus-profits' contracts employed on later large-scale wartime capital schemes which proved to be so highly satisfactory to a number of civil engineering firms and such a drain upon the public purse. There was, as the following extract from the second part of the above-quoted letter makes clear, an assumption that a financial agreement would eventually be made, but if it was not then the War Office would foot the bill for whatever costs were incurred anyway:

> I am accordingly to request that you will, pending agreement of the terms of remuneration, proceed forthwith with all necessary arrangements for the erection, ordering of material and work on the site, and the War Office undertakes, if agreement on the terms is not reached, to reimburse any expenditure you may incur in carrying out this instruction. I am to add that the Department requires separate and complete records to be kept by the Company of the expenditure on this service, these records being the property of the Government. As regards the purchase of land the Comptroller of Lands has been requested to keep in touch with your lands staff and to take the necessary executive action.

Survey and site levelling work began in April 1937 using directly employed labour under the supervision of ICI engineers. The site chosen for the factory proved a poor one. Its principal advantage, that services such as steam, compressed air and electricity could be taken from the existing Kemet factory, thus avoiding the cost of erecting dedicated service plant, boiler houses etc., was largely outweighed by the fact that the ground was inherently unstable. Subsequent tests indicated that the ground, which consisted mainly of reclaimed land formed by the deposition of sandy material dredged from the Manchester Ship Canal, had bearing qualities categorized as moderate to very poor with an extensive belt of running sand that greatly exacerbated the problem. The immediate effect of this largely unseen geological difficulty was that all the larger process buildings had to be built on piled foundations, while lighter forms of construction were necessarily employed for the less important structures. A certain degree of conflict arose between the War Office requirements for inter-building safety distances and the natural features of the site. In order to accommodate the War Office approved layout of weapons assembly buildings at Randle, the ICI engineers found it necessary to extend their site boundary to encompass a total of some 128 acres by the acquisition of a large dock previously used by the canal proprietors as a berth for their dredgers. This dock was then filled with rubble to form the foundation of two large assembly sheds. Within two years of construction both structures showed alarming evidence of subsidence which became so bad that one building had to be abandoned and demolished. Elsewhere on the site, despite the fact that there were concerns amongst the engineers about their long-term stability, most of the subsidiary buildings were put up without adequate foundations in order to expedite completion.

Work had hardly got under way when the War Office proposed the first of a series of huge extensions to the Randle scheme. ICI was asked to prepare designs for an additional 200 tons per week 'Runcol' plant at Randle. ('Runcol' was the code name for an alternative form of mustard gas formed by the reaction of crude thiodiglycol with hydrochloric acid. It was rather more expensive than Pyro to produce but exhibited much more stable characteristics.) Consideration was also given to the production of 'Syrup', an intermediary product containing approximately 90 per cent thiodiglycol. Further modifications to the factory scheme continued throughout 1937. The ratio of Runcol to Pyro was reversed, the revised demand being for only 50 tons of Runcol per week and 200 tons of Pyro 'M'. Standard Pyro consisted of mustard gas with a 15 per cent carbon tetrachloride content to depress its freezing point; the increased demand for this variant indicates the growing dominance of aerial bombs – which were subject to hazardous freezing of early formulations of mustard gas at high altitudes – over artillery-delivered weapons to which no such limiting conditions applied. Pyro 'M', in which the carbon tetrachloride content was largely displaced by monochlorobenzine, was developed by the Sutton Oak research team to provide a more stable form of vesicant agent. Some time later a third variant, Pyro 'B' was introduced, incorporating simple benzene in place of the more expensive monochlorobenzine.

Process plant at Randle was to consist of separate units capable of producing vesicant in daily batches of either 40 or 80 tons which could be operated in various permutations depending upon demand fluctuations. On 24 December 1937 the Director of Army Contracts gave approval for all the amendments made up to that date in the following letter:

> I am writing this to let you know at once the latest development on the gas scheme at Kemet. In brief, the scheme has been approved with the exception that in the case of one 80 ton unit, peacetime construction should be confined to the production of such services as would enable the factory to be rapidly completed in war. My object in writing this is to let you know that there is authority to proceed with everything that can be done to get on with the scheme without prejudice to the amendment mentioned above.

The extensions to the production facilities at Randle represented a quantum change in the scale of the factory. Earlier assumptions that services for the new factory could be tapped at minimal expense from the existing Kemet Works were, of necessity, discarded and in consequence the estimated costs including those for a new boiler house with ten Lancashire boilers and other ancillary plant, together with the multiplication of production units, increased the final cost by over a million pounds to £1,321,247. High-capacity pumping equipment was installed to extract process water from the long disused Runcorn and Latchford Canal and cooling water from the Manchester Ship Canal.

Up until August 1937 it had been supposed that the charging of weapons – i.e. filling with toxic chemical – would be undertaken at Randle but that final assembly, including the fitting of primers, detonators, smoke boxes, fuzes and other explosive or incendiary components, would be done elsewhere. Shortly after construction of the first weapon-charging plant, designated 'K.1', began in August, it was decided that final assembly should also be completed at Randle and that an area at the east end of the site, remote from the toxic section, should be put aside for this purpose. Some three months later authority was given for the construction of an additional charging house, designated 'K.2'.

Further extensions to the original scheme authorized throughout 1938 included a third charging house, 'K.3', additional Pyro and Runcol production plants, acid concentration plants, ethylene production units and a plant to produce quantities of the intermediate product sulphur dichloride above that which was already available from the Kemet factory. The first production plant, Pyro P.1, was completed on 14 March 1938, some six weeks behind schedule, under the supervision of the secret 'Z' Division of ICI's Castner-Kellner Alkali Company and produced its first batch of mustard gas on 13 April. The delay was due to the Porton design team taking an excessively long time to furnish the necessary working drawings. Major problems were quickly identified with leaking joints and corrosion of mild steel reaction vessels which resulted in the temporary shutting down of the plant in August after some 240 tons of mustard gas had been produced. Meanwhile, construction of Pyro plant P.2., Syrup plants S.1 and S.2, Runcol plant R.1, ethylene plants E.2 and E.3, sulphur dichloride plant SC.1 and charging buildings K.2 and K.3 was started between June and December 1938, while the last major units, Runcol plant R.2 and Pyro plant P.3, started in March 1939. The last vesicant production unit, Pyro plant P.3, came on line in February 1941. Except for a small larmine (phenyl bromo-acetonitrile) plant erected in November 1941 this marked the end of major building works at Randle. By the summer of 1944 the total cost of these works had reached £2,541,027. Originally, all contracts in connection with the gas warfare scheme were given the highest priority, but after 1942 this priority was reduced and this, together with the impossibility of obtaining sufficient skilled labourers, contributed to the numerous delays in construction.

Weapons Charging Facilities

The three charging unit buildings were vast structures designed to hold two weeks reserve stocks of empty bomb or shell casings, sufficient packing cases for five days continuous production, weapons painting, banding and stencilling equipment, and two weeks output of finished weapons. Charging machines, each built initially to a unique design to fill a particular projectile, were housed in individual concrete cubicles distributed across the centre of each charging building. After filling, bombs and artillery rounds were sealed and thoroughly inspected before despatch to the 'bonding' area where they would be left for forty-eight hours before final inspection to ensure there were no leakers. While it was thought that it would be safe to store filled, heavy-walled artillery shells unprotected in the charging buildings, the lighter cased aerial bombs and chemical drums were bonded in trenches with splinter-proof covers for protection against the risk of air raids.

Charging and assembly of 25-pdr shells, which began in October 1940 and continued for almost four years, was initially fraught with difficulty. The No. 1 pattern constant-volume charging machines, which were the result of many years of design and testing at both Porton and Sutton Oak, proved disastrous and simply did not work. The discharge heads were incapable of locating the filling holes in the shell castings and invariably dumped their charges on the floor of the filling sheds. A similar Porton-designed machine for filling BBC shells failed in a similar way. By March 1941 Porton had come up with a much modified device, the No. 2 charging machine. Although an improvement over the earlier design, the No. 2 vacuum charger was far too frail and complex for the continuous and arduous task allotted to it and it failed frequently. Eventually ICI's own engineers at the Springfield factory designed their own much simpler, more robust and reliable machine, the model 'JR'. This simple device filled the shells by gravity to a constant height and, as well as being more reliable than the Porton machines, was much faster, filling between 150 to 200 shells

Table 6   Capacities of Randle charging facilities

Charging building	Types of weapons filled	Weekly output
K.1	25-pdr shell	6,500
	6-in howitzer shell	11,000
	G.C. Bomb	2,500
	L.C. Bomb: 30 lb	10,000
K.2	L.C. Bomb 250 lb	1,600
	Livens drum	2,400
K.3	S.C.I. 250 lb	1,900 *or*
	S.C.I. 500 lb	900 *or*
	S.C.I. 1,000 lb	420
	Chemical lorries	22

per hour compared with 70 to 100 for the earlier patterns. The basic design of the 25-pdr chemical shell was found wanting, too. Of the 14,000 shells filled up until 3 October 1941 virtually every one was found to be leaking while in bond. Total production of 25-pdr chemical shells between October 1940 and September 1942 – the only period for which reliable figures survive – was 296,151.

Assembly Unit
The Randle assembly unit occupied a remote area of low ground at the east end of the site and consisted of thirty small, widely spaced buildings connected by 'cleanways' along which stores or finished weapons were moved from building to building on hand-propelled trucks. The assembly compound, which included storage magazines for gunpowder and fuzes, was physically separated from the rest of the site by a strong security fence and all the buildings within it complied with standard War Office minimum safety distance regulations.

Assembly of 30 lb aerial bombs began in March 1940 and 25-pdr artillery shells in October. Filling of 6″ and 5½″ howitzer rounds and a range of naval shells started in the late autumn of 1941. The decline in output of the assembly unit can be gauged from the numbers of staff employed (see Table 7).

By the end of 1942 it was apparent that demand for filled weapons did not justify the scale of the Randle assembly unit and a number of the buildings were put over to the filling of hexachloroethane smoke generators.

Randle was also contracted to supply 15,000 KSK lachrymatory grenades or tear gas bombs which were manufactured on site by adapting the glass envelopes of 100-watt electric light bulbs. The bulbs, without filaments, were filled by vacuum transfer and the necks were then closed by heating with a small blowlamp. To protect the seal a cardboard ring was fitted around the neck of the bulb where the bayonet cap would have been and filled with plaster of Paris.

Rocksavage Works
During the autumn of 1939 the Ministry of Supply authorized the construction of additional plants to be run as agency factories by ICI for the production of raw materials and intermediates required in the manufacture of vesicant war gases. The expanding gas warfare pro-

Table 7   Staffing levels at Randle

Year	Male	Female	Year	Male	Female	Year	Male	Female
1940	27	15	1942	85	362	1944	58	131

gramme meant that existing capacity for chlorine, which it was originally intended would have been supplied from the existing ICI Kemet works and the Ministry of Supply Hillhouse works, would be insufficient. A 48-acre site at Rocksavage, situated a quarter of a mile or so from Runcorn, was identified as a suitable location for a new electrolytic chlorine production plant and work on its construction was started in December 1937. The plant was extended in October 1938 to meet the increased demand for chlorine from the recently completed bromobenzyl cyanide unit at Randle and to supply the proposed new mustard gas factory at Rhydymwyn near Mold. Further extensions were authorized in 1939 to accommodate production plant for hexachloroethane, chlorinated rubber – used as a thickening agent for mustard gas – and for the mustard gas intermediate code-named 'syrup'. Bulk chlorine storage facilities were constructed in June 1939, and four months later a 20-ton per month phosgene plant was added. Later extensions to the phosgene unit increased its weekly output to 57 tons. In December, Treasury authority was obtained to build a phosgene charging plant on the site, equipped to fill 4.2" mortars for the Army, 250 lb and 500 lb bombs for the RAF, a small range of naval shell and 5" rocket-propelled bombs.

Hillouse and Springfield Works
Initially, the bulk of the raw materials required for the various grades of mustard gas manufactured at all the mustard gas factories were sourced from either ICI's own Kemet works or from the Ministry of Supply agency factory at Hillhouse. During the early autumn of 1939 it was proposed to build an extension to the existing Hillhouse works to process raw materials into intermediates and also to build an additional 300-ton per week vesicant plant on an adjacent plot. Site difficulties at Hillhouse prevented the vesicant plant coming to fruition and it was decided on 30 November 1939 that it should be developed for intermediates only. Eight possible locations were subsequently investigated for the new vesicant plant. Three were eliminated immediately and the remaining five surveyed in detail during December. A number of logistic advantages led to the selection of a site at Springfield, near Slawick station some 6 miles west of Preston:

- Proximity to the existing factories at Hillhouse and Runcorn.
- Availability of adequate rail and road transport links.
- Preston Corporation high-voltage power lines traversed the site.
- Proximity of the Ribble estuary as a conduit for toxic effluent after treatment in a delay chamber.
- Availability of copious water supplies from the nearby canal, from Fylde Water and from bore holes on site.

- Ample pool of labour in the vicinity.
- Good flat land at a suitable height above Ordnance datum.

The original Springfield scheme was planned on a large scale. It was proposed that there would be installed eight 'Pyro M' plants each capable of producing 72 tons of mustard gas per week along with four charging units in four widely spaced, discreet groups on the periphery of the site. Treasury funding was authorized on 2 January 1940 and the Ministry of Supply approved the final designs two months later, after which construction work immediately started, using building and engineering contractors recommended by ICI. Meanwhile, engineers at the Randle works, where similar plant was already operational, had modified the mustard gas reactors by incorporating stirring apparatus that effectively doubled the daily output of each unit. The Ministry of Supply therefore redesigned the Springfield layout around the new stirred-reactor design, thus reducing the number of separate vesicant plants required from eight to four, each of which would produce 144 tons per day. At the same time the requirement for four charging, filling and bonding units was reduced to three. Further developments in vesicant chemistry indicated that Pyro MD, the theoretically superior grade of mustard gas, could, by suitable modification to the plant design, be manufactured more economically than at first anticipated. It was therefore decided in November 1940 that the design modifications should be incorporated in the new plant under construction and that the four Springfield mustard gas reactors should produce Pyro MD. By early June of the following year, just as the first production plant was nearing completion, changes in the government's chemical weapons policy led to the abandonment of two more of the proposed vesicant installations at Springfield, leaving just two of the original eight, only one of which would now be converted for the manufacture of Pyro MD by the stirred-reactor process. On 8 May one of the three remaining charging buildings was abandoned and a week later, on 15 May, construction of stage two of the Springfield assembly section, amounting to ten buildings, was also cancelled.

Three factors affected the decision to restrict the scale of operations at Springfield. A change in emphasis in the War Cabinet's approved strategy for the use of chemical weapons, away from artillery weapons to aerial delivery systems, especially spray tanks and large capacity light-cased bombs, meant that the proposed charging units at Springfield, which were designed specifically for head-filling and assembly of artillery shells, were largely redundant. Experience at Rhydymwyn cast doubt upon the stability of mustard gas either in high volume, long-term storage or charged into weapons, and also put into question the policy of continuous production as the prospect of actual consumption

1. Porton Down research station. This view shows many of the completed buildings with Gas Wood, where the first chlorine experiments were conducted, in the middle background. The Porton railway appears to be under construction.

2. An early view of Porton Down research station showing a range of timber accommodation and laboratory buildings. Note the white painted flints that mark the edges of the pathways.

3. Experimental Livens bombs and mortar tubes in a storage compound at Porton Down during the First World War.

4. Toffee-apple mortar bombs undergoing trials at Porton Down.

5. Four of the five 24-inch gauge steam locomotives that provided motive power on the Porton Railway, lined up outside the engine shed.

6. Gas sentry in the trenches near Fleurbaix, early in 1916. The soldier ringing the gas warning bell wears a 'P' type respirator hood. Note the wind direction indicator in the background.

7. British soldiers injured by gas at the Battle of Estaires, outside an Advanced Field Dressing Station near Bethune.

8. Aerial photograph taken during a British gas attack in June 1916. German-held Montauban is to the upper left, with Carnoy behind the British lines at bottom right. Note that the clouds of gas appear to be rising higher and advancing less quickly than might be expected.

9. Loading gas cylinders into the Livens projector.

10. Women workers fitting eyepieces to gas masks at a British anti-gas factory during the First World War.

11. Makeshift protection against chlorine gas. British servicemen on the Western Front, 1915.

12. German troops using a variety of respirators, 1916.

13. Vickers machine-gun emplacement on the Western Front. Because of their exposed forward positions, machine gunners were given priority in the allocation of scarce respirators in the early years of the First World War.

14. Service pattern gas masks for man and mount. A lance corporal of the Household Cavalry at Windsor just prior to the outbreak of war.

15. Mustard gas bulk contamination vehicles (BCVs) in camouflaged, makeshift sandbag and corrugated-iron shelters at Shefford (No. 27 ASD) in Bedfordshire. The principal role of these vehicles would have been to contaminate roads and other approach routes in advance of German troops following an invasion of the United Kingdom in 1940/41.

16. Ammunition examiner inspecting 25-pdr mustard gas rounds in a field laboratory at Shefford Ammunition Supply Depot in Bedfordshire. Note the soldier's outdoor boots on the 'dirty' side of the demarcation line. On the 'clean' side he will be wearing felt boots made of the same material that is used to cover the inspection bench.

17. Gas filtration equipment installed in the basement of a famous department store in Oxford Street, London, in 1936. The scale of this plant indicates the seriousness with which government gas warfare propaganda was viewed during the years immediately preceding the Second World War.

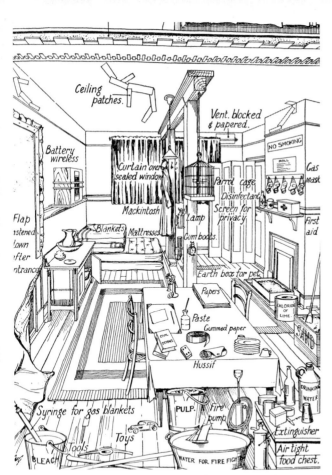

Ceiling patches.

Vent. blocked & papered.

Battery wireless

NO SMOKING

Curtain over sealed window

Parrot cage

Gas mask

Disinfectant

Screen for privacy

Mackintosh

Lamp

Flap fastened down after entrance

Blankets

Mattresses

Gum boots

First aid

Earth box for pet.

Papers

CHLORIDE OF LIME

Paste

Gummed paper

SAND

Hussif

DRINKING WATER

Syringe for gas blankets

PULP.

Fire pump

Extinguisher

Tools

Toys

Air tight food chest.

BLEACH

WATER FOR FIRE FIGHTING

18. Government recommendation for the layout of a domestic 'gas-proof room'. Such plans were much vilified by the left-wing press, much as the 'Protect and Survive' scheme was ridiculed during the cold war.

19. 'Always carry your gas mask' – evacuated children arrive in Somerset, September 1939.

20. Soldiers undergoing very public gas mask training in Bristol on the eve of the Second World War. Exercises like this were as much propaganda as practice.

21. More propaganda – part of a series of Air-Raid Precautions cigarette cards issued by W.D. & H.O. Wills shortly before the Second World War.

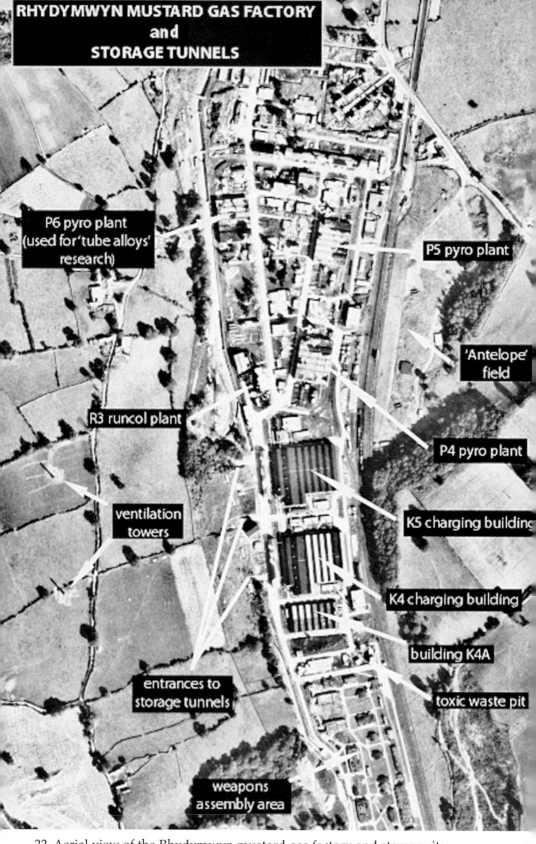

RHYDYMWYN MUSTARD GAS FACTORY and STORAGE TUNNELS

P6 pyro plant (used for 'tube alloys' research)

P5 pyro plant

'Antelope' field

R3 runcol plant

P4 pyro plant

ventilation towers

K5 charging building

K4 charging building

building K4A

entrances to storage tunnels

toxic waste pit

weapons assembly area

22. Aerial view of the Rhydymwyn mustard gas factory and storage site.

23. Rhydymwyn. No. 2 entrance tunnel to underground storage facility.

24. Rhydymwyn. Storage chamber 'A'. This tunnel would have contained charged mustard gas bombs and bulk mustard gas in drums. Note the drainage grilles in the floor. These served the dual purpose of draining away seepage water and extracting toxic spillage.

25. One of the LCTs operated by the Royal Army Ordnance Corps tied up alongside the military dock at Cairnryan being loaded with chemical munitions prepared for deep-sea dumping in Beaufort's Dyke.

26. A Tank Landing Craft (LCT) loaded with surplus chemical munitions leaving Loch Ryan en route for Beaufort's Dyke.

27. Surplus British chemical weapons being thrown overboard into Beaufort's Dyke.

28. Britain's only nerve-agent production facility, at Nancekuke on the north Cornwall coast. When this photograph was taken in 1976 sections of the factory had already been demolished. Visible in this view is the building containing the stabilization section and, to the right of the chimney, the artillery shell-filling plant.

29. Porton Down – the Chemical Defence Research Establishment in 1960. The range of single-storey buildings in the left foreground is the original headquarters building, constructed in 1918. The high-security 'Closed Area' occupies the north-east quarter of the site, its boundary clearly visible in this photograph.

30. 'And sheep may safely graze'. Britain's chemical warfare legacy. Bowes Moor, County Durham, autumn 2005.

MOD
DANGER
POISONOUS GAS AREA
KEEP OUT

Table 8   Springfield – Production units

Pyro No. 7	160 tons/week *or* 148 tons/week Pyro 'M' *or* 144 tons/week Pyro 'B'	Pyro No. 8	148 tons/week Pyro 'MB' *or* 144 tons/week Pyro 'BD'

Table 9   Springfield – Bulk storage

Lead-lined steel tanks fully below ground	250 tons Pyro 180 tons lewisite 360 tons Pyro
Steel tank semi-buried or earth-mounded	65 tons BBC
Concrete tank below ground	500 tons Pyro

Table 10   Springfield – Charging units

K.6	25-pdr shell 5.5″ howitzer shell 65 lb L.C. bomb	K.7	25-pdr shell 5.5″ howitzer shell

of filled weapons in a chemical exchange receded. Finally, the acute difficulties of finding sufficient skilled labour for construction of the chemical factories were becoming insoluble. At its peak, some 2,300 men were engaged on the construction of the Springfield plant and it had been found necessary to withdraw labour from other pressing contracts, to conscript labour from south Wales and the north-east region, and to import neutral labour from Ireland, all of whom were subsequently found compulsory billets in the vicinity of the works. Throughout the Springfield contract there were serious delays and constant disorganization due to changing government requirements as policy or the course of the War fluctuated.

Wade and Roydmill
The works at Wade near Nantwich in Cheshire were originally built as a shadow factory in 1938 to be held in readiness but not to come into operation until wartime. It was intended to produce chlorine, bleaching powder and chlorine-based intermediates for consumption in the other Ministry of Supply chemical weapons factories. The factory first came into production in April 1940. After the War the Wade plant was acquired from the government by ICI and gradually developed into a huge complex producing a wide range of materials based upon chlorine produced in its Gibbs cell generators. Products included vast amounts of ethylene for the ICI polythene plant at Winnington, chlorinated rubber and the notorious pesticide DDT, which was produced at the

113

rate of 4 tons per week. An important development at Wade during the latter part of the War was the production of vinyl chloride as a starting point for polyvinyl chloride which became of increasing importance in the electric industry as a replacement for rubber insulation after the loss of Malayan rubber supplies following the Japanese occupation.

Valley Works, Rhydymwyn

With arrangements in place for the manufacture of mustard gas and derivatives at Randle, the government turned its attention towards the end of 1938 to the problem of providing secure, bomb-proof storage for its reserve stocks of chemical weapons. The initial requirement was for storage capacity for 1,500 tons of bulk mustard gas and filled bombs. Facilities were to be provided immediately adjacent to the storage areas for filling projectiles if necessary and, at a later date, possibly for the manufacture of vesicants. The essential design parameters were that the site should be secure from enemy attack – with the storage facilities underground if possible – close to the main mustard gas manufacturing factory at Randle, and that there should be sufficient land available for the construction of the necessary filling unit and proposed Pyro and Runcol production plants. It was not envisaged that a thiodyglycol plant would be required as supplies of this intermediate product would be sourced from Randle.

Five potentially attractive sites in north Wales, close to the Dee estuary, were surveyed by the Department of Industrial Planning (DIP) and staff from the Geological Survey in conjunction with representatives from ICI's Special Products Division. Eventually, the valley of the River Alyn at Rhydymwyn was selected as the most suitable on account of the steep limestone hills to the west and the relatively broad, flat, valley bottom. The only drawbacks of the site were that a 6-mile-long effluent pipeline would be required to dispose of toxic waste generated by the factory and, of apparently lesser perceived importance, that the Alyn was prone to overflow its banks during periods of particularly inclement weather.

Plans for the layout of the proposed development were prepared following prolonged consultations between ICI engineers and the various government departments that lasted from April well into June 1939. The initial scheme was that a series of three parallel tunnels should be excavated in the precipitous limestone escarpment on the western edge of the valley and that the meandering course of the Alyn should be straightened and contained within a deep concrete culvert that would redirect its flow along the western edge of the valley, close to the tunnel entrances, in order to leave the whole of the valley floor free for construction of the factory. Access to the tunnels would be via three concrete bridges spanning the culvert. It was hoped that the much straighter and deeper artificial culvert would give the added advantage of greatly reducing the risk of flooding from the Alyn under storm conditions. The plans provided for the erection of a number of large buildings required for mustard gas production at the broad, northern end of the valley with the assembly unit, which consisted of a much larger number of widely spaced small buildings, concentrated in the narrow southern end.

No definite decision had yet been made regarding the provision of manufacturing facilities at Rhydymwyn, so in order to allow ground-work to proceed as quickly as possible, development was divided into two stages. Stage one, for which Treasury approval was granted in October 1939, consisted of:

- Underground storage for 1,500 tons of bulk mustard gas.
- Facilities for charging, bonding and storing 250 lb light-cased aerial bombs.
- Similar facilities for charging, bonding and storing SCI units (Smoke Curtain Installations, or aircraft spray apparatus).
- Construction of all the necessary office, workshop, canteen and service plant.

Stage two, the realization of which was initially in some doubt, was to consist of:

- Construction of two 80-ton per week Pyro plants.
- Construction of two 75-ton per week Runcol plants.
- Provision of Pyro mixing facilities.
- Construction of two six-furnace ethylene production units.
- Provision of oil and alcohol storage.
- Construction of charging facilities equivalent in capacity to those provided at Randle by charging units K.1, K.2 and K.3.
- Facilities for reconditioning recovered SCI bombs.
- Weapons assembly facilities equivalent to those provided at Randle.

Construction of the Storage Tunnels

Although the hillsides along the valley of the Alyn were riddled with old limestone quarries none were felt suitable for conversion for the storage of toxic gases, so the Halklyn United Mining Company was contracted to excavate new tunnels for this purpose at Rhydymwyn. Employing the Halklyn United Mining Company had several advantages for the government in that the company had wide experience of such work in the locality, it maintained an existing, skilled labour force and it had all the necessary plant and management personnel close to hand.

Three parallel pilot headings, each 6 feet square and approximately 760 feet in length and 150 feet apart were driven into the hillside. Once the pilot headings had proved the stability of the rock strata they were enlarged to 36 feet in width and 14 feet high. At the same time, work began on the excavation of the four main storage chambers, designated A, B, C and D, each 535 feet long, which intersected and ran at right angles to the three access tunnels. Storage chamber 'D' was positioned at the furthest extremity of the access tunnels with the other three storage tunnels parallel to it but separated from one another by some 20 feet of solid rock. Ventilation shafts fitted with extraction fans were sunk from the surface to the inner extremities of access adits 'A' and 'C'. By working simultaneously from three entrance shafts the mining company was able to proceed at a prodigious rate, extracting in excess of 1,000 tons of rock during each 24-hour shift, all of which was dumped on the valley floor and subsequently levelled. It had originally been intended that chambers 'C' and 'D' – those furthest into the hillside – should be used for the storage of bulk vesicants, while the two tunnels nearer the hillside edge, which were somewhat narrower, would be used to store filled light-cased bombs and mustard gas stored in drums. The bulk vesicant would be stored in forty-eight huge, lead-lined steel tanks each with a capacity of 65 tons, arranged in rows in the tunnels. In May 1940, however, some time before tunnelling was completed, the Ministry of Supply increased the storage requirement at Rhydymwyn from 1,500 tons to 3,120 tons. To meet this requirement it was necessary to enlarge chamber 'C', which had been designed to hold aerial bombs, in order to accommodate an additional twenty-four bulk storage tanks. The bomb- and drum-storage capacity consequently lost was made up for by extending chambers 'A' and 'B' by 222 feet and 272 feet respectively.

The necessity for the increased storage capacity for bulk supplies of vesicant was made clear in Ministry of Supply Memorandum 226/39:

When Randle and Valley Works [Rhydymwyn] become operational it will be necessary to increase storage to over 2,000 tons to account for the lag between charging and manufacture. So long as gas warfare is uncertain, factories will operate at a low rate until stocks are sufficient and they will then stop. If usage increases production will have to be increased and, because charging is quicker than manufacture, a reserve of some seven weeks full output, i.e. 4,200 tons, will be required. For technical reasons it is not wise to hold charged weapons for more than six or eight weeks.

The increased reserve can best be provided by additional transverse tunnels off those at Valley – (Extra 1,500 tons for £53,000 tunneling and £53,000 for plant) but work must be commenced without delay.

Meanwhile, in October 1939, before much preliminary work had got under way on the limited charging and storage facilities envisaged in Stage 1 of the development at Rhydymwyn, Treasury funding was

Table 11   Production Plant rated weekly output

No. 4 Pyro	120 tons Pyro *or*
	110 tons Pyro 'M' *or*
	108 tons Pyro 'B'
No. 5 Pyro	120 tons Pyro *or*
	110 tons Pyro 'M' *or*
	108 tons Pyro 'B'
No. 3 Runcol	50 tons Runcol
No. 4 Runcol	50 tons Runcol
Nos 5/6 acid concentrators	To meet plant requirements
Nos 7/8 acid concentrators	To meet plant requirements

Table 12   Charging Units

K.4	25-pdr shell	K.5	No. 6 chemical drum (65 lb)
	5.5" shell		30 lb aerial bomb
	6 lb aerial bomb		250 lb aerial bomb
	500 lb aerial bomb	K.5/F.2	Assembly of 400 lb S.C.I. tanks

obtained for the manufacturing facilities outlined in Stage 2 of the scheme. This, initially, was to consist of a group of Pyro 'M' plants with a combined output of 200 tons per week, a 100-ton per week Runcol plant and a small lewisite plant with a capacity of 10 tons per week, but capable of rapid enlargement to 100 tons per week if required, together with charging and assembly units equal in capacity to those existing or under construction at Randle. There was some debate over the requirement for the proposed lewisite plant at Rhydymwyn and in November it was dropped from the schedule. The arrangement of separate production and charging plants is shown in the Tables 11 and 12.

Plans for a further Pyro process unit (Pyro.6) and a diphenyl cyanoarsine plant were abandoned.

'Woodside' and 'Antelope' Satelite Storage Sites

Although the decision had been taken to erect a manufacturing facility at Rhydymwyn the principal function of the site was to act as a reserve store for the output of the Randle factory and to supply toxic gases to the charging units there and at Springfield. Soon after production began at Randle it became obvious that a considerable lack of synchronization was developing between the output of the mustard gas reactors and the capacity of the charging plants to absorb this output. Unforeseen problems with leakage and excessively rapid deterioration of filled weapons exacerbated this problem and led to an unwillingness to fill such weapons, particularly light-cased bombs, while there was no foreseeable likelihood of them being used. The immediate provision of additional bulk storage, beyond that available in the 100 5-ton pots at Randle and before completion of the tunnels at Rhydymwyn, was urgently required. To at least partially meet this requirement the Ministry of Supply suggested that ten of the lead-lined mild steel tanks destined for the tunnels at Rhydymwyn, which were on site but as yet uninstalled, should be buried in waste ground adjacent to the factory site to provide temporary storage until the tunnels were completed. Consequently an area south of the London Midland and Scottish Railway line that bordered the eastern perimeter of the site, formerly used as a racetrack and known as the 'Antelope' field after the nearby 'Antelope' public house, was acquired by the Ministry of Supply for this purpose in May 1940. Excavations were made and ten of the 65-ton tanks were buried in two separate lines approximately 200 feet apart. Earth removed from the excavations was heaped on top of the tanks to give additional protection. The advantage of this scheme was that storage would be available for 650 tons of Pyro or Runcol in the immediate future, enabling production to continue unhindered at Randle. Following further discussion it was also agreed, in June 1940, that temporary charging facilities should be made available at the Antelope facility and, to meet this requirement, two charging buildings, TK.1 and TK.2, were erected and fitted with charging machines to fill 30 lb and 250 lb aerial bombs and 400 lb S.C.I. tanks. Special incorporation facilities were also provided for mixing chlorinated rubber or ground Perspex (methyl methacrylate) with the Pyro used to fill S.C.I. tanks in order to increase its viscosity.

With little apparent likelihood of chemical warfare becoming a reality, but with the War Cabinet and Chiefs of Staff still unwilling to accept that Germany would not resort to the use of such weapons and thus authorize a reduction in the rate of production of toxic gases, the storage position became increasingly precarious. Highlighting these difficulties, ICI wrote to the Ministry of Supply stating that 'It is evident that until gas warfare breaks out it is going to be difficult to keep our factories working even to minimum capacity unless you can arrange further bulk storage facilities in the immediate future.'

To relieve pressure on the factories it was decided that further storage capacity for bulk vesicants should be constructed and that this should be provided at a location remote from the main works. The attitude of the Ministry of Supply, heavily influenced by pressure from the War Office, was somewhat at odds to that of ICI. In a letter to ICI dated 18 July 1940 the Ministry justified its acceptance of the company's demand for extra storage capacity thus:

The basic idea behind the emergency storage is that should the enemy decide to use gas, then it is highly probable that he will first attempt to disable Randle by air attack, and the services feel that the possession at other places of stocks of gas might in certain circumstances prove extremely important.

The initial requirement was for storage capacity for an additional 540 tons of mustard gas. A suitable 12-acre site, later known as 'Woodside', some 3½ miles from the factory near Northrop on land belonging to Gwern-y-Marl farm was quickly requisitioned and work put in hand to bury nine lead-lined steel tanks each of 55-ton capacity. The Woodside scheme was continuously expanded as a satellite site to both Rhydymwyn and Randle, and by 1943 the nine original tanks had been supplemented by two more identical units for the storage of Larmine and, in September 1940, by the addition of a further nineteen 65-ton tanks for vesicant storage. Finally a 250-ton lead-lined concrete bulk storage tank was also added. This was to be the progenitor of the bulk tanks provided in 1943 at the RAF Forward Filling Depots described in a later chapter. A concrete ring road was constructed within the 12-acre site and the storage tanks positioned at approximately 100-foot intervals around the outside of this road. In June 1940 it was decided that as an additional emergency measure two temporary charging plants similar to those at the Antelope site should be built at Woodside, inside the perimeter road.

Progress at the Factory Site

Building and technical work continued at the factory site through the autumn and winter of 1940. The first completed production plant, Runcol R.4, was commissioned and handed over to the process department in November and it was thought likely that the first of the charging buildings, K.5, would be ready by the end of the following January. Meanwhile, work was progressing well on the second Runcol plant, R.3, but progress with the Pyro units was falling behind target due, in part, to the continuing schedule of modifications resulting from ongoing research and development at Randle. Progress was retarded generally in February 1941 when much of the valley was flooded by the River Alyn which rose to its highest recorded level following a sudden thaw after heavy snow, breaching the recently constructed concrete culvert and destroying foundations for many of the process buildings then in course of construction. In the same month ICI was ordered to stop work on fitting out Pyro process building P.6, although the main building was to be completed and made weatherproof for use as a store. Modifications made to P.4 and P.5 upon principles developed at Randle meant that the combined output of these two plants would exceed that of the three unmodified reactors as first specified. Towards the end of the War further radical improvements were made to the process plant at Rhydymwyn involving the installation of brass distillation units to enable implementation of the newly developed 'direct' process for the manufacture of mustard gas.

Factory Services

The copious amounts of water required at the factory were taken from three separate sources. Water for domestic use, firefighting and boiler feed was taken from the Birkenhead Corporation Alwen aqueduct, but cooling water for the factory's numerous condensers was normally abstracted from the River Alyn. Factory process water was pumped from deep underground via vertical shafts connected with old mine workings belonging to the Halklyn District United Mines Company located below the factory area. Water from this source was also used to supplement that from the Alyn used to cool the condensers during the summer months when the Alyn was prone to run dry.

The greatest perceived difficulty when designs for the factory were prepared – although others appeared later – was that of disposing of process effluent and toxic leakage from the plant. All toxic effluents arising from the factory and from the drainage pits and vacuum system exhausts in the tunnels were routed into a huge, 60-foot diameter, 30-foot deep effluent pit sunk near the middle of the works. From Rhydymwyn the contents of the pit were pumped via an underground pipeline for approximately 6 miles into the estuary of the River Dee near Flint. The pipeline was of cast-iron construction, 15 inches in diameter for the first 3,000 yards which were on a steep up-slope, reducing to 12 inches on the downgrade towards the Dee. The outfall into the estuary on the foreshore was constructed on short screw piles as the bearing quality of the mud was very poor.

The Tunnels Commissioned

Transfer of the steel tanks from the Antelope field into the storage tunnels began in November 1940 and on 11 December the first tanker load of Pyro 'M' arrived from Randle for transfer into underground tank No. 1. The weather was so cold that day that it was necessary to light braziers around the transport tank in order to thaw it out before pumping could commence. This was to become a common practice at Rhydymwyn. By 20 December the first Pyro tank was full and two weeks later, on 4 January, the first delivery of Runcol arrived from Randle. On the same day the first production batch of Runcol from Rhydymwyn's R.4 reactor was transferred to underground storage by means of the complex vacuum transfer system using a system of buried pipework. Within the tunnels, tanks containing Pyro were identified by broad horizontal yellow bands.

All twenty-four tanks in the innermost chamber 'D' were full by the end of June, after which the transfer of Pyro 'M' from the remaining Antelope tanks began, a task that was completed on 5 October. Thereafter the tanks were dug up from the Antelope field and put into their final positions in chamber 'C', the last one being emplaced in February 1942. Following the storage of high benzene content Pyro underground, certain fire precautionary measures were put in place including the use of copper-beryllium spark-proof spanners.

Bulk transport of toxic chemicals between Rhydymwyn and Randle or the other poison gas factories was undertaken by road, rail or special road/rail tankers. The factory was linked directly to the LMS main line and had a comprehensive internal railway system. Road tankers consisted of special 7½-ton tanks mounted on Foden diesel chassis. Road convoys must have presented a sinister sight in the local lanes of north Wales, with each tanker accompanied by two police vehicles with warning loudspeakers blaring, closely followed by an emergency decontamination vehicle.

Manufacture of Runcol at Rhydymwyn
'Runcol' is the product of the chlorination of crude thiodiglycol by gaseous HCL (hydrochloric acid) in the presence of water to give a mixture of dichlorodiethyl sulphide (codenamed 'H') and chlorethyl-thiodyethyl ether (codenamed 'T') with a light aqueous layer saturated with HCl.

Manufacture of Runcol involved six discreet stages:

1. Generation of gaseous HCl.
2. Concentration of sulphuric acid to absorb water from HCl solution.
3. Reaction of HCl with 'syrup' (crude thiodiglycol).
4. Separation of Runcol from residual toxic acid.
5. Drying of Runcol.
6. Disposal and/or recovery of acids.

Gaseous HCl was driven off a 35 per cent solution by the addition of concentrated sulphuric acid in a generator plant consisting of one tank (for the sulphuric acid) mounted above another. Each Runcol plant was provided with two Evans Bowden coke-fired sulphuric acid concentrators for acids recovery, located in separate buildings. The hydrogen chloride from the generator was then used to chlorinate 'syrup' in batches of 53–58 gallons in a 110-gallon reaction vessel. This process took about fifty minutes and was highly exothermic, generating sufficient heat to boil the resultant Runcol, the vapour from which was contained by water-cooled reflux condensers. Once the reaction was complete compressed air was blown through the vessel for three minutes to remove excess HCl. Two consecutive charges of Runcol were led into a settling tank fitted with a sight glass and after about twenty minutes the toxic acid was drawn off. The raw Runcol was then passed to a drying still which was similar to a large laboratory retort surrounded by a steam jacket. Finally, the finished product was drawn off into two 5-ton pots mounted on weighing machines, after which it was transferred to the underground storage tanks by pipeline or tanker wagon.

Bulk supplies of raw thiodiglycol were delivered from Rocksavage or Wade works in eight steel-bodied railway wagons, while hydrochloric acid was obtained from either Wade or the ICI works at Wigg, and delivered by rail in eleven purpose-built ebonite-lined tank wagons. Sulphuric acid, which was always in short supply throughout the War, was delivered by rail from the ICI works at Widnes.

Problems at Rhydymwyn
As the War progressed it became increasingly evident that whilst Rhydymwyn was an ideal location for the secure storage of chemical weapons, it was poorly suited as a manufacturing site. The original design brief called for a vacuum distribution system for the transfer of all finished vesicants and intermediate products. It was thought that, due to the high toxicity of most of the chemicals involved, a positive pressure-pumping system would present too great a risk; a leak anywhere in the system might result in the widespread contamination of the whole works. Thus, vacuum pumps and a network of underground pipes were installed at an early stage of the factory's construction linking the reactors, filling plants and main bulk storage tanks in the tunnels. Alternate means of toxic transport was available in the form of railway tanker wagons on the factory's internal railway system, but this was, at least at the planning stage, seen only as an emergency contingency measure.

The first problems appeared almost as soon as the factory became operational and were due to the fact that the buildings, many of which were massive constructions, were built on quarry waste deposited on the valley floor during the excavation of the tunnels. At the peak of construction this limestone waste was being dumped at the rate of 1,000 tons per day. The uncompacted waste settled quickly and, despite the fact that all the buildings and plant were erected on concrete foundations, many of them showed serious settlement cracks and distortion. The No. 4 Runcol reactor delay chamber, in particular, tilted so alarmingly that it had to be demolished and rebuilt. As a result of this settlement many of the underground pipe runs became broken, and it was soon evident that both finished mustard gas and acid effluents were seeping into the substrata. The acid leakage was of particular concern as it was found to be leaching away the limestone substrata, thus further weakening the support for the buildings. Ruptures in many of the underground pipelines due to ground settlement resulted in large sections being abandoned and resort was made instead to railway wagons for transport of finished products from the factory into underground storage.

Another problem, never completely overcome, was a result of rushed and faulty planning that caused the decontamination and toxic waste incineration plant to be built in the middle of the site. This location, in conjunction with the restricted natural airflow in the narrow valley, resulted in surrounding buildings regularly being blanketed in a fog of toxic gases.

Rhydymwyn Post-war

Production ceased at Rhydymwyn on 29 April 1945 but the factory remained under ICI control until 30 June 1948 when it was transferred to the Ministry of Works and put under care and maintenance. Much of the plant was subsequently purchased on favourable terms by ICI. The tunnels were put under control of the Air Ministry and retained for the bulk storage of toxic material under ICI management.

Dismantling and decontamination of the factory site began in July 1948. The satellite storage site at Woodside had been reinstated, at a cost of £25,970, in 1946 and the Antelope field had been cleared of plant and decontaminated by February 1948.

Disposal of vesicant stocks from Rhydymwyn began immediately after the end of the War, but by 1951, in response to increasing East-West tension, the process was temporarily halted and for a few years there appears to have been a policy of increased reliance upon chemical weaponry in response to the perceived Soviet numerical superiority in conventional troops and weapons. By the early 1960s, however, the UK had, overtly at least, abandoned chemical weapons and certainly by the end of the previous decade the storage tanks at Rhydymwyn had been emptied and removed. Much of the bulk toxin was returned to Randle for destruction, while thousands of filled munitions were dumped at sea.

Although production at Valley Works ceased in April 1945 the site continued, and indeed still continues, to be bathed in a sinister aura of mystery. This is due in part to the relatively high level of security that is still maintained on account of the health and safety risks still existing on site, the result of the wartime ground contamination caused by leaking pipe work and questionable disposal and decontamination procedures. But there are other factors, too, that perpetuate Rhydymwyn's air of mystery. The improvements in plant efficiency, developed while the factory was under construction, meant that the target output could be achieved with a much lower capital outlay on plant than was at first anticipated, resulting in the abandonment of one of the proposed Pyro units. However, as we have seen, building P.6, a large prestressed reinforced-concrete structure and one of the largest on the site, was almost completed before this decision was made. The changes coincided with major developments in the Anglo-American atomic bomb programme, known in the United Kingdom as the 'Tube Alloys' project and operated under the umbrella of the Department of Scientific and Industrial Research (DSIR).

By the spring of 1942, 'Tube Alloys' research had reached a point where it was necessary to erect a large-scale pilot plant for the separation of uranium isotopes by the gaseous diffusion method developed by Professors Simon and Pierls. A location of the utmost security was required to house this plant and on 2 March 1942 the disused P.6 building was identified in a letter from DSIR to the Ministry of Supply as the ideal site for 'this scheme, project "X", which is of a very special nature'.

A contemporary ICI narrative of works undertaken under project 'X' records that:

> At the request of CD2, ICI Special Products Department have carried out certain modifications and additions to P6 building in order to make it suitable for a plant being developed by Tube Alloys (DSIR). The modifications have been made on the basis of information supplied by the Clarendon Laboratory, Oxford; Messrs Metro-Vickers, Manchester; and at a later date by ICI (Fertilizer and Synthetic Products), Billingham. The plant will be operated by ICI (F&SP) personnel.

The presence of the highly sensitive Tube Alloys research unit at Rhydymwyn caused a great deal of friction between the various security organizations there, including the Military Police, uniformed civilian police service, Special Branch and the Home Guard, none of whom were particularly keen to have their sphere of competence trespassed upon. The official policy regarding security was to maintain as low a key as possible, giving the impression that building P.6 was just an ordinary factory laboratory looking after day-to-day quality control in the works. Managers there, however, were worried about the viability of maintaining this fiction, writing to their superiors at the DSIR in September 1942 that:

> We feel that if the Factory Inspector dealing with Valley Works concerns himself officially with the P6 operation he would take a fairly close interest in our affairs in view of the unusual nature of some of the equipment, coupled with the fact that it is on a 'plant' rather than a research scale. Moreover, the electrical load is on the scale of a small factory.

Table 13   Output of Rhydymwyn charging unit (total production of filled weapons), 1941–1944

Start of production		Type	No. filled
1941	4 April	30 lb Mk II bomb	38,784
	3 May	250 lb L.C. bomb	3,998
	18 June	30 lb bomb Mk III	38,734
	28 June	30 lb Mk I(M) bomb	2,788
	29 June	25 lb Mk I shell	1,602,196
	29 June	25 lb Mk II shell	116,683
	31 July	1,000 lb S.C.I. bomb	150
	17 August	6″ howitzer shell	123,765
	3 September	65 lb L.C. bomb	114,786
	15 October	Glass bomb	1,424
	12 November	No. 6 drum	97,855
1942	31 March	50/60 gallon drum	2,452
	26 April	65 lb L.C. bomb	148,841
	29 April	GS 18	509,118
	6 July	4.2″ mortar	322,414
	6 July	4.2″ C.S.A.	19,804
	6 July	4.2″ C.9	198,287
	12 September	6 lb bomb	173,661
	10 November	G.S. 24	982,246
	16 November	Chemical mine	4,115
	5 December	400 lb bomb	29,667
1943	3 March	5.5″ shell	28,157
1944	14 February	G.S. 28	105,670
	3 March	American drum	2,133
	1 May	500 lb L.C.	5,312
	29 September	3″ mortar	246

All Tube Alloys work had ceased at Valley Works in February 1945, some two months before the last batch of Runcol was pumped from reactor R.3 at the end of June, but building P.6 was kept under care and maintenance by ICI on behalf of DSIR for many years and security remained high, with both a military police and a shadowy MI5 presence at all times, which sometimes caused a degree of conflict. Rhydymwyn's high and overt level of security kept firmly at arm's length the public and other inquisitive or acquisitive government departments. Such security served the site well through the forty subsequent cold-war years when the underground chambers were designated as Macadam, the alternative site to Burlington in Wiltshire for the Emergency Government War Headquarters in the event of nuclear war. It was not until the turn of the new millennium that its secrets were finally and fully revealed.

Chapter 7

Tabun, Sarin, Soman and the 'V' Agents

As the Allied armies closed in on Berlin in 1945, disconcerting discoveries were being made by intelligence and scientific officers investigating the many captured arms factories and ammunition dumps overrun in Germany and western Poland. The system of marking German artillery shells to distinguish their different fillings was well known to the Allies, but when British troops captured the principal German chemical weapons research establishment at Raubkammer near Munster they discovered a small stock of bombs carrying marks – a green ring where a white ring, indicating mustard gas, might have been expected – that implied something rather more sinister. At much the same time more considerable stocks of similar bombs were found in an ammunition depot west of Berlin. Analysis carried out by staff from Porton Down, with the co-operation of German scientists on site, revealed that these shells were filled with tabun, an organophosphate nerve agent a thousand times more lethal than mustard gas.

The more or less accidental discovery of tabun, the first of the so-called nerve agents, was a chance result of the enormous advances made in academic and industrial chemical research, principally in Germany but also in Britain and the United States, during the interwar years. Most of this research was purely commercial in initial orientation but, inevitably, all discoveries that might have military applications were avidly followed up. Typical of these attempts at technological transfer from the industrial to the military field was the interest expressed in Germany in the discovery of tetraethyl lead, the anti-knock additive for gasoline. It was quickly appreciated in military scientific circles that not only did tetraethyl lead prolong the life of aircraft engine bearings but that it was also an exceedingly toxic compound and, moreover, that it was highly liposoluble, which gave it much potential as a chemical weapon easily absorbed through the skin. Although work on tetraethyl lead as a chemical warfare agent came to nothing, investigations into its properties led German investigators into a remarkable, lateral line of research. This, too, proved to be something of a scientific cul-de-sac, but is worthy of at least a cursory review.

The scientists argued that if tetraethyl lead could be used to increase the octane number of gasoline, and thus reduce its propensity to the

126

over-rapid, premature detonation that caused so much damage to internal combustion engines, then a modest degree of application on their part should throw up a compound with exactly the opposite characteristics. What they hoped, but ultimately failed, to find was a substance which, if loaded into anti-aircraft shells and released by means of a time fuze in the path of enemy aircraft, would be drawn into the aircraft engine's induction system and would so decrease the octane value of the fuel that the engine would literally rattle itself to bits within seconds. Similarly, satisfactory consequences were hoped for from the ground-burst detonation of identically charged shells amongst enemy armoured vehicles.

CS Gas

In 1928, research undertaken in industrial laboratories into the properties of benzalmalonitriles led to the highly sternutatory benzyldine derivatives. That there might be some chemical warfare potential in these substances was first suggested in 1934, but little more was done until the early 1950s when military scientists re-evaluated previous research while investigating alternatives to the existing CN (chloroacetophenone) tear gas. British research indicated that 2-nitrobenzalmalonitrile was the most effective candidate, although perhaps somewhat too aggressive in its effects for its intended purpose. In the United States, further research by two American chemists into certain 2-cyano, 2-bromo and 2-hydroxy analogues proved conclusively that the sternutatory characteristics of 2-chlorobenzalmalonitrile perfectly matched the military requirements and the new material quickly replaced CN as the standard tear gas. The two men responsible for the discovery were R.B. Corston and R.W. Stoughton, and the product was CS gas.

Tabun

By far the most important interwar discoveries, however, were those made in Germany during the 1930s relating to methyl fluoroacetate and its related compounds. Methyl fluoroacetate was discovered by an I.G. Farben research team investigating insect repellents during the late 1920s. Its commercial value was quickly identified and a patent upon its manufacture and use obtained in 1930. Further work upon more refined derivates which indicated great commercial promise as systemic insecticides was undertaken at the Wuppertal-Elberfeld (Bayer) branch of I.G. Farben from 1934 under the direction of Dr Gerhard Schrader who had previously been deeply involved in research into obscure fluorine compounds. During Schrader's examination of a range of 2-fluoroethanol derivatives, manufacturing processes for which had been developed at I.G. Farben's Ludwigshaven laboratories under Dr Ufer, it was discovered that 2-fluoroethanol was highly toxic to warm-blooded animals. Evidence collated by Dr Schrader indicated that the presence of fluorine atoms conferred remarkable toxicity to organic molecules containing them. Schrader went on to produce a series of 2-fluoroethyl esters and, in due course, fluoroacetic acid, all of which exhibited intense toxicity. Development of these laboratory agents into commercial insecticides, however, was held back by seemingly insurmountable difficulties in designing suitable large-scale production plant.

Meanwhile, Polish chemical warfare researchers in Warsaw working on aliphatic fluorine compounds had independently discovered the high toxicity of 2-fluoroethanol and embarked upon a parallel course of research to that undertaken by Schrader and his team in Wuppertal. In September 1939, following the German invasion, one of the Polish scientists escaped to the United Kingdom to collaborate with a team investigating a series of aliphatic fluorine compounds which showed promise as candidate chemical warfare agents. Investigation of these compounds continued throughout the War, yet, despite considerable optimism based upon evidence that in laboratory rats at least, fluoroacetic acid exhibited potent toxicological properties, it was finally established in 1944, as a result of an heroic piece of self-experimentation on the part of a British worker, that the human body was remarkably resistant to fluoroacetate poisoning.

By 1935 Schrader had already exhausted the toxicological capacity of the organofluorines and had moved towards an intensive study of a range of fluorophosphate compounds. By 1938 he had proved conclusively that *nn*-dimethylamidophosphoryl fluoride was an effective insecticide and patents were immediately taken out in Germany, Switzerland, the United States and Great Britain to protect I.G. Farben's interests in the discovery.

Following upon this successful line of inquiry Schrader's team went on to synthesize a huge range of organophosphorous compounds through the years leading up to the Second World War. Amongst these was a group of *p*-acryl derivatives of the alkyl esters of *nn*-dimethylamidophosphoric acid. Included amongst these was a member of a subgroup of extraordinarily toxic compounds in which the acyl substituent was a cyanide radical. This, the most deadly chemical compound then known to mankind, was ethyl-*nn*-dimethylphosphoramidocyanidate, or tabun, which was first identified on 23 December 1936.

In compliance with the government decree of 1935 which required all scientific discoveries that might have military significance to be reported to the state laboratories, samples of tabun along with details of its preparation, were sent to the chemical warfare section of the Army Weapons Office in May 1937. I.G. Farben had by that time already obtained patent protection for tabun. The German government

128

took immediate steps to make the patent secret and all discussion of it, or of any organophosphorous research, in scientific periodicals was suppressed.

Further development was distributed amongst a number of German academic laboratories although the most important work was undertaken at the army chemical warfare establishments. By 1939 research was sufficiently advanced to warrant the construction of a pilot production plant at Munster Lager in order to produce supplies of tabun for field testing at the Raubkammer proving ground. Meanwhile, plans were being prepared for a remote, large-scale production facility at Dyhernfurth with a projected output of 1,000 tons per month. The factory became operational in April 1942 and it is estimated that, according to the post-war US Strategic Bombing Survey, 12,000 to 15,000 tons of tabun were manufactured there before it was overrun by Soviet forces in 1945. Some doubt remains as to exactly what state the factory was in when the Soviets captured it. Some reports suggest that such existing stocks of filled weapons and bulk toxins were evacuated before the Soviets arrived, and that much of the plant had been either dismantled or destroyed. Others suggest that the plant was captured intact, along with some 12,000 tons of tabun. One British estimate, which tallies reasonably well with that made later by the French, is limited to the quantity which was recovered from various locations in filled weapons, which amounted to approximately 15,000 tons. Unverifiable and somewhat dubious sources suggest that Soviet scientists recommissioned the factory and resumed production there, at least for a short time in 1946, although more recent evidence suggests this was unlikely.

Sarin
Schrader continued research on fluorine containing organophosphorous compounds at Wuppertal-Elberfield and, by 1938, his team was investigating such agents incorporating carbon-phosphorous bonds. Eventually they isolated isopropyl methylphosphonofluoridate, which, it was proved, possessed a toxicity many times greater than tabun. The new compound was named sarin after the four members of the team responsible for its discovery: Schrader, Ambros, Rüdiger and Van der LINde. Samples of sarin were despatched to the army chemical warfare laboratory at Berlin-Spandau in June 1939 where its military significance was immediately seized upon. Very small-scale pilot plants were erected at Spandau, Munster Lager and Dyernfurth but the translation from pilot to full-scale production was fraught with difficulty. Several methods of preparation were investigated but all involved the use of hydrofluoric acid for final fluoridation and hydrofluoric acid is amongst the most corrosive of chemicals. The acid dissolves most

metals, glass – so it cannot be stored in glass vessels – and concrete and, uniquely, also dissolves most inorganic oxides. It reacts strongly with water, other acids, alkalis, oxidizers and most combustible materials and is, in most particulars, a remarkably inhospitable compound. Quartz and the noble metals – gold, silver and platinum – are more or less impervious to its depredations, so it was found necessary to construct most of the process plant for the manufacture of sarin from silver components.

Once the practical difficulties were overcome plans were prepared for a full-scale manufacturing plant at Falkenhagen near Furstenburg, south-east of Berlin, where construction began in September 1943. Work on the factory progressed only haltingly due to prolonged controversy between the Army and I.G. Farben over which organization should control the completed plant. There was also open opposition to its construction from the increasingly powerful Schutzstaffel (SS), conservative elements within which foresaw little immediate military use for nerve gases other than the inevitable initiation of catastrophic retaliation on the part of the Allies. Furthermore, the SS, cognisant of Germany's dwindling industrial resources, pressed for priority to be given to a range of obscure projects which they actively promoted. High amongst these SS schemes was a factory adjacent to the Falkenhagen sarin plant currently being built for the production of *N-stoff* or chlorine trifluoride.

Chlorine trifluoride is a most remarkable chemical agent which, if it were a little less indiscriminately ferocious in character, might have had many military applications. Its very ferocity, however, is probably what gave it immediate appeal to the SS which, as a body, rather coveted its reputation in the field of brutal ferocity. Contact with either liquid or high-density vaporous chlorine trifluoride causes almost any organic material, from hair, fur or fabric to paper, wood, carbon or even the asphalt that paves the streets, to burst spontaneously into flame. The German Army briefly toyed with the idea of loading it into artillery shells as a means of destroying the charcoal elements in the most efficient of the allied gas masks but gave up the idea in the face of the trifluoride's unpredictable malevolence. Despite its rejection by the German Army, it was subsequently re-evaluated by the SS, seemingly upon Hitler's specific instructions, and construction of the Falkenhagen plant pushed ahead in preference to the sarin facility. The factory, with a rated output of 50 tons per month, was completed just a few weeks before it was overrun by the Soviets, by which time some 22 tons of chlorine trifluoride had been produced.

Cyclosarin
Cyclosarin, the last of the wartime organophosphate nerve agents to emerge from Schrader's research, is markedly different from the pre-

130

viously discovered agents in that it has a much lower vapour pressure, evaporating some seventy times more slowly than sarin and twenty times as slowly as water. This made it a potentially promising persistent chemical weapon, much more so than sarin which is classified as a non-persistent agent.

Despite its apparent promise, cyclosarin was not followed up by the German authorities, partly because the War was drawing to a close at the time of its discovery, which rather altered the priorities of the German scientific community; partly because the valuable persistent attributes of cyclosarin were somewhat negated by its slightly lower toxicity and by the relative costliness of the precursor chemicals required for its preparation; and, thirdly, because of its inflamability, which put it at a distinct tactical disadvantage in war situations where fire and flame are seldom far removed.

There was a resurgence of interest in cyclosarin in both the United States and Great Britain during the early 1950s when both countries were engaged in intensive reviews of the organophosphate nerve agents and their successors. The conclusions of this transatlantic research, however, varied little from those of the earlier German investigations – the slight advantage in persistency was more than outweighed by the expense of its manufacture and its inferior toxicity. Attempts were made to develop a combination of sarin and cyclosarin that exhibited to advantage the most murderous properties of each ingredient, but the results were lacklustre. It had been hoped that the whole would be greater than the sum of its parts but, in fact, experiments upon animals revealed that sarin/cyclosarin mixtures had relative toxicities that fell midway between the two. CIA evidence which, like all other American intelligence gathered before, during and immediately after the Iraq wars, should be accepted only with the greatest circumspection, suggests that the Hussein regime deployed chemical weapons utilizing sarin/cyclosarin mixtures, partly in order to increase the persistency of 'straight' sarin but principally on account of the shortages of sarin intermediates caused by years of trade sanctions.

Soman

While undertaking research for the German Army in late 1944 upon various analogues of the nerve agents previously discovered by Schrader and his team, the Nobel Laureate, Dr Richard Khun, isolated 1,2,2-trimethylpropyl methylphosphonofluoridate, the pinacolyl analogue of sarin, which he named soman. It was soon established that soman was considerably more toxic than sarin but further development was held back, like that on cyclosarin, by the end of the War and a shortage of the raw materials, particularly pinacol, required for its manufacture.

The exceptional toxicity of soman, compared to the earlier nerve agents, is due to the ease with which it is able to penetrate the blood-brain barrier into the central nervous system. This characteristic also appears to give soman far greater resistance to the effects of atropine and oxime, the standard antidotes administered to nerve gas victims.

Properties of Sarin

Sarin, in common with the other so-called nerve gases, works by disrupting the transmission of nerve impulses at nervous synapses, and at the junctions between nerve endings and muscle tissue. Nerve impulses are transmitted across junctions in the nervous system and at nerve endings by means of a chemical known as acetylcholine. A single molecule of acetylcholine can perform its function only once, after which it is rapidly destroyed by the enzyme acetylcholinesterase and thus, in the case of a nerve that activates a muscle, allowing the muscle to relax. The action of sarin and the other nerve gases is to inhibit the function of acetylcholinesterase allowing acetylcholine to accumulate at the nerve endings, which very quickly causes uncontrolled over stimulation of the muscles and organs of the body.

The enzyme acetylcholinesterase is vital for normal bodily function but is present in the tissue in only minute quantities; the crucial property of the nerve gases is that they combine with few, if any, chemicals that occur in the human body and thus the tiniest trace will be sufficient to swamp the acetylcholinesterase within a few minutes, particularly if it is able to penetrate the blood stream. The body readily absorbs nerve gases through the skin and the thin membranes of the eyes, respiratory and digestive systems. In liquid form they easily penetrate clothing and in this way pose the most serious threat in that, being in their pure state almost odourless and exhibiting no immediate irritant effect upon the skin, contamination may go unnoticed until the fatal symptoms of nerve-gas poisoning appear.

Typically, sarin entering the respiratory system in the form of vapour or aerosol will lead to death within about thirty seconds. Liquid sarin absorbed through the skin will prove fatal within fifteen minutes. The immediate symptoms of sarin poisoning are an asthma-like tightening of the chest and difficulty in breathing, pain in the eyes and occluded vision, together with a sudden runny nose. These are rapidly followed by vomiting, diarrhoea, uncontrollable sweating, dribbling and involuntary urination. The victim becomes giddy and the whole body twitches and convulses as the nervous system randomly stimulates muscles and organs. Soon the muscles become weak through continuous contraction and death occurs usually through suffocation and congestion of the lungs.

By the early 1950s sarin's physical and toxicological characteristics had identified it as by far the most promising of the nerve agents from the military standpoint. Although, in absolute terms, expensive to produce it was relatively the least expensive and technically the least complicated to manufacture on an industrial scale. The astonishing speed at which death follows exposure to a lethal dose, and the high potential mortality that might be produced by very small quantities released under optimum environmental conditions were attractive features, but were countered to some extent by the facts that recovery from non-lethal doses was equally quick, and environmental conditions are rarely conducive to the effective use of any chemical weapon. Due to its rapid rate of evaporation sarin presents an immediate but short-lived threat, the immediacy of which can be of immense military advantage. The absence of odour or other sensory evidence of sarin's presence, coupled with its almost instantaneous effect, leaves little or no overhead between exposure and detection during which countermeasures, particularly the injection of atropine antidote, might be taken. As an offensive weapon sarin is particularly valuable in that it is highly – though not equally – effective as both a respiratory and a cutaneous poison, which means that personnel under attack need effective gas masks and whole-body impermeable protection, with all the sensory deprivation and logistic overload that such protection imposes.

The principal drawback of sarin is that it is unstable, particularly when manufactured from precursor materials that are not absolutely pure, and its shelf life can in some cases be no longer than a few weeks. Stringent quality control through every stage of manufacture improves stability, but long-term storage, which is a prerequisite for a weapon that is intended to function primarily as a deterrent, remains problematic. An elegant technique developed in the United States during the 1970s to overcome this problem culminated in the M687 155 mm binary howitzer shell. The principle of the binary shell is that within a conventional artillery round two chambers are loaded, each containing relatively stable and relatively innocuous late-stage precursors which, when mixed, rapidly form a toxic agent. In the M687 one chamber contained a mixture of isopropyl alcohol and isopropyl amine (known as 'OPA') while the second chamber, which would normally be inserted only immediately prior to deployment, contained methylphosphonyl difluoride. When fired the shock of acceleration up the gun barrel ruptures a frangible disk separating the two chemicals which are then free to mix, a process aided by the spinning motion of the projectile. When combined the chemicals in the M687 form sarin, which is aerosolized by a small burster charge at the point of impact. Manufacture and filling of M687 binary shells began at Pine Bluff Arsenal on 16 December 1987 and continued uninterrupted until shortly before

June 1990, following agreement upon a weapons destruction programme with the Soviet Union.

Nerve Gases in the Post-war Era

Further investigations into organophosphorous compounds and their commercial, insecticidal possibilities continued in academic and industrial laboratories after the Second World War, with little immediate reference to their implications as chemical warfare agents. During 1952 and 1953 several industrial laboratories, including Imperial Chemical Industries in the United Kingdom and the international pharmaceutical firm Sandoz Ltd, independently but simultaneously discovered a series of substituted 2-aminoethanethiol organophosphate esters that demonstrated astonishing potency as anti-mite insecticides. These discoveries were to result in a rush for patent protection that soon descended into acrimony and litigation. Ranajit Ghosh and J.F. Newman isolated the first of these compounds, diethyl S-2-diethylaminoethyl phosphorothiolate at the ICI research laboratory in 1952 (patented in November 1952) and published their findings in the journal *Chemistry and Industry* three years later in 1955. Marketed under the trade name *Amiton,* the new insecticide was a clear, colourless liquid. Offered as its hydrogen oxalate salt it was also available from ICI as an insecticide in the form of a white powder under the trade name *Tetram.* Sandoz Ltd applied for a British patent for their insecticidal compound in May 1953.

Concurrently, research was under way at a number of European academic laboratories into the interrelationship between various analogues of the newly discovered amiton-type compounds and the process of cholinesterase inhibition. Dr Gerhard Schrader, now heading a team at the Bayer A.G. laboratories, researchers at the I.M. Sechenov Institute in Leningrad and at the Swedish Chemical Warfare laboratory under Dr Tammelin, were all investigating alkyl alkylphosphonothiolate analogues, working upon the theoretical assumption that compounds of the sarin type, with an alkylated phosphorous atom in the side chain, should exhibit an extraordinarily high level of toxicity.

Further commercial research on the new compounds, however, ceased abruptly around the middle of 1955 when it was discovered that *Amiton,* ICI's new insecticide, was lethal to humans and was immediately withdrawn from the market. Clearly the higher analogues then under development, despite their even greater insecticidal properties, had no commercial future.

The very properties of Ghosh's new compounds and their derivatives that ruled out any commercial potential they may have possessed as insecticides corresponded exactly with those sought by chemical weapons researchers at the British government's Porton laboratories.

Scientists at Porton and in the United States had made headway in the field of organophosphorous compounds during the Second World War but their research fell far behind that of Schrader and his associates in Germany. Allied chemists were, in fact, greatly surprised by the advances made in Germany that were revealed following the Allied occupation. Appropriated German science formed the basis of future chemical warfare programmes in Great Britain and the United States, where a production facility for sarin nerve gas was erected at Rocky Mountain Arsenal near Denver, Colorado, in the early 1950s. The principal precursors for sarin were sourced from the Muscle Shoals Army Chemical Plant in Alabama. Production began in 1954 and finished in 1956.

While sarin was adopted by the United States, and later by NATO, as the standard military nerve agent, and while the United Kingdom toyed with the idea of erecting its own sarin manufacturing facility, scientists in the United States were already looking forward to the next generation of ever more toxic war gases. And this is exactly what was handed to the Porton scientists in 1954 when preliminary details of Ghosh's discoveries were passed to them. This new generation of nerve gases, soon codenamed the 'V' agents, seemed to fulfil all the current criteria. They were some fifty times more toxic than sarin and in physical characteristics seemed akin to almost clear motor oil. Moderately to highly viscous and with a low vapour pressure, they evaporated only slowly and adhered tenaciously to surfaces with which they came in contact, rendering them excellent medium- to long-term persistent agents, which is exactly what was required. One variant, codenamed 'VX' was identified as the most suitable for military purposes and information concerning this was quickly passed to the United States. The British government decided not to progress further with development of VX but in the United States it was followed up with some vigour. Why Great Britain should not wish to pursue VX is unclear although it has been suggested that, with resourses already committed to development of a sarin plant in Cornwall (see below) and with a possibility of the complete renunciation of offensive chemical warfare in the near future, VX offered a valuable bargaining tool with the United States over nuclear technology. Construction of a factory for the large-scale manufacture of VX at the Newport Chemical Plant in Alabama started in 1959. Production began in April 1961 and continued until June 1968 when the factory was mothballed.

The British Nerve Gas Project – Llandwrog and Nancekuke
We have noted already that during the Allied advance through Germany alarmingly large quantities of tabun-filled aerial bombs, bulk nerve gas and other smaller weapons charged with organophosphorous

nerve agents were discovered in dispersed German ammunition depots. Eventually some 71,000 filled 250 kg tabun bombs were located, along with nearly 250,000 tons of other chemical weapons, and the question was raised as to what to do with this lethal hoard. The matter was discussed at length by both the British and American Chiefs of Staff who eventually telegraphed to the Joint Chiefs of Staff Mission that:

> We have considered the disposal of stocks of German chemical warfare material and have come to the conclusion that the general policy governing their disposal should be as follows:
> - Toxic chemicals in bulk should be destroyed except for stocks of high quality mustard gas and tabun.
> - Chemical shell and mortar bombs other than those charged with tabun should be destroyed.
> - Stocks of aircraft bombs charged with tabun should be safeguarded for the present.

The telegram went on to say that 'Stocks of this material both in bulk and in charged weapons should be retained for possible use in the Far East.'

Agreement was reached with the United States government that Britain should take charge of the 71,000 filled tabun bombs, the Americans declaring that they were more interested in the infinitely more toxic, and, crucially, more stable, nerve agent sarin, development of which was already making hesitant progress in the United States. The most important factor, according to the US Chiefs of Staff, was that the weapons should be retained by the West rather than be allowed to fall into the hands of the Russians.

The transfer and storage of this 14,000-ton lethal stockpile presented a logistic problem the resolution to which was a year in the planning. Location of a suitable storage site was the first difficulty. Any sort of contained storage like the underground reserve bomb stores was quite out of the question for the most minute of leaks would in all probability mean instant death to any staff working nearby. The ideal site would be a remote location on the west coast of Britain where the bombs could be kept in open storage in order that any leakage would be carried out to sea by the prevailing westerly wind. A disused airfield, of which there were many by the summer of 1946, would meet most of the other parameters: a large tract of open land with secure boundaries, already owned by the government where unusual activity would be unlikely to raise much concern and with concrete runways that would provide ideal stacking grounds at minimal cost. One site presented itself immediately: Llandwrog airfield, 5 miles south of Caernarvon on the very edge of Caernarvon Bay.

No. 277 MU, RAF, was formed at Llandwrog in August 1946 and began preparations to receive the bombs. Shipments began in October

1945, the bombs travelling via Hamburg to Newport docks from where they were transported by rail in batches of 500 to 31 MU Llanberis. Llanberis was an underground RAF bomb store near the shore of Llyn Padarn in the shadow of the Snowdon range that had something of a tragic history. Built to a unique and questionable design during the early war years it collapsed suddenly on the morning of Saturday, 25 January 1942, burying 14,000 tons of bombs which at that time represented some 14 per cent of the entire RAF stockholding. Although the site was later partially rehabilitated it never thereafter fulfilled its intended role as a strategic reserve depot. The compact underground depot sat within an RAF estate that extended over more than 350 acres composed primarily of disused slate quarries, some of which were several hundred feet deep. Taking advantage of these quarries the RAF used Llanberis during the latter years of the War and the immediate post-war period as a dumping ground for obsolete ammunition. Thousands of tons of bombs, bullets, shells and grenades of all descriptions were simply tipped into the bottom of the deepest of the remote slate quarries and conveniently forgotten about.

Llanberis was chosen as the primary reception centre for the German tabun bombs partly because it had become the RAF's de facto surplus ammunition disposal centre and partly because there already existed suitable RAF rail transfer facilities. Staff there were well experienced in the handling of weapons earmarked for disposal or long-term storage and there was suitable heavy lifting equipment easily to hand. The weapons were given a cursory examination and stored briefly at Llanberis before being shipped by lorry to Llandwrog. The last of the 71,000 bombs, sealed in their original German packing cases, were finally transferred to Llandwrog at 5.30 pm on 13 July 1947, where they were stored in widely separated stacks along the runways.

Almost as soon as the first bombs arrived at Llandwrog realization of the folly of the entire operation began to dawn. The only real justification for their retention – the possibility of their employment in the swift termination of the war with Japan – had been eclipsed by Little Boy's atomic flash over Hiroshima on 6 August 1945. Thereafter, for nearly a decade the Chiefs of Staff deluded themselves that the 71,000 mouldering time bombs stacked in the open at Llandwrog, as the crates and cases rotted in the salt air and the nerve agent within decomposed, were a viable deterrent to the expansionist threat of the Soviet Union. The fact that the bomb's fusing systems, mounting lugs and brackets, were incompatible with fittings on any British aircraft and would require complex re-engineering was completely overlooked – and no engineer who valued his own mortality was likely to treat lightly the prospect of welding new brackets to the side of a thin-walled canister containing a couple of hundredweight of the most deadly cocktail known to toxicology.

But in July 1947 there were more immediate problems. Staff at Llandwrog were horrified to discover, first, that the entire consignment had been shipped with fuses still inserted and, second, that the already corroding cases had a disconcerting propensity to leak at the joints. The first task, then, was to remove the fuses and nose caps (in the open air) and the next to seal the cases against the risk of leakage and further corrosion. The technique adopted at Llandwrog consisted of dipping the bombs in a large tank of lanolin-based preservative which effectively encapsulated them in a thick resilient wax that offered a high degree of protection from the harsh coastal environment, and also sealed the vulnerable welds to prevent outward leakage. Processed at the rate of 500 bombs per week, the task took three years to complete. Open storage, however, continued to take its toll and towards the end of the decade it was decided to erect twenty-one Bellman hangars on the runways to give added protection to the now ageing nerve gas bombs. The advantage of offshore winds carrying away leaking vapour was immediately lost with inside storage and the risk to personnel increased substantially. Previously leakers were detected by the presence of the distinctive ripe fruity smell of monochlorobenzene which had been added to the tabun during manufacture, but in the confined space of a hangar it was likely that once the odour was detected a fatal dose would already have been ingested. By this time, however, scientists had designed efficient detection instruments that could give remote warning of very low levels of tabun in the atmosphere which offset the risks of inside storage.

During the eight years that the stockpile remained at Llanwrog seventy-two irreparable leakers were disposed of on site. The disposal method was surprisingly simple and effective. Leaking bombs were transferred by a team of six men wearing full body protection and breathing apparatus to an area of sandy beach in a remote corner of the airfield where a 6-foot-deep pit was dug and partially filled with caustic soda crystals. Wooden beams were then laid across the opening and the bomb rolled over them. The filler plug was then removed and the nerve agent allowed to drain over the caustic soda which completely neutralized it. The hole was then filled with sand and the empty bomb case and the surrounding land doused with caustic soda solution.

By the early 1950s it was evident that the process of corrosion and chemical decay was accelerating and that the entire stock of bombs at Llandwrog was of little or no military or scientific value. Reluctantly, in June 1954, it was decided that the site should be cleared and the bombs, which were by now a serious liability to the RAF, should be dumped at sea.

Operation Sandcastle

Disposal of the bombs, under an operation code-named *Sandcastle*, was a risky, two-stage process involving the initial transfer of the weapons to the military port at Cairnryan in south-west Scotland and thence, aboard three rotting hulks, to a point 120 miles north-west of Ireland just beyond the continental shelf where the ships and their lethal cargos would be scuttled in 6,000 feet of water. Detailed plans for the operation were prepared by No. 42 Group RAF in January 1955. Six LCTs were assembled at the nearby port of Fort Belan towards which a new access road from Llandwrog was under construction during the spring. Weather conditions were critical to the success of the scuttling operation and it was intended that during the few suitable summer months of 1955 16,000 bombs would be disposed of.

Loading trials with the landing craft which were to transport the bombs to Cairnryan, conducted on 13 June, indicated that no more than 400 could be safely loaded in each vessel, far fewer than anticipated, the limitation lying not with the weight of the bombs but with their overall dimensions. It was then realized that each bomb could be reduced in length by some twenty inches by cutting off the tail fins, a job that, if done manually, would represent perhaps a further year's work. RAF technicians quickly got to work and designed a hydraulic guillotine that successfully accomplished the task of de-tailing each bomb in seconds, although foreshortening the wooden packing cases still required time-consuming manual carpentry. Once completed, however, it was possible to load 800 bombs on each landing craft and by mid-July the requisite 16,000 weapons were delivered to Cairnryan without undue incident.

Meanwhile the first of the scuttling ships, SS *Empire Claire,* was being prepared for her final voyage. Non-essential salvageable machinery was removed, which unfortunately gave her a pronounced list to starboard, and during the week prior to Saturday, 23 July the cargo of 16,000 bombs was safely stowed aboard ready for departure that morning. It was noted with mild concern that careless loading had rather exaggerated the starboard list. The ship's crew for the one-way trip to the North Atlantic consisted of her Master and six engineers, together with a two-man Royal Navy scuttling crew consisting of Lieutenant Commander Healey assisted by an able seaman. Three TNT scuttling charges, two main charges and a reserve, were strategically positioned to blow holes in the ship's bottom in such a way that she would sink steadily and horizontally. *Empire Claire* and her three escort vessels, RASCV *Mull* and RASCV *Sir Walter Campbell,* together with the ocean-going Clyde tug *Forester*, were scheduled to depart early on the Saturday morning, but this was postponed first by inclement weather and then by industrial action by the Clyde boatmen which kept *Forester* in port all weekend.

The convoy eventually set sail on Monday morning, but was hardly out of the Loch before *Empire Claire*'s main bearing overheated to the point of seizure and a pump failure stopped fuel flowing to the main and auxiliary engines. *Forester* took the ship in tow but without auxiliary power her steering gear was unworkable and the ship wallowed wildly. Fortunately the engineers were eventually able to restart the auxiliary engines which restored the steering gear and thus avoided the ship capsizing before she reached the edge of the continental shelf. *Empire Claire* reached her final destination at 6.00 am on Wednesday, 27 July, but held position for four hours in increasingly poor weather conditions while an RAF photo-reconnaissance aircraft arrived to record her departure below the waves. When the main scuttling charges were fired at 10.00 am the ship lurched even further to starboard and she seemed destined to capsize, scattering her cargo of nerve gas far and wide across the North Atlantic. The emergency charge was quickly fired, blowing out the vessel's stern, after which she sank quickly with her bows in the air.

Subsequent cargoes were dispatched with markedly less drama. MV *Vogtland* went down on 30 May 1956 with 28,737 tabun bombs aboard and two months later, on 21 July, SS *Kotka* was successfully scuttled with her cargo of 26,000 bombs, 330 tons of arsenical toxin and fifty unidentified packing cases reputedly filled with anthrax.

Nancekuke

The United Kingdom's investigations into the military possibilities of the organophosphorous compounds, which had previously only made halting headway, received an enormous post-war impetus from the stockpile of captured German nerve agent and, more particularly, from recovered German research documents concerning tabun and sarin which made their way to Porton. Sarin was immediately identified as the most suitable agent for the United Kingdom services and by 1950 development was sufficiently advanced for production to begin at the pilot plant stage. At this point it was realized that neither Porton nor the existing experimental production facility was suitable. Porton had never been envisaged, since its inception, as more than a research establishment and Sutton Oak, it was thought, was unsuitable due to its location. Close to large centres of population and industry it was thus ill positioned on two fronts – it was too vulnerable to unwanted observation and, more importantly, the risk of leakage and subsequent local contamination was too great. A new, remote location was therefore sought, the criteria being similar to those required a few years earlier for the storage site for stocks of German tabun. Once again, the solution was a remote and abandoned coastal airfield far from prying eyes and in a particularly sparsely populated area of the Cornish peninsula, facing out into the Atlantic Ocean. The site was the disused Portreath airfield, situated on the cliff tops a couple of miles to the east of the village of the same name. RAF Portreath had opened in March 1941 under the control of No. 10 Group, Fighter Command and at the cessation of hostilities was put under care and maintenance in December 1945. The following year it was briefly reactivated for use by a Polish Resettlement Unit under the RAF Technical Training Command. This did not last long, however, and the airfield was finally abandoned in 1946. After several years of disuse the derelict airfield with its four large, concrete runways was taken over by the Ministry of Supply on behalf of the Chemical Defence Establishment, Porton, and renamed Nancekuke.

For ten years after the end of the Second World War the United Kingdom maintained an active, offensive chemical warfare programme and the planned development at Nancekuke was to be central to this. It was intended that the huge site, extending to several hundred acres, should initially be home to a pilot scale sarin production plant undertaking process research work, but plans were already being prepared to build a vast, fully automated sarin production and weapon-filling plant there. The rationale behind the Nancekuke scheme was explained in a surprisingly frank Ministry of Defence press release issued in October 1970 which stated that:

> In the years immediately following the end of the Second World War, Europe was far from settled and it was considered possible that this country might become involved in another major war. Against this background and bearing in mind the time it takes to design and, if necessary, erect a complex chemical plant, it was decided to undertake a design exercise against the event of the UK requiring a retaliatory capability as a deterrent. It was also necessary to produce sufficient quantities of newly discovered agents (now known as 'G' agents) to enable them to be properly evaluated and to support research and development of protective measures. To meet these needs a pilot plant was required and, since Sutton Oak was not a suitable site for this purpose, the establishment was transferred to Nancekuke in 1951. The pilot plant was built and from 1953 to 1955 it produced sufficient GB (sarin) to prove the process and to meet the requirements for assessment trials and the testing of defensive equipment under development at Porton. Subsequently international tension relaxed to the point where it was not judged necessary to proceed with a production plant.

The pilot plant, which at full capacity could produce approximately 6 kg of sarin per hour by a continuous process, purportedly ceased production in 1955 by which time a stockpile of some 16 tons had been accumulated. Thereafter, according to Ministry of Defence sources and reports from outside observers, small-scale batch manufacture continued on a large, laboratory-bench scale, producing sufficient sarin for defensive research purposes until the establishment closed in 1976. This apparatus could produce approximately 1.5 kg of sarin or its derivatives per day. Unsurprisingly, Nancekuke also had a laboratory scale, continuous-flow 'V' agent plant which, according to a scientist who worked there, was last run in February 1968 to produce about 10 kg of VX for defensive experiments.

Although the proposed sarin factory was never built at Nancekuke, another, non-nerve gas chemical warfare agent, the irritant agent CS, was manufactured there on an industrial scale since about 1960. The CS plant produced the agent on a batch process at the rate of 30 kg per day and by the time the plant closed down in the mid 1970s had manufactured some 33–35 tons. Although sarin and CS are the agents that immediately come to the public mind when Nancekuke is discussed, the establishment was in fact involved in the development and manufacture of a huge range of chemicals, many of them therapeutic, as well as defensive equipment, much of which can be only guessed at from the titles of files lodged in the National Archives, the contents of which remain classified. Amongst the latter was a 40 kg per day production plant for the oxime-based nerve-agent antidote P2S, and a facility for the manufacture of carbon-impregnated protective clothing. Some insight into the post-1956 activities at Nancekuke can be gleaned from a parliamentary answer given by the Secretary of State for Defence in January 2000 when questioned about Health and Safety issues at the site:

> The pilot plant was decommissioned and, from then on, the work at Nancekuke was carried out solely in support of the defensive programme seeking to address the services' requirements for equipment to detect nerve agents in the field, for prophylaxis and therapy for nerve agent poisoning, for the protection of individuals and facilities, and for monitoring decontamination and residual contamination of terrain and equipment. Various nerve agents were produced but only on a laboratory bench scale.
>
> The House should be aware, however, that the work at Nancekuke was more wide-ranging than just the small-scale production of chemicals and agents for research and studies into the stability of those materials. There were many activities that did not involve working with nerve agents at all. For example, some production and development was concerned with riot control agents, chemicals for detectors, drugs for development as countermeasures, training stimulants and charcoal cloth for NBC – nuclear, biological and chemical – protective suits.

The closure of Nancekuke was announced in 1976 and by 1978 the site was completely abandoned as an operational facility although strict perimeter security was maintained. Some two years later, in 1980, the site was handed back to the RAF who established a Ground Control Intercept radar station there. Although the British government renounced offensive chemical weapons in 1956 and ceased all manufacture of toxic agents – except for small quantities for defensive research – the legacy of the 1950s programme continues to haunt them.

The most public of these recurring spectres is the ethical question posed by the attitude of the Ministry of Defence regarding personal injuries incurred by staff at its chemical defence research facilities. Two celebrated cases – which have been widely publicized over recent years and which, in consequence, will be only briefly touched on here – illustrate this attitude, which is fuelled by an unwholesome combination of institutional secrecy within the MoD and fear of the financial cost of litigation should the murky truths be eventually revealed. The first case concerns Tom Griffiths who worked as a fitter at the Nancekuke factory in the 1950s and who, during the dismantling of some pipe work in a disused sarin storage cubicle was contaminated by one small drip of nerve gas from a broken pipe joint. Griffiths had previously been assured that the equipment he was working on had been certified free from contamination and was advised that no protective clothing was necessary. The effects were immediate: Griffiths fell seriously ill, his eyesight was affected and his blood cholinesterase level dropped alarmingly. Although he was put under observation for several weeks no medication was administered. The problem was that on account of the secrecy surrounding Tom Griffiths' work he could not tell his own doctor about the events preceding his illness and thus organophosphate poisoning was never suspected. Griffiths was never fully fit for work again, but it was not until 1969, some eleven years after the event, that information leaked out about the sinister purpose of the Nancekuke factory and the true cause of his illness realized. Applications were made for a disability award, supported, by 1971, by no less than six independent medical reports confirming the diagnosis that his illness was due to sarin poisoning, but these were met by continued government denial and obfuscation. Finally, in 1975, a medical tribunal dismissed the evidence from Tom Griffiths' own doctor and rejected an earlier suggestion that he should be awarded £467 compensation, reducing this to £1.75 for 'lack of vision'.

For over thirty years servicemen were offered the opportunity to volunteer as guinea pigs in a programme of medical research at the Porton Down research station which, they were told, was to investigate the cause of the common cold. The reward was a few pounds supplement to the serviceman's standard pay and a few days extra leave, just sufficient, so it seems, to have attracted about 3,000 men by the time the project was wound up in 1989.

In fact, the work had nothing to do with the common cold but was concerned with testing the tolerance of the human body to a range of chemical warfare agents including the nerve gases sarin and VX. At least one of these experiments went horribly wrong. In May 1953, one of the volunteers, a twenty-year-old RAF engineer named Ronald Maddison, was exposed to a dose of 200 mg of sarin deposited onto a patch of uniform material on his arm. Within fifteen minutes he had died a horrific death. News of the incident was confined within the Porton establishment; under pressure from the War Office, the then Home Secretary, Maxwell-Fyffe, requested the Wiltshire coroner, Harold Dale, to hold his inquiry into the death in secret, 'on grounds of national security'. On 16 May the inquest concluded that Maddison died due to 'misadventure' and, as far as the government was concerned, that was that. The victim's family, however, were not satisfied with the inquest verdict and fought tenaciously for fifty years to lever the truth about Ronald Maddison's death out of an unwilling Ministry of Defence.

They made little progress until 1999 when the Wiltshire Police Force launched a criminal inquiry into the whole conduct of human experiments at the Porton Down research establishment. The investigation, launched in July 1999, was code-named Operation Antler and was undertaken by a full-time staff of twenty-six investigators. While Operation Antler was under way, the findings of the original inquest were quashed by Lord Chief Justice Woolf in November 2002 and a new inquest demanded. The substance of the claim made by Maddison's supporters was that the Ministry of Defence or its predecessors acted outside the ethical guidelines of the Nuremberg Code, a set of guidelines rooted in international law and established at the time of the Nuremberg war crimes trials.

Dr Ulf Schmidt, speaking as an expert witness on behalf of the Maddison family, stated in his evidence to the new inquiry, held in July 2004 at Trowbridge Town Hall in Wiltshire:

> I am trying to ascertain whether they were informed that it was nerve gas that was being tested on them, or were they just invited to take part in some experiments. Some volunteers who gave evidence at the Maddison inquest say they were told they were being tested for a cure for the common cold. This is now called 'the common cold issue'. Obviously, if that was the case, they didn't give informed consent.

Schmidt pointed out that 'informed consent' was a key principle of the Nuremberg Code, dismissing a MoD claim that the United Kingdom had no written rules regulating such matters and that consequently no law had been broken.

At the inquest Alfred Thornhill, who had been a young ambulance driver at the time of the incident and had been called to Maddison's aid, recalled what he had seen on the morning of Maddison's death:

> It was like being electrocuted, his whole body was convulsing . . . The skin
> was vibrating and there was this terrible stuff coming out of his mouth, it
> looked like frogspawn or tapioca. I saw his leg rise up from the bed and I
> saw his skin turning blue. It started from his ankle and started spreading
> up his leg. It was like watching someone pouring a blue liquid into a glass,
> it just began filling up.

After hearing sixty-four days of evidence the inquest jury concluded
that Ronald Maddison's death was due to the 'application of a nerve
agent in a non-therapeutic experiment'. Dismayed at the outcome, a
MoD spokesman commented that 'the Ministry of Defence notes the
jury's findings and will now take some time to reflect on these'.

Outside of the town hall 74-year-old Terry Alderson, who had been
another Porton volunteer in the 1950s, told reporters gathered there:

> It was Russian Roulette, Ronald Maddison was just the first. Reading
> between the lines they have got away with murder. Our health was never
> monitored afterwards and nobody knows how many died.
>   This shows what liars the MoD were, nobody volunteered for these
> tests, we were sent in there like sheep.

The second restless nightmare waiting in the wings for the Ministry
of Defence was that created by the environmental consequences of their
chemical weapons disposal policy. In Chapter 8 we will discuss in some
detail the methods by which the United Kingdom's stockpile of wartime
chemical weapons – which consisted primarily of RAF mustard gas
bombs – was disposed of, but here we will look just at the way the
debris of the nerve gas era was hidden away.

Throughout most of the 1950s it was thought that deep-sea dumping was a legitimate means of disposing of all types of toxic or otherwise dangerous military detritus. Immediately after the War tens of
thousands of tons of high explosive and chemical weapons were taken
offshore to be dumped in deep water where, at depths of 2,000 feet or
more it was confidently asserted that it could cause no harm. From
the mid-1960s this assertion has been questioned by the increasingly
vociferous environmental lobby, their arguments being regularly substantiated in concrete, or at least in rusty iron, by the alarmingly
frequent appearance on the Cumberland coast of sundry chunks of
corroded Second World War ordnance. By 1971 deep-sea dumping was
accepted as an untenable option and thereafter the Ministry of Defence
took to concealing its cast-offs.

Following the closure of the Nancekuke complex small quantities
of toxic material were transferred to Porton Down; some chemicals
were either neutralized on site or returned to the commercial chemical

industry, but a considerable volume was buried on site along with debris from dismantled plant and buildings. At the time, as with the deep-sea dumping of a decade earlier, this was considered to be an environmentally acceptable procedure. Material was dumped in five clearly defined and widely separated locations within the boundary of the Nancekuke site. One, which consists of an old quarry some 40 or 50 feet in depth, was filled with rubble and steelwork from the demolished factory along with similar material from surviving Second World War airfield buildings. Close to the cliff edge four specially excavated pits each 2 metres in depth were excavated and filled with waste chemicals from the factory. Nearby, the ground level of a shallow valley leading to the cliff edge was raised by about 20 feet by the deposition of building rubble, waste chemicals and quantities of asbestos from demolished buildings. More worryingly, two deep, long-abandoned tin-mine shafts within the factory perimeter were used to dump surplus equipment from the Sutton Oak research establishment at the time that its function was transferred to Nancekuke. The exact nature of this equipment is a matter of conjecture.

The problem with landfill is that what goes under the ground inevitably comes out in the water. Currently, in the United Kingdom, just as in the United States, the problems of serious ground and water contamination from buried military waste are having to be addressed. The only safe solution is to recover these contaminants and treat them by chemical or physical means to ensure that their future environmental impact will be neutral. This process is just beginning at Nancekuke at the time of writing and is expected to be completed by the end of the decade.

United States Post-war Policy

American chemical warfare policy between the end of the Second World War and the beginning of the 1970s is characterized by an attitude of vague obfuscation on the part of central government that gave no clear indication as to its position with regard to either international convention or the will of the people. Certainly, public attitude during the 1960s was hardening against chemical warfare as it had done in the 1930s; the old, gung-ho attitude of 'you can cook 'em better with gas' had somewhat moderated as the American public realized that the line of differential between cooker and cooked had diminished to invisibility and that they were no longer the only cooks in the kitchen. The axiomatic problem had been that, throughout the ambiguous twenty-year vacuum created by central government's inattention to chemical warfare policy, the military had, as it always will when not strictly corralled by its civil leadership, expanded its options and capabilities, unhindered by specific directives to the contrary.

146

Towards the end of this period, however, there at last emerged tangible evidence of the acceptance of a 'no-first-use' deterrent policy. The US Secretary of State for Defence announced in April 1969 that:

> The United States does not have a policy that requires a single and invariable response to any particular threat. In the field of chemical warfare, deterrence is the primary object of the United States.
>
> Chemical weapons, in many situations, may be more effective than conventional (high explosive and projectile) weapons. Accordingly it is believed wise to deter their use.

A year later, in March 1970, Ambassador Leonard Spoke reiterated the Nixon doctrine during the course of a speech in which he stated that:

> At the present time, some states believe that a chemical warfare capability is important for their national security. States maintain chemical warfare programs and stockpiles to deter the use of these weapons by others and to provide a retaliatory capability if deterrence were to fail. Unlike biological weapons, whose very doubtful retaliatory value has already been discussed, the inability of an attacked nation to retaliate with chemicals could give a significant military advantage to any government which might decide to violate the prohibition on the use of chemical weapons.

The United States finally ratified the Geneva Protocol in 1975 with the reservations that the treaty did not apply to the first use of defoliants or riot control agents, both of which were used regularly during the Vietnam campaign, and that the United States retained the right to retaliate in kind with anti-personnel chemical weapons if deterrence failed. Production of nerve gas weapons continued unabated after American ratification of the Geneva Protocol.

Moves had been made to bring the chemical warfare programme to an end in the early 1970s. In May 1973 Congress had been requested to abolish the Army Chemical Corps but this was not proceeded with at that time. Meanwhile, action was being taken to dispose of the first batches of obsolete blister agents currently decomposing at Rocky Mountain Arsenal. Legislative approval was given for the sale to the chemical industry, rather than destruction by chemical neutralization, of some 1,294 tons of phosgene stored there. Meanwhile, phase one of 'Project Eagle', the disposal of 3,407 tons of mustard gas was under way, along with phase two, the destruction of 21,115 type M34 sarin cluster weapons which began in October 1973. In the same month the US Secretary of Defense authorized the disposal of the entire retaliatory stockpile of filled sarin weapons and bulk nerve agent at Rocky Mountain.

The true end of the United States chemical warfare programme was a somewhat halting and irresolute process which began in 1985 with the passing by Congress of Public Law 99-145 which required the Army to destroy its stockpile of obsolete chemical weapons. This requirement was extended in 1992 to include the remaining chemical materiel including binary weapons and production plant. In 1993 the United States signed the UN-sponsored Chemical Weapons Convention, an agreement which it finally ratified in October 1996 and which came into force on 29 April 1997. Under the terms of this convention the United States agreed to a ten-year disposal timetable that would see the entire stock of legacy unitary weapons, modern binary weapons, manufacturing and assembly facilities and, crucially, dumps of previously discarded obsolete weapons, completely destroyed by 29 April 2007.

The 1985 announcement was in some respects a red herring in that the bulk of the weapons scheduled for destruction did not represent a definitive reduction in America's active chemical weapons stockpile, rather the necessary destruction of obsolete ordnance that was rapidly becoming too unstable to safely retain. In 1984 a National Research Council report entitled *Disposal of Chemical Munitions and Agents* noted that at that time all the chemical agents in the army stockpile were at least sixteen years old, some were more than forty years old, and none had been manufactured after 1968. The report went on to explain that much of the stockpile was deteriorating, many filled weapons were leaking, and that maintenance and security were proving prohibitively expensive. Following upon this report the Committee on Demilitarizing Chemical Munitions and Agents recommended that 'the stockpiles of obsolete or unserviceable toxic chemical agents and munitions, including bulk stocks, should be destroyed as soon as possible. For the present time, however, storage is the only option.'

Prior to the Chemical Weapons Convention the accepted disposal process for obsolete or surplus chemical weapons was that of burial at a range of military sites throughout the United States and by deep-sea dumping. A report issued by the National Academy of Science (NAS) in 1969 which highlighted the environmental consequences of deep-sea dumping led directly to the 1972 Marine Protection Act which prohibited all further ocean disposal. While the NAS was compiling its report the Army was engaged in what were to prove to be the last of a series of deep-sea dumping exercises code-named 'Chase' (Cut Holes in 'em And Sink 'Em) which, copying current British practice, involved loading obsolete weapons aboard surplus naval hulks and scuttling them beyond the continental shelf. Although most of the 'Chase' operations concerned the disposal of conventional weapons, four – numbered VIII, X, XI and XII – subsequently achieved considerable notoriety when it was revealed that the hulks were loaded with chemical weapons. Each vessel contained approximately 7,500 tons of surplus chemical weaponry and was scuttled approximately 200 miles off the

New Jersey coast in 7,200 feet of water. The four operations, confusingly numbered in the order in which they were planned rather than implemented, are shown in Table 14.

The M55 rocket, which was designed as a long-range, large area battlefield nerve gas weapon, proved to be a dangerous liability to the US Army. The 7-foot-tall rockets were manufactured during the late 1950s at the Newport Army Ammunition Plant in Indiana and were propelled by a 13 lb double-base (nitro-glycerine and nitrocellulose) propellant contained within an aluminium-bodied motor unit. Shortly after production ceased it was discovered that instability of the propellant, possibly caused by a complex chemical process initiated by a supposed stabilizing agent reacting with the aluminium propellant container, might cause spontaneous combustion while in storage. Whilst propellant instability was the prime motive for the first round of disposals (Chase X and Chase XI) in the late 1960s and was to remain a problem for the following quarter of a century, further unforeseen difficulties arose when the remaining stockpile of almost 250,000 rounds came up for disposal as a consequence of the Chemical Weapons Convention. Inspections undertaken in 1999 revealed that in many cases the liquid sarin had, through reaction with the aluminium inner lining of the rocket, become gelatinized thereby rendering the process of dismantling hugely more hazardous, time consuming and thus expensive. Non-gelled rockets disassembled at the Anniston facility were processed at the rate of thirty-two per hour; gelled rockets, by comparison, could be processed in no less than one hour.

The disposal process had continued for some forty years and by 1997, when the Chemical Weapons Convention came into force, detailed records of many of the landfill sites had been lost and personal recollections were hazy. By the end of 1999 some ninety-nine locations in thirty-eight states had been positively identified and it was estimated that 229 discreet dumping grounds existed, many of which remained to be rediscovered.

Table 14   Operation Chase

CHASE VIII	SS *Corporal Eric Gibson*	June 1967	Bulk mustard gas
CHASE X	SS *LeBaron Russell Briggs*	August 1970	M55 rockets charged with sarin, sealed in concrete
CHASE XI	SS *Mormactern*	June 1968	M55 rockets charged with sarin. Sarin in ton containers. VX in ton containers.
CHASE XII	SS *Richardson*	June 1968	Bulk mustard gas contaminated with water

Table 15   US land service chemical weapon stocks, 1997

	Type	Loading	Note
M60	150 mm artillery	Mustard gas	
M360	105 mm artillery	Sarin nerve gas (1.6 lb)	Unitary charge
M104	155 mm artillery	'H' or 'HD' mustard (11.7 lb)	
M110A1/A2	155 mm artillery	'H' or 'HD' mustard (11.7 lb)	
M121/A1	155 mm artillery	Sarin or VX (6.5 lb)	Unitary charge
M122	155 mm artillery	Sarin (6.5 lb)	Unitary charge
M426	203 mm artillery	Sarin or VX (14.5 lb)	Unitary charge
M687	155 mm artillery	Sarin	Binary charge (see text for details)
M23	Landmine	VX nerve gas (10.5 lb)	13″ diameter
M55	Rocket	Sarin (10.7 lb) or VX (10 lb)	Introduced c.1950 (see text for details)

Disposal of the estimated stockpile of 250,000 155 mm M687 binary artillery shells received much media attention in the last years of the twentieth century. For reasons of security the two principal components of M687 shells were, during peacetime, stored in separate chemical weapons depots, a system which to some extent simplified the disposal process. Disassembly was undertaken at Hawthorne Army Depot, Nevada, approximately 140 miles south-east of Carson City. Projectiles, complete with burster charges and OPA canisters, were transported by road from the various storage sites for dismantling, as many of the components as possible being recycled for non-military

Table 16   US Chemical weapons storage sites (stock levels, 1997)

Location	Total capacity	Material stored
Umatilla Chemical Depot	3,717 tons	Mustard gas in bulk
		Nerve agents in filled weapons
Pueblo Chemical Depot	2,611 tons	Mustard gas in filled weapons
Deseret Chemical Depot	13,616 tons	Mustard gas in bulk
		Mustard gas in filled weapons
		Nerve agent in filled weapons
Johnston Atoll	2,031 tons	Mustard gas in bulk
		Mustard gas in filled weapons
		Nerve agent in filled weapons
Pine Bluff Arsenal	3,850 tons	Mustard gas in bulk
		Nerve gas in rockets and landmines
Anniston Arsenal	2,254 tons	Mustard gas in filled weapons
		Nerve gas in filled weapons
Blue Grass Arsenal	523 tons	Mustard gas in filled weapons
		Nerve gas in filled weapons
Edgewood Arsenal	1,625 tons	Mustard gas in bulk
Newport Arsenal	1,269 tons	Nerve agent in bulk

Table 17   Stockholding of US land service chemical weapons, 1997

Type	Number of filled weapons							
	Anniston	Blue Grass	Pine Bluff	Pueblo	Deseret	Umatilla	Johnston	Total
Mustard								
105 mm	23,065			383,418			46	406,529
155 mm	17,643	15,492		299,554	54,663		5,779	393,131
4.2″ mortar	258,912			97,106	63,568		43,660	463,246
Sarin								
105 mm	74,040				798,703		47,735	920,478
155 mm	9,600				89,141	47,406	6,387	152,534
203 mm	16,026	3,977				14,246	13,020	47,269
M55 rocket	42,738	51,716	90,231		17,353	91,375		293,413
VX								
155 mm	139,581	12,816			53,216	32,313	42,682	280,608
203 mm						3,752	14,519	18,271
M55 rocket	35,636	17,733	19,582		3,966	14,513		91,430
M23 landmine	44,131		9,378		22,690	11,685	13,302	101,186
Grand total								3,168,095

use. At Hawthorne the OPA cylinders were removed, punctured and the chemical agent drained off into drums for reprocessing. Some material was recovered and sold to the chemical industry while any surplus was destroyed. The contaminated cylinders were then shredded and buried as landfill. The steel shell castings were cut apart using high-pressure water-jet technology in order to remove the aluminium exploder canisters, after which the explosive was melted out, reprocessed and subsequently sold for mining, demolition and other similar purposes. The aluminium containers were melted into ingots and sold for scrap. Similarly, the cut-up shell castings were sold as scrap steel. By the first deadline of 29 April 1999, 201,728 M687 binary shells had been destroyed with the balance, including secondary fillings, additional components and manufacturing facilities, scheduled for destruction by April 2007.

Stocks of VX nerve agent were disposed of in a number of ways both prior to and as a consequence of the UN Chemical Weapons Convention. Large quantities of VX were incinerated at the Johnston Atoll facility where the agent had been stored both in filled weapons and in bulk containers. Johnston Atoll served as a test bed for future nerve gas disposal facilities at other chemical ordnance depots. Many options were considered for the destruction of these stockpiles, although in the first instance incineration was the favoured method. Other possible techniques considered were: chemical neutralization followed by either super-critical water oxidation, gas phase chemical reduction or electrochemical oxidation. Preparatory to the start of the disposal programme obsolete weapons from US bases in the Pacific Basin and West Germany were despatched to Johnston over a period of twenty years, starting in 1971. The Reagan administration agreed to remove all chemical weapons from Germany by the end of 1992, a process subsequently brought forward to September 1990 by President Bush the elder. Under a highly secret plan, the stockpile of 100,000 VX and sarin nerve gas shells were transported by road convoy from the depot at Clausen in West Germany to Miesau, from where they were taken by freight train to the port of Nordenham and thence to Johnston Atoll.

Construction of the necessary incineration plant on Johnston Atoll began in 1985 and by the end of November 2000 the last of the 400,000 weapons accumulated at the depot, containing 400,000,000 lb of mustard gas, sarin and VX nerve gas, had been destroyed. Experience gained at Johnston Atoll highlighted the environmental disadvantages of the incineration technique and has led to widespread public concern about the erection of similar incineration plants at the eight remaining homeland chemical weapons storage facilities. In response to the concerns raised by a small but increasingly influential congressional organization known as the Chemical Weapons Working Group over the incineration plants at Umatilla, Tooele and Anniston it was decided to implement the more costly but less environmentally damaging neutralization and super-critical water oxidation process at Blue Grass Army Depot in Richmond, for which a preliminary contract was let in June 2003. Sustained pressure from the vociferous environmental lobby, demanding much more scrupulous control over potentially harmful emissions, has caused costs to spiral and has pushed the 2007 deadline on to at least 2012, although it is generally accepted within US military circles that the programme may not be completed until the year 2020.

Soviet Chemical Weapons in the Cold War Era

Following joint development with Germany at Shikani during the inter-war years, Russia built her first mustard gas plant at Trotsk, near Samarsa, in the early 1930s and, before the outbreak of the Second World War, had established at least three more at Bandyuzhsky on the River Kama, Kuibyshev and Karaganda. American intelligence assessments prepared in the immediate post-war years suggest that there might have been as many as thirty factories in the USSR producing a total output of 35,000 tons of mustard gas by the end of the War, and thirteen lewisite plants along with others manufacturing a comprehensive range of lesser toxic agents. At the height of the Russian campaign, German intelligence estimated Soviet chemical agent capacity at 8,000 tons per month.

Reliable records of post-war Soviet chemical warfare activity are sparse and to create an approximate image of Soviet capacity at the beginning of the cold war we must turn to American intelligence analyses of the period, the credibility of which, unfortunately, are somewhat variable. It is presumed that vesicant production facilities were mothballed but retained, and that existing stocks of mustard gas and other casualty and irritant weapons were kept in long-term storage. Meanwhile, based upon information gleaned from captured German material the Soviets were able by 1958 or 1959 to produce sarin on an industrial scale. A probable, theoretical timescale for the Soviet development of nerve gas weapons was put forward by H. Swyter, a Department of Defense official, at the DoD Conference on Chemical and Biological Warfare on 25 July 1969. Swyter's thesis was that:

> The Soviet nerve gas capability came into existence in the early or mid 1950s because it wasn't until then that the Russians could afford anything. The Russians, when they started spending money and getting a conventional land force capability in the early 1950s were faced with American nuclear weapons, and they figured that a chemical capability was a second best thing. When they got a little richer in the early 1960s they went ahead and bought the tactical nuclear capability. Once you have it, it doesn't cost you much to maintain these stockpiles, and they have all the doctrine and training programmes set up anyway.

By 1960 the US Congressional Committee on Defence Appropriations was being told by General Trudeau, head of Army Research and Development, that 'We know that the Soviets are putting a high priority on development of lethal and non-lethal weapons, and that their stockpile consists of about one sixth chemical munitions.' This claim was made at a time when the Army Chemical Corps was fighting hard not just to maintain its existence but to increase its power in the wider defence field, and in consequence was not averse to overstating the Soviet threat in order to justify its own existence. The figure of one-sixth had been bandied about as a rough estimate, based upon no concrete evidence, since the mid 1950s, its origin obscured by the mists of time, swathed, for added security, in veils of secrecy and buried by obfuscation. Nevertheless, having once been stated it was thereafter accepted as fact and maintained its groundless irrefutability until at least 1969. Then, on 29 June of that year, an article by S.M. Hersch in the *Washington Post* sensationally exposed the shaky foundations upon which Trudeau's statistics, and thus the whole US chemical weapons policy, were built. Hersch wrote:

> A responsible government official who provided reliable information in the past told me how the Trudeau statistic, which is cited by the Army

even today, came to be. 'In 1963 or 1964,' the source said, 'the Army issued a request to send a large shipment of nerve gas to West Germany under US control. Their argument was that the Russians have it in Russia; therefore we need it in Germany,' the source recalled. The request was turned down. To back up its plea, the Army presented evidence supporting Trudeau's statement. This consisted of analysis made from aerial photos of Russia that showed large storage sheds similar to those used for storing warfare gases at the US Army's depot at Tooele, Utah. 'The Army computed the roof size of the Russian sheds, figured out how many gallons of nerve gas could be stored in a comparably sized shed in Utah, added a 20 percent "fudge" factor and came up with the estimate,' the source said.

Several years earlier, in December 1962, the insidious process of disinformation had already increased the Soviet Union's tally of poison gas factories from thirty or forty to well in excess of 100. In the transcript of a speech made in December 1962 and subsequently published in the *Armed Forces Chemical Journal* under the title 'Is Russia outstripping us in Weapons of Mass Destruction?' Admiral Coggins, former Chief of ABC in the US Navy and later at Supreme Headquarters, Allied Powers in Europe asserted that:

A few years ago the Soviet Union had 106 chemical plants in operation, of which one half were either producing, or were capable of producing, the later war gases. His stocks greatly exceed the combined stocks of the free world, being quite sufficient for three or four major offensives on a wide front. His present stockpile is reported as enormous, comprising fully 15 per cent of the total of the Russian military munitions.

He then went on to delineate the make-up of this stockpile, suggesting that it included some 50,000 tons of tabun recovered from Dyhernfurth – though the earlier consensus was that no more than 15,000 tons were unaccounted for – and that the greater part of the remainder consisted of mustard gas. Throughout the 1960s and early 1970s the figures of Trudeau and Coggins were widely accepted as the barely minimal estimate of the true magnitude of the Soviet chemical arsenal. The head of Army Research and development told Congress in 1969 that 'we do not know precisely what agents they have developed and deployed and [. . .] we are not positive in terms of precise quantities,' but his department was quite happy to see a swathe of European periodicals quote hugely inflated estimates, which of course reinforced the urgency of the US Army's demand for an increased chemical warfare budget to counter the Soviet threat, without itself being perceived as warmongering. By early 1969 regular media reports, based upon only vaguely attributed NATO sources, estimated the Soviet chemical stockpile at 300,000 to 350,000 tons. By December, *Der Spiegel* had doubled this to 700,000 tons, 15 per cent of which was nerve gas. Shortly afterwards the Swiss periodical *Allgemeine Schweizerische Militarzeitschrift* suggested a full third of Soviet weapons were chemical.

The most reliable evidence from Russian sources suggests that the American proposition that nerve gas production along the tabun-sarin route started in 1958–9 was correct and also indicates that soman was being produced industrially by 1967 and certain 'V' agents (particularly the Soviet equivalent of VX) by 1972. By the early 1980s nerve gas manufacturing and storage sites were reputed to have been built at a number of locations including Zaporozhye, Pavlodar, Volsk and Novocheboksarsk. Estimates of total stockpiles of all chemical weapons including nerve gases and blistering agents varied between 40,000 and 50,000 tons.

The end of the old Soviet chemical warfare programme and the commitment to destroy the entire declared stockpile of weapons which, since the collapse of the Soviet Union had come under the control of the Russian Federation, came in 1987. In that year President Gorbachev announced that with the closure of the Novocheboksarsk nerve gas factory, chemical weapons production in Russia had ceased. On 23 September 1989 foreign minister Edward Shevardnadze and US Secretary of State James Baker signed a document that was to become known as the Wyoming Memorandum of Understanding which marked a key waypoint on the route to full implementation of the Chemical Weapons Convention, which was intended to be a verifiable, global ban on all chemical weapons. The first phase of this agreement, which had been a central goal of US foreign policy since 1984, was completed in February 1991 and opened the way for a full exchange of data on each country's chemical weapons capabilities. Phase two, which was implemented in 1994, allowed for more detailed data exchange and for mutual inspection of each party's declared chemical weapons sites. Parallel with these inspection arrangements, Presidents Bush and Gorbachev signed the Bilateral Destruction Agreement in Washington on 1 June 1990, under the terms of which both agreed to reduce their stockholding of chemical weapons to no more than 5,000 tons by 31 December 2002.

In Russia, the Dumas passed the relevant legislation to authorize the destruction programme on 27 December 1996 but this was blocked by the Council of the Russian Federation the following January amidst concerns about the ecological safety of the proposed disposal programme. The problems facing the Russian government are strikingly similar to those that arose in the United States. Previously acceptable sea dumping and landfill disposal techniques became environmentally untenable and proposals to transfer stockpiles of chemical weapons to remote incineration or destruction plants were turned down on account

Table 18   Declared Russian stockpile, 1997

Nerve agents (soman, sarin and VX)	32,000 tons
Lewisite	6,800 tons
Mustard gas	800 tons
Mustard/lewisite mixture	400 tons

Table 19   Storage/disposal locations

Kambarka	blister agents	bulk storage	6,360 tons
Gomy	blister agents	bulk storage	1,160 tons
Maradykovsky	nerve agents	aerial delivery	6,960 tons
Pochep	nerve agents	aerial delivery	7,520 tons
Kizner	nerve agents	rocket and conventional artillery rounds	5,680 tons
Shchuche	nerve agents and phosgene	rocket and conventional artillery rounds	5,440 tons
Leonidovka	nerve agents	aerial delivery	6,880 tons

of the dangers inherent in moving vast quantities of toxic material, much of it in an unstable, dubious condition, through populated areas. The only acceptable solution seemed to be local destruction at the storage depots by chemical decomposition and neutralization. Even this, though, has been resisted by local representation fearful of the effects of the programme upon nearby residents. The 1997 declared Russian stockpile is shown in Tables 18 and 19.

All Russian nerve gas agents were stored charged into weapons, although, unlike US practice, these weapons were not fitted with their explosive components (fuzes, gaines and burster charges) until the time of issue. This, to some extent, simplified the process of dismantling and disposal, although the benefit was offset by the fact that most Russian weapons were of welded rather than screwed construction and thus required more hazardous procedures for emptying their nerve gas contents. Blistering agents were stored in large-capacity bulk containers similar to those previously utilized in the United Kingdom.

The Soviet Union had built a large plant at Chapayevsk as early as 1989 for the chemical destruction of toxic weapons, purportedly by treatment with ethylene glycol and ethylene amine, but the factory was closed soon after in response to sustained public opposition. There are also reports that a mobile neutralization plant was built, initially for the destruction of faulty weapons but later adapted for full-scale disposal. The plant was claimed to have been able to neutralize toxic agents at the rate of 90 kg per hour and that for the decade up to 1990 had destroyed 4,000 munitions containing a total of 200 tons of nerve gas.

Russia's problem has been that in the country's new economic climate there simply have not been sufficient funds available to fulfil its obligations under the Chemical Weapons Convention. Financial assistance has been forthcoming from the European Union and from the United States under the Co-operative Threat Reduction programme but, even with this aid and a five-year extension up to 2007, it is unlikely that the target for disposal will be met.

Chapter 8

United Kingdom – Storage and Disposal of Second World War Chemical Weapons

It quickly became apparent that during the Second World War, chemical weapons, if they were to be used at all, would be used primarily as aerial weapons, and that such weapons, to be effective, would necessarily be large-scale devices. Although many hundreds of thousands of land service artillery rounds were manufactured for army consumption – though the majority were retained in reserve depots as unfilled shells for safety's sake – the chemical weapons plants were largely geared up to fill high-capacity aerial bombs and aircraft spray tanks. The greatest storage burden for such weapons fell upon the RAF, whose history of ammunition storage throughout the War was a continuous tale of tragedy. Rather late to grasp the scale of stockholding that would be required by a modern air force, by the time the need arose to provide deep underground storage for its reserve stockpile in order to protect it from German bombing, the RAF found that the Army had already mopped up the best and cheapest of the United Kingdom's underground storage capacity. Eventually, however, the RAF was able to provide itself with five huge, underground reserve depots. Of these, two were 'artificial' in character in that they consisted of networks of concrete tunnels constructed in deep, abandoned quarries that were then covered with an overfill of waste stone to depths of 40 or 50 feet. One such depot was established in a slate quarry in Llanberis in north Wales, the other in an old limestone quarry at Harpur Hill near Buxton in Derbyshire. The three other reserve depots were built in existing underground mineral mines: a gypsum mine at Fauld near Burton on Trent; a limestone mine at Linley, north of Birmingham; and a Bath-stone quarry at Chilmark in Wiltshire which had long ago provided the stone to build Salisbury cathedral. A series of catastrophic collapses during the construction of the Linley depot led to its abandonment even before it was completed, and less terminal but still serious collapses at Chilmark further weakened the Air Ministry's faith in underground works in general. This disquiet was well founded for in January 1942, shortly after it was opened, the 'artificial' underground depot at Llanberis spectacularly collapsed, burying 14,000 tons of bombs.

158

Inspection of the Harpur Hill depot, which had been built to the same overall plan, revealed that it, too, was on the point of collapse, resulting in its rapid emptying and reconstruction. Realizing that it was on, or rather under, shaky ground as regards its large-scale storage facilities, the Air Ministry gave orders that its chemical weapons reserves and other particularly sensitive ammunition should no longer be stored underground.

RAF chemical weapons storage policy underwent a continuous process of metamorphosis during the first three years of the War as, with experience, depot staff gained a better understanding of the handling and storage characteristics of filled weapons, and plans for their tactical and strategic use were resolved. At first, the basement area of the tunnels at 21 MU Harpur Hill was designated as the main reception and storage point for RAF mustard gas bombs, and in June 1940 staff there were busy examining thousands of bombs hurriedly returned from France by the British Expeditionary Force following the fall of France. These weapons had been dispatched as a precautionary measure to operational units direct from the factories some months earlier and were subsequently returned via Fowey docks, and thence by rail to Buxton.

Towards the latter part of 1940 limited holdings of gas bombs were held at all underground reserve depots and surface forward ammunition depots, usually at specially prepared sub-sites staffed by one corporal and four airmen who had undergone a course of instruction in the handling and care of such weapons. At some locations such holdings were substantial: at 100 MU South Witham, for example, provision was made for 6,000 tons of chemical weapons. Up until December 1942 only a small number of operational squadrons were trained in the use of chemical weapons. No. 88 Squadron at Attlebridge, 226 Squadron at Swanton Morley and 107 Squadron at Great Massingham practised low-spray (SCI) techniques flying Bostons, while 15 Squadron at Bourn, 149 Squadron at Lakenheath and 214 Squadron at Chedburgh practised dropping 65 lb LC and 400 lb SC bombs flying Stirlings. As the prospect of the invasion of the European mainland grew nearer it was thought increasingly likely that the Luftwaffe would try to deflect the Allied effort with the unrestricted first use of chemical weapons, so plans were laid for a massive retaliation in kind. Stocks of mustard gas bombs were enormously increased at all forward depots, more squadrons were hastily trained in, and detailed orders issued for, their use. Air Council instructions, issued on behalf of the War Cabinet, stated quite unambiguously that 'Should the enemy initiate chemical warfare, HM Government intends to retaliate in kind [...] with unrestricted heavy-scale bombing against centres of German population best calculated to bring about a collapse of German morale.' The intended attacks would take one of two tactical forms:

1. High-explosive and incendiary bombs followed by phosgene, which would force huge swathes of the population into the open escaping from burning buildings, where they would be killed or incapacitated by phosgene, which was a toxin lethal in its effect but relatively non-persistent.
2. High-explosive bombs followed by mustard gas, which would open up buildings and render rescue efforts, clearance and reconstruction almost impossible due to the long-term persistence of mustard gas.

Bowes Moor

That the storage of large numbers of mustard gas bombs and other chemical weapons in the same depot as conventional weapons, and particularly their storage in ill-ventilated and, as was later to be revealed, structurally questionable underground depots, was unsatisfactory soon became evident, and in September 1940 it was suggested that a remote, open site, ideally on moorland in the north of England, should be found for the establishment of a dedicated CW reserve depot. A suitable site was found on Bowes Moor, just to the north of Bowes station, 10 miles south-west of Barnard Castle in County Durham, and by early December 1941 development was sufficiently advanced for the first receipts of mustard gas bombs to be made. The moorland location, with bombs stored either under tarpaulins in the open or in lightweight, widely dispersed wooden sheds, had both advantages and disadvantages. The most serious disadvantage was that in the first year or so of operations sheep were allowed to roam freely among the storage sheds and open stacks of bombs. These sheep, true to their reputation for eating almost anything that confronted them by way of gastronomic experiment, quickly consumed the tarpaulins covering stacks of 65 lb LC bombs and then attempted to make alfresco meals of the bombs themselves, puncturing many of the thin-cased weapons, much to their – the sheep and the bombs – ultimate disadvantage. Similar depredations occurred at the army ammunition depot at Drymen on the banks of Loch Lomond, where tarpaulins were routinely consumed by roaming livestock, though the thick-cased artillery shells stored there tested the resolution of the herds of highland cattle rather more severely. The problem at Bowes Moor was eventually overcome by the erection, on RAF account, of many miles of sheep-proof fencing and gates.

Later in the War, Bowes Moor was largely rebuilt with covered accommodation for most categories of weapon except for 250 lb and

160

1,000 lb LC bomb components, which were simply stacked on hard-standings. A range of fifty new buildings were put up in 1942 to store 'special' 250 lb bombs to the east of the main access road. Special gas-proof air-raid shelters were provided at Bowes Moor to protect people working there in the event of an enemy attack bursting any of the stored bombs.

Mustard-gas-filled bombs and the strategic limitations that might or might not determine their pattern of use presented an intractable long-term storage problem. Experience up to 1941 indicated that the reliability and safety of filled bombs stored under even the best conditions became unsatisfactory after little more than six or eight weeks. These thin-cased weapons were easily punctured and required great care in handling, and, despite the care taken in bonding the weapons after manufacture, they were too readily prone to leakage at joints. More seriously, it was discovered that the fillings tended to react with the outer casing, resulting in pitting and the risk of perforation of the case, and also of contamination of the vesicant by chemical reaction with impurities in the metallic case. Had the turnover of CW bombs occurred at the same rate as high-explosive bombs then the problems would have been negligible, but, in accordance with government policy of no first use, filled bombs were both accumulating and decaying at the forward depots in alarming numbers. The fragility of these weapons also made them vulnerable to damage in transit, particularly over long distances, which was inevitable as long as the reserve stocks were maintained in central depots. To overcome this difficulty and also to provide extra flexibility and security to the weapon-filling capacity should a sudden surge in demand require it, the Air Ministry considered a scheme for the construction of local filling plants, or Forward Filling Stations, at the end of 1941.

Forward Filling Stations
The concept of forward filling stations was first proposed in 1938 in circumstances very different from those that led to their eventual construction in 1942. At the time of Munich it was generally feared that chemical weapons would be extensively used from the outset by both sides in the war which was by then considered inevitable. Basing their projections on a wildly inaccurate analysis of the strength of the German Air Force, the British government also expected that the country would be subject to a massive assault – a knockout blow – in the first few days of the War, aimed at the seat of government, RAF aerodromes and war factories. To ensure continuity in the supply of poison gas, it was proposed to disperse bulk storage tanks of mustard gas and head-filling apparatus to disparate areas of the country to avoid destruction. This plan was not followed up, but, following the success

of the Woodside satellite scheme at Rhydymwyn, it was revived in 1941 to meet a different contingency. The pivotal aspect of the Woodside scheme, which made the later forward filling stations viable, was the design of the bulk-storage tanks there, which was of lead-lined concrete construction with a capacity of 250 tons. Originally built in this form to overcome the shortage of material required for conventional mild steel tanks with loose lead liners, the large concrete design allowed the quick construction of high-volume bulk storage at an economical cost.

The forward filling depot concept was considered by the Air Ministry at the end of 1941 and a suitable satellite site at Barnham was surveyed in January 1942. Preliminary plans were prepared in April and costings presented to the Air Council in October. Approval to proceed with Barnham and two other sites at Melchbourne Park and Norton Disney was granted the same month. In December 1942 estimates were approved for two further sites at Lord's Bridge and West Cottingwith and construction work at all five began in February 1943.

Building work at Barnham and Melchbourne Park had not progressed far when it was announced that, when completed, these two forward filling depots would be handed over to the USAAF and that alterations would be needed to their design to meet American requirements. The original plan called for two 250-ton underground storage tanks at each site, but the USAAF, which intended to employ high-capacity M33 mustard gas spray tanks, requested a bulk storage capacity of 1,500 tons at each site, which was provided by three concrete tanks each 34' 10" in diameter and 15' 6" deep. Norton Disney, West Cottingwith and Lord's Bridge were retained by the RAF and were built to the original specification with two 24-foot-diameter tanks. Weapons charging houses were built adjacent to each storage 'pot' and fitted with simplified versions of the Porton-designed and Randle-modified charging equipment employed successfully at Randle and Rhydymwyn. Operational simplicity was achieved by resorting to positive pressure vesicant transfer in place of the more complex but inherently safer vacuum arrangements used in the factories. Design and construction of all five sites was overseen by ICI staff, and all instrumentation and charging machines were assembled and installed by ICI engineers.

Additional accommodation was provided at each site for the storage of thousands of empty cases and packing material and for bonding filled weapons. Extensive decontamination equipment was also provided at each site and extreme measures taken to ensure an adequate supply of water including, at Norton Disney, the sinking of a 1,000-foot-deep borehole.

There were long and serious delays in the building and fitting out of the Forward Filling Depots, due partly to an acute shortage of labour and also to the fact that in the final years of the War the provision of poison gas slipped increasingly far down the Ministry of Supply list of priorities. Barnham, the first site to be completed, was not handed over to the USAAF until 29 January 1944 and the last, West Cottingwith, until the beginning of June. Although the storage pots at all five sites were filled with vesicants the sites were never used in anger and their capital cost of £732,971 was, like so much of the cost of all wars, money dissipated to no purpose.

Clearance and Closure

At the end of the Second World War the British Army found itself burdened with something in excess of 1,200,000 tons of surplus ammunition for which it had neither any immediate or foreseeable requirement nor the facilities to store. Similarly, the RAF possessed over 250,000 tons of surplus bombs filled with either high explosives or chemical warfare agents. A small proportion of this stockpile was returned to the filling factories to be broken down and similarly small quantities were disposed of by sale to minor foreign powers, but the bulk was simply shipped out to sea and thrown overboard.

Immediately after the end of the War in Europe it became obvious that the vast reserves of bulk mustard gas and, more importantly in the first instance filled gas weapons, was going to be a major liability thrown upon the RAF. By August 1945 it was estimated that there were some 150,000 filled 65 lb LC mustard gas bombs in the RAF inventory. These were delicate, thin-cased weapons renowned for their fragility and propensity to leakage, and also prone to corrosion of the case by contact with the toxic filling. It was considered that within six months the entire stock would become so unstable that it would be impossible to transport them safely for disposal. The stockpile of larger, more sturdily constructed 300 lb, 400 lb and 1,000 lb bombs, amounting to an approximate total gross weight of 14,000 tons presented less of a problem and it was considered that these could safely support the rigour of transport for dumping at sea. While the Air Ministry was unconcerned about the long-term toxicological consequences of dumping high explosives and incendiaries at sea there was at first a degree of apprehension about using this technique with chemical weapons. Other means of destruction, including incineration and chemical decomposition, were implemented, but the relatively tiny quantities that could be disposed of within a viable time span using these methods made dumping the only practicable option.

Earlier in March experiments had been conducted at Bowes Moor under the supervision of Professor Peacock, Senior Scientific Officer at the Ministry of Aircraft Production, to determine the most efficient means of disposing of the large quantities of mustard gas. Peacock's experiments indicated that a cheap and efficient plant could be built to burn vesicants at the rate of about 150 gallons per hour, but this process involved first decanting the mustard gas from the bombs which was a tedious and hazardous process which the RAF was anxious to avoid. A quicker and cruder alternative was then decided upon: 65 lb bombs would simply be stacked in the storage sheds at Bowes in huge quantities, intermixed with a small number of incendiary bombs; the whole would then be ignited, the intense heat generated completely destroying the mustard gas and at the same time decontaminating the remains of the buildings. Ad hoc modifications to this system were later employed at other RAF ammunition dumps. At Harpur Hill, for example, chemical-filled bombs were stacked on a concrete pad in a remote corner of the site, intermixed with a few incendiary bombs and thoroughly doused in petrol. A few hundred rounds of tracer ammunition from a Bren gun would then be blasted into the stack to puncture the bombs and ensure ignition. Later in the autumn the same system was approved for the incineration of larger calibres of CW bombs at Bowes Moor.

Meanwhile Bowes Moor had been designated as the central disposal point for RAF chemical weapons which were now accumulating there in vast numbers. In October 1945 no less than 2,500 tons were received from various forward depots, and similar quantities continued to arrive throughout the rest of 1945 and the following year. Bowes' incineration capacity was quickly overwhelmed, so preparations were made for deep-sea dumping of the residual stocks. Some time earlier a joint services committee had been charged 'to ascertain what harbours, if any, in the UK are sufficiently remote from populated areas to avoid serious danger to life and property from an explosion and where harbour facilities are not vital to shipping.' The ideal port would be one from which surplus ordnance of all types could conveniently be despatched to the depths of Beaufort's Dyke, a 700–1,000-feet-deep chasm some 50 miles in length and 3 or 4 miles wide in the bed of the northern Irish Sea. Reporting its findings, the committee noted that 'only one harbour of this type can be found and that is Cairnryan.'

Cairnryan, on the eastern shore of salt-water Loch Ryan, north of the port of Stranraer in south-west Scotland, was indeed ideal in every respect. The military port at Cairnryan had been built in the early years of the Second World War to provide reserve capacity should the southern or east coast ports be closed by enemy action. It was particularly well suited as a port for deep-sea dumping operations as its deep waters could accommodate ocean-going vessels at berths remote from commercial vessels, yet close to the Beaufort's Dyke dumping ground. Apart from its function as the primary port of departure for surplus ammunition, Loch Ryan was also home to a large ship-breaking undertaking that was the graveyard of countless German submarines and, more famously, of several British capital ships including the aircraft carrier HMS *Ark Royal*.

Disposals of conventional weapons began in June 1945 when 242 tons of 4.2" mortar bombs were thrown overboard from LCT (Landing Craft Tank) 1119. Throughout June and July a further 1,500 tons of surplus army ammunition was dumped. The first RAF weapons to be disposed of in Beaufort's Dyke were 5" rocket heads filled with phosgene, over 14,600 tons of which had been dumped by the end of October. During September four more surplus LCTs were adapted for RAF ammunition dumping and in November No. 275 MU RAF was formed to oversee the operation. It was hoped that the LCTs could dump 150 tons of bombs per voyage but when loading and handling difficulties reduced this to only 100 tons, two more LCTs and two RAOC coasters, SS *Malplaquet* and SS *Sir Evelyn Wood*, were added to the unit's fleet, increasing its capacity to 500 tons per day; 2,000 tons were disposed of in this manner during the first month of the operation. By 27 January the total disposal had reached 4,500 tons and by the end of February 9,300 tons. By 30 April Cairnryan had dumped a total of 42,000 tons of chemical weapons, including large quantities despatched from Brafferton earlier in the month, and in May alone this total was increased by a further 13,500 tons, consisting mainly of small, 65 lb bombs. Meanwhile 30,000 similar weapons were incinerated at Bowes Moor. In July deep-sea dumping of Pyro-filled bombs started from Barry Docks in south Wales, with 31,000 tons scuttled in the first month and a further 1,000 tons per month scheduled for disposal in subsequent months. Dumping of phosgene bombs from the Cumbrian port of Silloth also started in July. Conventional dumping techniques, with individual bombs lobbed over the ship's side, was proving too slow and labour-intensive to keep pace with the enormous quantities of bombs arriving daily at the dockside, so it was decided that a fleet of decrepit merchant ships should be acquired by the RAF, packed with thousands of tons of surplus ordnance, sailed or towed out into the Irish Sea and scuttled in Beaufort's Dyke. The first ship to be sacrificed in this way was SS *Empire Peacock* which set sail from Barry Docks in August laden with 3,186 tons of 400 lb SCI bombs. She was followed in September by *Kindersley*, laden with 1,227 tons of mustard gas, which made the longer journey to deep water off Skagerrak where, along with at least eighty-eight other ships scuttled by the Allies and containing tens of thousands of tons of German chemical weapons including mustard gas, phosgene and the nerve gas tabun, she has continued to poison Norwegian waters for the last sixty years.

During October the penultimate mustard gas scuttling ship, *Empire Woodlark*, went down carrying 1,378 tons of CW bombs, after which

Table 20 Vessels scuppered laden with chemical weapons aboard

Date	Latitude	Longitude	Vessel	Depth (metres)
2/7/45	58.00.9	11.00.00	*Empire Fal*	2,000
11/9/45	55.30.00	11.00.00	*Empire Simba*	2,500
1/10/45	55.30.00	11.00.00	*Empire Cormorant*	2,500
30/10/45	55.30.00	11.00.00	*Wairuna*	2,500
30/12/45	55.30.00	11.00.00	*Botlea*	2,500
25/8/46	47.57.00	08.33.24	*Empire Peacock*	750
3/9/46	48.03.00	08.09.00	*Empire Nutfield*	500
1/10/46	47.54.00	08.21.00	*Kindersley*	1,000
2/11/46	59.00.00	07.40.00	*Empire Woodlark*	800
11/11/46	48.00.00	08.21.00	*Lanark*	850
5/2/47	47.40.00	09.22.00	*Dora Oldendorf*	4,000
27/7/47	47.55.00	08.17.00	*Empire Lark*	800
9/8/47	56.22.00	09.27.00	*Leighton*	1,300
8/9/47	47.47.30	08.21.00	*Thorpe Bay*	1,500
3/11/47	47.36.00	09.31.00	*Margo*	4,100
1/3/48	47.55.00	08.58.00	*Harm Freitzen*	2,500
22/8/48	47.16.30	09.24.00	*Empire Success*	4,200
22/9/48	47.23.00	09.24.00	*Miervaldis*	4,000
20/6/49	47.52.00	08.51.00	*Empire Connyngham*	2,000
Operation Sandcastle				
27/7/55	56.30.00	12.00.00	*Empire Clare*	2,500
30/5/56	56.30.00	12.00.00	*Vogtland*	2,500
23/7/56	56.31.00	12.05.00	*Krotka*	2,500
Final operation (*probably* the disposal of nerve-gas stockpile ex Nancekuke)				
?/6/56	56.00.00	10.00.00	not recorded	2,000
?/9/56	56.00.00	10.00.00	not recorded	2,000

the RAF resorted once again to tipping weapons overboard from its little fleet of Silloth coasters, 1,272 tons being disposed of in October, 1,278 tons in November, then 305 tons, 620 tons and 837 tons in subsequent months. Plans to close Bowes Moor finally and draw a line under the RAF filled-weapons disposal programme were put on hold in November when it was discovered that due to an administrative oversight, the Air Ministry had unintentionally sold the last of the proposed scuttling ships, SS *Empire Rhodes,* which had been purchased a few months earlier for the not inconsiderable sum of £120,000. Bowes Moor was finally declared clear of chemical weapons in July 1946. Huge stocks still remained elsewhere, but until 1956 these were retained as part of the RAF active inventory.

Operation Inkpad

By the summer of 1947 the large surplus of M33 mustard gas spray tanks held by the USAAF at Melchbourne Park was causing considerable concern. In excess of 9,000 of these weapons, which consisted of increasingly leaky 55-gallon pressurized tanks, were in semi-open storage at Coppice Wood, a sub-site a short distance to the north of the main filling depot. The method of disposal approved by the Air Ministry involved the excavation of eight shallow concrete-lined burning-pits into which the spray tanks were decanted via long pipelines. The low viscosity 'Y3' mustard gas, dissolved in benzene, burnt at a high temperature and was completely destroyed. Ministry of Supply scientists reassured the press that, despite the copious volume of oily black smoke that almost continuously blanketed the area during the eight months required to complete the incineration process, there was no risk to public health. The incineration process proved much slower than anticipated, so, in contravention of avowed Air Ministry policy, it was decided to dump at sea large numbers of spray tanks that were deemed after inspection to be sufficiently safe to survive the journey to Cairnryan intact. Vesicant incineration at Coppice Wood was completed by the end of March 1948 after which the empty drums were decontaminated in a specially designed furnace, the process being completed the following January. Meanwhile a similar incineration procedure was adopted at FFD West Cottingwith for the disposal of the few 65 lb LC bombs initially scheduled for retention but now found to be rapidly deteriorating there.

By June 1948, when the majority of the excess or unserviceable filled bombs had either been destroyed or were scheduled for destruction, it was decided that, in response to the deteriorating situation in Berlin, filling capacity at all the FFDs would be retained and the plant overhauled. Site inspections showed that only Lord's Bridge remained immediately serviceable, all the others requiring spare parts or repair. All the underground storage pots were full except at Barnham where the three pots, with a capacity of 1,500 tons, held only 300 tons. West Cottingwith still held a stock of 26,000 empty cases at its Acaster Mabis sub-site.

Chemical weapons policy turned about-face briefly towards the end of 1948 when it was decided that all existing filled weapons in safe condition would be retained, but by the following June disposal began again and by December 1950 all chemical weapons sites with the exception of the forward filling depot bulk storage units were, in some cases somewhat prematurely, certified free from toxic material.

Operation Pepperpot

During the early 1950s considerable quantities of the nation's mustard gas stock was returned from Rhydymwyn and elsewhere to the ICI agency factory at Randle where small-scale filling of 1,000 lb aerial bombs continued until at least 1954, most of the filled weapons being either stored at the factory or dispatched to Norton Disney. Vesicant reserves were still maintained at the five forward filling depots, but no weapon filling was undertaken at these sites, where the consequences of their age and hasty wartime construction were beginning to cause concern. A routine inspection of the storage pots at Norton Disney in October 1951, for example, indicated that the mustard gas had eaten through the lead lining of one of the pots and contaminated the concrete sump below.

It was decided early in 1953 to decommission all the forward filling depots in an operation code-named 'Pepperpot', and on 14 July the first stage of this operation began at the Little Heath site at FFD Barnham. Preparatory work took several months but by October the Ministry of Supply had arranged for the first special tanker train to begin the transfer of 1,500 tons of mustard gas from Barnham to Randle where it was to be reprocessed. The first train left Barnham on 21 October 1953 accompanied by an armed military escort and arrived at the factory several days later after a hazardous journey over a railway system still in a parlous state following nearly fifteen years of minimal maintenance under government control. Due to problems with decanting the type 'Y3' vesicant stored at Barnham, subsequent transfers were delayed until the following spring. In April two further trains removed the remaining content of pot 'A', after which the decontamination process began. During May pots 'B' and 'C' were finally emptied and the last of five special poison gas tanker trains was despatched to Randle. All the residual plant and pipework was then broken down and decontaminated with bleaching powder after which the scrap metal and other suspect materials were dumped in the empty pots which were then sealed with concrete. The entire site was then ploughed to a depth of eighteen inches and sprayed with bleach solution before being finally declared safe by the Ministry of Supply in November.

Clearance of FFD5 at West Cottingwith began in the late summer of 1954, the first 124-ton train load of poison gas from the site arriving at Randle on 12 August followed by a further consignment on 29 August. Work finished in October 1955 after which all contaminated pipework was cut into short lengths using oxy-acetylene equipment and dumped in the empty pots. Empty pipe ducts on the surface were treated with bleach and then filled with earth and rubble, while the surrounding land was harrowed to a depth of 12 inches and treated with a strong concentration of bleach paste. Once the pots were completely filled with debris and rubble the steel lids were refitted and sealed with a layer of concrete. FFD3 at Norton Disney was decommissioned in a similar manner between August 1954 and July 1957, but here all the suspect plant was dismantled and transferred to Randle for decontamination and disposal.

Engineers began dismantling the pumping equipment and ancillary plant at FFD4, Lord's Bridge, in January 1955, work having started on emptying the storage tanks early the previous December. Shortly before 10 o'clock on the morning of Tuesday, 11 January, while workmen were using oxy-acetylene to cut up steel pipework near the 'K' pot filling plant, there occurred an enormous explosion that ripped the concrete top from the underground storage tank, throwing it several yards to one side and shattering the upper section of the tank's concrete shell. The explosion was followed by a major fire which spread a pall of toxic black smoke over the surrounding countryside and which was only brought under control by the courageousness of a small RAF firefighting team working in the most hazardous circumstances. The particular bravery of Corporal John Saunders, who stood on the very edge of the shattered tank for thirty minutes directing a jet of foam over the inferno inside the pot until the flames were finally quelled resulted in the award of a George Medal. There was widespread fear of the toxicity of the cloud of smoke and vapour from the fire that was by now drifting towards Cambridge, and civilian police loudspeaker vans toured the area warning local inhabitants of the hazard. For several weeks after the incident civilian employees and local residents thought to have been at risk from exposure were subjected to rigorous medical checks, but no ill effects were revealed. Similarly, no ground contamination or contamination of watercourses was discovered.

Some 20 tons of mustard gas was destroyed in the explosion which was presumed to have been caused by a spark from the oxy-acetylene cutting process igniting highly inflammable benzene vapour – used as a solvent to reduce the viscosity of certain grades of Pyro – leaking from pot 'K'. Thereafter the utmost vigilance was exercised to contain the vapour in the now badly damaged and completely exposed underground tank. A thick layer of foam was maintained on top of the remaining mustard gas until pumping equipment could be installed to transfer it into the adjacent 'J' pot.

The remaining vesicants were eventually transferred from Lord's Bridge without further incident and decommissioning of the last forward filling depot at Melchbourne Park was completed between July 1957 and December 1958. The entire bulk stock of mustard gas, some 4,200 tons, was eventually destroyed in a large-scale, high-temperature incineration plant at Randle designed and built by ICI engineers with assistance from scientists from the government's chemical defence research establishment at Porton Down. During the incineration process the toxic compound was broken down into sulphur dioxide, hydrogen chloride and small amounts of carbon dioxide, the greater parts of which were captured by a sophisticated effluent scrubbing plant.

This, however, was not the end of the forward filling depot saga. As early as July 1954 there were concerns voiced within the Air Ministry over the decontamination techniques employed at Norton Disney, and ground contamination at Melchbourne Park was found to be so serious that it was thought for a while that the whole site might have to be retained by the Air Ministry in perpetuity. Some four years later, in March 1958, it was reported that an area within the Marsh Close sub-site at Lord's Bridge was found to be seriously contaminated with mustard gas. The ground there was again treated with bleach paste, but no serious effort was made to trace the source of contamination. A schedule of regular inspections of all five sites by government scientists was subsequently established which still continues today. In 1985 a soil and water analysis at Melchbourne Park revealed very high levels of toxic materials and a decision was taken to break open the pots there, which had been sealed for thirty years, to make a thorough investigation of the source of the contamination. This operation, which was undertaken jointly by the RAF and a Royal Engineers detachment, was wittily codenamed 'Coleman Keg' – Coleman's having, for a century or more, been a household name famous as manufacturers of mustard as a table condiment. When the lids were removed from the three underground tanks on 11 July 1985 it was discovered that pot 'A' contained two skips filled with heavily contaminated scrap metal and seven leaking cylinders of mustard gas, pot 'B' also contained two skips of scrap together with thirty-three containers of mustard gas, while pot 'C' held seven skip loads of waste material and no less than eighty-three decaying cylinders of mustard gas. A prolonged and delicate operation was required to remove this highly toxic material which was eventually taken away for disposal, after which the pots were thoroughly decontaminated, filled with rubble, sealed with concrete and finally covered with earth.

The End of Chemical Weapons in the United Kingdom

We have seen, in Chapter 7, that the United Kingdom's flirtation with offensive nerve gas weapons came to a somewhat abrupt and premature end with the cessation of manufacture at Nancekuke in 1955 when, in the words of the establishment's official historian, 'international tension relaxed to the point where it was not judged necessary to proceed with a production plant.' Similarly, the country's involvment with the earlier generation of cutaneous chemical weapons seemed to dwindle away at much the same time without an apparent, overt policy for its official abandonment. Even today it is difficult to be precise about the exact date of the demise of Britain's offensive chemical warfare capacity; the consensus of official and secondary sources seems to offer no more precision than that British interest in chemical weapons finally lapsed in 1956 or 1957.

What is obvious, however, is that by the mid 1950s Britain was, for reasons of national pride and international prestige, absolutely committed to expenditure on nuclear weapons which she could ill afford, and all other military expenditure was secondary to this. Alignment with the United States in opposition to the largely chimerical threat of Soviet expansionism in Europe demanded a hugely expensive air defence infrastructure. The passive element of this alone – the 'ROTOR' radar detection system – was to prove the most costly single defence contract ever made by the British government and expenditure at this level, together with that of developing an independent nuclear deterrent, left no contingency for the older conventional or chemical means of waging war. It was freely admitted that in the event of a war against communist forces in Europe the United Kingdom, as recompense for her nuclear contribution to NATO, would expect the United States to pick up the tab for her shortfall in conventional capability. Similarly, it was implied that the gift to the United States of Britain's early research into VX and the other advanced organophosphorous nerve agents in the early 1950s should be compensated for, in the event of war, by the supply by the United States of the necessary sarin and VX bombs, mortars and artillery ammunition.

Under these conditions it was easy for the British government to give up chemical weapons and thereby both ease the strain on its purse strings and clear its concience. There never had been any great enthusiasm within the military for chemical weapons and public opinion had always viewed them with no more than ill-veiled disgust. Chemical warfare had, for years before the defence white paper of 1957, slipped by default into the background of military thinking, overshadowed by the atomic and then the nuclear bomb. Although the white paper, entitled *Defence: An Outline of Future Policy,* made no specific reference to chemical weaponry and, indeed, was published shortly after the final demise of the chemical warfare programme, its contents give some insight into the military debate during the years that led up to its publication:

> Over the last 5 years defence has on average absorbed 10 per cent of Britain's gross national product. Some 7 per cent of the working population are either in the Services or supporting them. One eighth of the metal using industries, upon which the export trade largely depends, is devoted to defence. An undue proportion of qualified scientists and engineers are engaged on military work.
>
> In order to make an adequate contribution to the North Atlantic, Southeast Asia and Baghdad alliances, Britain must possess an appreciable

element of nuclear deterent power of her own, including thermonuclear weapons.

Britain has been bearing a disproportionately large share of the total burden of Western defence and reductions must be made accordingly both from the standpoints of finance and manpower.

A little more than ten years later, justifying the decision to abandon chemical weapons, the Secretary of State for Defence told the House of Commons Select Committee on Science and Technology in July 1968 that:

> In the field of chemical weapons we have a very good defence capability indeed so far as our services are concerned. It is not so easy to conceive of the use of chemical weapons against a civil population in these islands. Their use against soldiers in Europe is something which one must almost expect if there were a war in Europe. We have not felt it necessary, nor indeed did the previous government, to develop retaliatory capability here, because we have nuclear weapons, and obviously we might choose to retaliate in that way if that were the requirement.

This view was repeated and expanded upon in May 1970, when the Secretary of State informed the House that:

> NATO as a whole has chemical weapons available to it because the United States maintains an offensive chemical capability. However, I believe that both the former and present government in Britain were right not to stockpile offensive chemical weapons in the United Kingdom. If the House really considers the situation, I believe it will recognize that it is almost inconceivable that enemy forces would use chemical weapons against NATO forces except in the circumstances of a mass invasion – in which event more terrible weapons would surely come into play.

Chapter 9

Conclusion

What seems clear from the albeit slightly selective evidence that we have examined with varying degrees of discrimination in the previous chapters is that the acquisition of chemical weapons was never a high priority amongst the mainstream of military men, that chemical warfare was never seen as a viable means of attaining a meaningful military end, and that the whole concept of chemical warfare aroused universal public vilification. Yet every advanced (and many not-so-advanced) nation in the world squandered huge industrial resources on the development of such weapons for almost half a century. Why then, if, as it seems, no one wanted them, did the whole world pursue chemical weapons with such sustained vigour?

The answer to this question, like the answer to the concomitant question of why, if the stuff was assembled in such vast quantities in so many countries with so many varying military and political pressures and constraints, was it never used, involves psychology as much as the study of rational policy and is, therefore, largely unsupported by written record. Four factors seem to have driven the development of chemical weapons: self-interest and, to a lesser extent national interest, on the part of the chemical industry; the narrow, detached, personal ambitions and jealousies of a small minority of scientists; the absolute and irredeemable ineptitude of the intelligence services; and, particularly in the United States, an instinctive urge for self-perpetuation amongst the military class whose careers became dependant upon the Chemical Warfare Service.

The question as to why chemical weapons were not used is best answered by a brief examination of the two events in modern history when they might have most readily been unleashed. The first occasion when the fragile structure of constraint might have broken down is a matter of hypothesis only, being at the time of the anticipated German invasion of the United Kingdom had Operation Sealion gone ahead in the spring of 1940. The second occasion was when Germany rather than the United Kingdom was in extremis, during the Normandy invasion of 1944. The differing constraints that existed at the beginning and end of the Second World War are instructive and worth examining in a little more detail.

It is probable that, despite Britain's avowed no first use policy, chemical weapons would have been deployed against German troops attempting to land on the beaches of southern England. German commanders certainly expected to be faced with chemical weapons, as was made clear by General Ochsner who later wrote:

> We had to reckon with the British, in the defence of their homeland and in an attempt to defeat our invasion, using every weapon and all means available to them that might hold out even the slightest hope of success. We had to allow for the possibility of our troops being attacked while approaching the English coast with non-persistent agents as well as with vesicants sprayed from aircraft. Another possibility was that immediately after landing our troops would come up against large scale vesicant barriers and that they might be subjected to further gas attacks from the air and by gas shells fired by artillery.

This same scenario seemed to be in the mind of General Alan Brooke, later Lord Alanbrooke who replaced General Sir Edmund Ironside as General Officer Commanding Home Forces in July 1940. In his diary for 22 July 1940, after criticizing Ironside's static rear-defence system of pillboxes and anti-tank ditches, he comments:

> I visualize a light defence along the beaches, to hamper and delay landings to the maximum, and in the rear highly mobile forces trained to immediate aggressive action intended to concentrate and attack any landings before they had time to become too well established. I was also relying on heavy air attacks on the point of landing, and had every intention of using sprayed mustard gas on the beaches.

Military expediency might have required such action in that it may perhaps have been the only effective way to slow the German landings given that conventional weapons were so thinly spread following upon the recent losses at Dunkirk. In the use of chemical weapons British forces would have been at a distinct advantage. The recent build-up of such weapons meant that there were at least 1,000 tons of chemical bombs or artillery shells immediately available which, although not an overwhelming quantity, was quite sufficient to hold an enemy advance. A large part of this chemical arsenal consisted of mustard gas filled into SCI spray tanks and, fitted to Blenheim IV bombers, these spray tanks would have represented a formidable threat to German troops exposed on the beaches of Kent and Sussex and beyond. Britain would also have held the logistic advantage in that her dense and efficient transport infrastructure and short defensive supply lines would have rendered the bringing up of additional supplies an easy task. The use of gas as an offensive weapon did not figure in the German invasion plan, nor had it figured in the planning of the assaults against Poland and France. Blitzkrieg tactics and chemical weapons, the main functions of which are inevitably to slow down the frontal battle and hamper mobility in the rear on account of its added logistic burden, were quite inimical.

So, there existed compelling incentives for the United Kingdom to use gas against an invading Germany army, and these were probably not sufficiently outweighed by contemporary restraints to prevent its use. The two principal forces acting against British first use of gas were the threat of retaliation in kind and the possible alienation of popular opinion abroad. Retaliation, if it had come, would probably have been confined to counter-force attack and in that situation the Germans, on account of the logistical burdens previously referred too, would have been seriously disadvantaged. In the spring of 1940 there still existed on both sides a strong ethical disinclination towards launching indiscriminate attacks against civilian targets and, indeed, there were frequent high-level debates about the legitimacy of even targeting civilian factories involved in war production. The probability of large-scale air bombing of London with mustard gas, despite the fact that the Luftwaffe outnumbered the RAF in bombers by four to one, was sufficiently remote at that time for it not to act as a disincentive. Both sides were restrained by the fact that both the German and British intelligence organizations had grossly overestimated the sizes of their opponent's chemical weapons stockpiles and both were in consequence very keen to avoid the risk of escalation. What British intelligence did not know at the time was that the Germans were afraid that the United Kingdom already possessed nerve gases in a more advanced state of development than their own, which acted as a major disincentive. A further restraint upon unrestricted use of chemical weapons by Germany was their awareness of the superiority of Britain's anti-gas air-raid precautions organization compared with that which existed in Germany throughout the War. In the United Kingdom everyone had been issued a gas mask and had been thoroughly trained in its use, the urban population was more than adequately provided with gas-proof air-raid shelters, there were plenty of decontamination centres and everyone had been encouraged to arrange their own gas-proof rooms at home. The German government, by contrast, had almost completely overlooked its own civil defence requirements in the early years of the War because at that time attacks upon the homeland seemed inconceivable. Later, as the War drew to its conclusion and German cities were being bombed into submission, it had neither the time nor the industrial resources or raw materials to provide such protection for its population. Towards the end of the War, when Germany had lost superiority in the air, fear of retaliation in kind was without doubt the dominant constraint on German use of poison gas.

Any fears the British government may have had concerning international opprobrium had they been compelled to resort to chemical weapons to repel a German invasion centred upon the likely response of the United States, to which Britain looked for succour and support. The majority opinion in the War Cabinet, however, was that first use in such a situation of *extremis* would be regarded as legitimate. On the other hand, there was a strong body of opinion suggesting that a subsequent retaliation by Germany against British civilians in response to the first use of gas by the British against invading troops might bring America into the War, even if the invasion itself was not a sufficient impetus.

The second occasion in which chemical weapons might have been used was during the Allied invasion of Normandy. Within the German High Command the possibility had certainly been discussed, as General Ochsner makes clear:

> Were gases a suitable weapon for this purpose? At first glance the answer must be in the affirmative. Entire sectors of the coastal front could have been rendered impenetrable for the enemy, or at least untenable unless he decontaminated them. To do so, however, he would have needed enormous quantities of decontaminants, innumerable vehicles, specialized units and forces, and these could only have crossed the channel at the expense of combat forces . . . there was the added factor that the morale of the landing troops would have been seriously affected.

For the Allies it was a major worry and many commanders were both fearful that the Germans would employ gas and surprised that they did not. General Omar Bradley notes in his memoirs that:

> While planning the Normandy invasion we had weighed the possibility of enemy gas attack and for the first time during the war speculated on the probability of his resorting to it. For perhaps only then could persistent gas have forced a decision in one of history's climactic battles, for even a light sprinkling of persistent gas on Omaha Beach would have cost us our footing there.

The fact that Allied forces involved in the Normandy landings were particularly well provided with anti-gas protection and supported by substantial reserves in the supply line indicates how seriously the threat was taken. The disincentives preventing the Germans from resorting to gas were, however, compelling. With the loss of air superiority the fear of retaliatory attacks against her cities and civilian population which, by the autumn of 1944 were effectively devoid of air protection or civil defence facilities, ruled out all prospect of Germany using gas against Allied forces in Europe, as Albert Speer confirmed at Nuremberg: 'All sensible Army people turned gas warfare down as being utterly insane since, in view of your superiority in the air, it would not be long before it would bring about the most terrible catastrophe upon German cities, which were completely unprotected.'

Speer's evidence at Nuremberg points to a third occasion when chemical weapons might have been used, and that perhaps the most dangerous of all, during the encirclement of Germany in the autumn of 1944 when, to some extent, the rational thinking upon which the principle of deterrence depended was in partial suspense in certain quarters. Amongst those advocating the chemical option, according to Speer, were 'a certain circle of political people ... mostly Ley, Goebbels and Bormann, always the same three, who by every possible means wanted to increase the war effort'. Speer describes the following conversation with Robert Ley who, in peacetime, was a professional chemist of some standing, during a meeting near Sonthofen in the autumn of 1944:

> As usual, our conversation took place over glasses of strong wines. His increased stammering betrayed his agitation: 'You know we have this new poison gas – I've heard about it. The Fuehrer must do it. He must use it! Now he has to do it! This is the last moment. You must make him realize that it's time.'

Deterrence prevailed, however, and indeed throughout the War both sides involved in the conflict went to great lengths to ensure that chemical weapons were not used and that no excuse for retaliation should be offered. During the German invasion Russian commanders were warned by their superiors to be circumspect in the use of screening smoke lest the Germans should view this as first use of chemical weapons and thus be provoked to retaliate in kind. Following the Battle of the River Plate, during which the German Battleship *Graf Spee* sought refuge in the neutral harbour of Montevideo, there was some consternation on board, stirred up by a ship's surgeon, that many of the crew were suffering from injuries very similar to those that might be expected from mustard gas exposure. It was well known at the time that British warships included amongst their weaponry a small proportion of gas shells. There was, consequently, much speculation in both the German and neutral press that the British had fired mustard gas shells at the *Graf Spee*, an action which would have at least partially explained the mystery of why the German battleship had sought the rather dishonourable safety of a neutral port despite her relatively minor damage. The risks of retaliatory escalation associated with unfounded allegations on the part of a German ship's doctor were, of course immense, and the German authorities were quick to quash the rumour once it was discovered that the injuries were caused by coolant leaking from a refrigeration system damaged during the sea battle.

There were other restraints upon the first use of chemical weapons that were psychological rather than immediately military in character and are thus difficult to quantify. Some of these are personal: Hitler's distaste for chemical weapons, for example, due apparently to his having been gassed during the First World War, is well known. Roosevelt, too, was contemptuous of chemical warfare and through his personal opposition contained the less restrained ambitions of some members of the Chemical Warfare Service. Admiral Leahy, who became President Truman's Chief of Staff, also exercised a restraining influence on the proponents of chemical weapons in the United States, 'weapons which,' he once said, 'violate every Christian ethic I have ever heard of and all the known laws of war'.

Clearly, from the very start of the Second World War it was realized by all right-thinking parties that chemical weapons, which had anyway been foisted upon unwilling military establishments, were and would only ever be deterrent in nature and function. There was, however, a constant escalation in their accumulation, contained in a kind of isolated vacuum detached from the mainstream of war, fuelled by the strange, intellectual insecurity that seems always to cause the scientific community of one nation to presume that scientists in the enemy camp have not only followed the same research path but have also travelled it faster. This phenomenon is easily compounded by the work of the respective intelligence services whose entire raison d'etre seems to be to run rings around the truth. This proved to be the case with chemical weapons and even more vividly so in the field of biological warfare during the Second World War, where the intelligence community created a labyrinthine structure of research projects and production facilities that simply did not exist in the real world. The process was that, first, a primary scientific study, maybe in Britain, would indicate that a certain organism was a likely biological warfare candidate; scientific intelligence would then conclude that because Britain had discovered this organism then it was inevitable that the Germans had not only also discovered it but had already developed it to the weapon stage. Military intelligence would then institute a search for production facilities hidden in the enemy homeland and would, of course, fail to find them. The failure would be blamed on the fact that the new weapon was so secret and so vital to the German war effort that it was concealed by the most stringent and impenetrable veil of secrecy. The de facto assumption would then be that the Germans had built networks of secret underground pharmaceutical factories turning out the relevant organism, be it botulinum or anthrax, or some other abominable organism, by the bucketful daily. In response, Britain would devote immense resources to the development, first of an antitoxin that probably would work, and then of an organism even more virulent that probably would not. Finally, all parties would congratulate themselves on having thwarted another iniquitous German scientific initiative.

Despite the decades of declaration by purportedly disinterested scientists that they have developed a higher form of killing that does away with the pointless physical destruction and dissipation of national wealth that are the inevitable consequences of conventional warfare, their despicable offspring, for all their genius, have never been released upon the world. They have, nonetheless, wreaked their vengeance upon the world in more insidious ways, and in some respect it is justice that they should do so. The Second World War should have provided sufficient evidence of the utter futility of chemical weaponry and for many nations it did. Even the United Kingdom learned its lesson – though it took ten years to fully comprehend – but some countries never did, and continued to stockpile ever more fearful mountains of chemical ordnance throughout the half century of the cold war. The United States and the former Soviet Union were the worst offenders and now, in an age of open government and environmental enlightenment, they are paying the price.

Index

181